Advance praise for *Countering Violent Extremism in Pakistan*

Anita Weiss, a prolific expert on Pakistan for some 40 years, has written a "must read" groundbreaking book on the role of religion and the exponential increase of religious extremism in Pakistan. Based on exhaustive on-the-ground research, she provides a unique window on how and why people have responded to and what they have done and are they doing to stop the spread of violent extremism.

> – John Esposito, Professor, Religion & International Affairs and Islamic Studies, Georgetown University; Founding Director, Prince Alwaleed Center for Muslim–Christian Understanding, Georgetown

Anita Weiss brings to the fore the voices of Pakistanis who have long struggled to counter extremism, intolerance, and terrorism in all its forms. Going beyond the urban areas, she has located people and organisations in smaller cities, towns, and rural areas, where change is happening daily. The diversity of approaches of these change makers is exhilarating: from the non-violence of Bacha Khan to the science focus of the Zoya schools, the stirring and resilient emerging Pashto and Sindhi poetry, to the urban initiatives in art for peace and open spaces. Making a strong case for a hopeful and forward-looking Pakistan, Weiss has certainly opened an important avenue of study.

> – Yaqoob Khan Bangash, Director, Centre for Governance and Policy, ITU, Lahore; Founder, Afkar-e-Taza ThinkFest, Pakistan

Anita Weiss shows how people are in fact countering hatred and violence through art, music, poetry, education, and religion itself. This is a masterful work of insightful analysis and engaging writing. Readers who do not know Dr Weiss will appreciate nevertheless that they are in the hands of one of the world's most perceptive and engaged scholars of social forces in Pakistan.

> – Christopher Candland, Professor, Political Science; Founding Director, South Asia Studies, Wellesley College

Anita Weiss shows that violence can be fought more effectively than in deradicalisation camps by music, poetry, education and religion! This is a fascinating book based on multifaceted, plurilingual fieldwork.

> – Christophe Jaffrelot, Senior Research Fellow, Sciences Po (Paris); Research Director, CNRS; and Professor, Indian Politics and Sociology, King's India Institute (London)

Dr Weiss's groundbreaking new work identifies and amplifies the voices of Pakistanis young and old, expressing their resistance to extremism and offering a vision for a new Pakistan rooted in religious harmony and local culture.

> – Farahnaz Ispahani, Journalist, former MNA, Pakistan, and author of *Purifying the Land of the Pure: Pakistan's Religious Minorities*

The extremism problem of Pakistan is well known and continues to be covered by scholars, journalists and policy wonks. But there is a larger, invisible story that has escaped attention mainly due to the decades-long securitization of global discourses around Pakistan. This is where Anita Weiss, a longtime scholar and observer of the country, has made a tremendous contribution to existing literature by presenting a compelling narrative on how myriad groups, communities and individuals are fighting extremist doctrines that were once used by the state for (geo)political imperatives. As Weiss shows us, the heroic efforts of Pakistan's poets, musicians, educationists, and community organizers—spread across the regions—bespeaks the formidable resistance to state policies of the past and their tragic fallout. The style is accessible, empathetic and the range of initiatives covered underscore the pluralistic nature of Pakistan's society that remains the greatest organic antidote to ideologies of exclusion and hate.

> — RAZA RUMI, Policy analyst, journalist; Director, Park Center for Independent Media; Professor of Journalism, Ithaca College, and author of *Being Pakistani: Society Culture and the Arts*

COUNTERING VIOLENT EXTREMISM IN PAKISTAN

LOCAL ACTIONS, LOCAL VOICES

COUNTERING VIOLENT EXTREMISM IN PAKISTAN

LOCAL ACTIONS, LOCAL VOICES

Anita M. Weiss

OXFORD
UNIVERSITY PRESS

OXFORD
UNIVERSITY PRESS

Oxford University Press is a department of the University of Oxford.
It furthers the University's objective of excellence in research, scholarship,
and education by publishing worldwide. Oxford is a registered trade mark of
Oxford University Press in the UK and in certain other countries

Published in Pakistan by
Oxford University Press
No. 38, Sector 15, Korangi Industrial Area,
PO Box 8214, Karachi-74900, Pakistan

© Oxford University Press 2020

The moral rights of the author have been asserted

First Edition published in 2020

ISBN 978-969-734-014-9

Typeset in Adobe Garamond Pro
Printed on 68gsm Offset Paper

Printed by Kagzi Packages, Karachi

To
the courageous souls—the sparks of hope—who have sought,
in their own paths, to stand up to hatred,
destruction, and evil in Pakistan

Contents

Preface

My life has been entwined with South Asia as far back as I can recall. When I was ten, I had pictures of India hanging all over my room, but little did I realize then that they were stylized representations of western images of the subcontinent. My first sojourn outside of the United States was to India my sophomore year in college and I have sought to return to South Asia annually ever since. Yet that 'India' of my youth was not the nation-state, but the larger cultural area that comprises much of South Asia, including Pakistan. There is no place in the world that captures 'home' to me more than Pakistan; thinking of Pakistan evokes that warmth and love for place, people, and setting that can only be found 'at home.'

I was fortunate to travel to Pakistan a year before Zia ul Haq proclaimed his Islamization programme in February 1979. I saw Lahore as a city of gardens, a place where life is lived on the streets and, in my naiveté, a place where everyone was welcome. Within a year, between the promulgation of the Hudood Ordinances, the Soviet invasion of Afghanistan that unleashed havoc upon Pakistan, and Zia ul Haq pushing his Wahhabi agenda, the social cohesion and celebrations I had witnessed in Pakistan, albeit limited, were becoming unhinged. I could still visit a village and swim in a tube well, take a hike along a mountain trail, and get henna applied to my hands on Eid. But along the way, I saw changes happening in my 'home' which I cannot walk away from. Was the advancing anger and despair giving way to violence, or were there other forces feeding that violence?

I know that this question remains unanswerable at this time. But more important is what I see occurring now, which is my inspiration for writing this book. I see something exciting happening all around the country: people asserting they want their cultural identity back, their society intact, and throw off the bondages of hatred, violence, and fear that at least for a while seemed to break out at any time in Pakistan. In effect, they are cleaning their house—and my house—and I am documenting the exciting acts in which they are engaged.

After I completed my doctoral dissertation over thirty-five years ago,[1] I asked a friend, a social activist, what I could do to give something back to Pakistan as I had conducted the field research there that ultimately resulted in my doctorate in sociology. She advised me to strive to give a voice to people who are not readily listened to; this led me to research working women's lives in the Walled City of Lahore.[2] I feel that I have been engaged in this ever since then: struggling to understand what is happening in Pakistan and giving voice to it. But of all the research and writing that I have ever done, nothing is more important to me than giving voice to the amazing people who are recapturing their identity—Pakistan's identity—and asserting that 'this is who we truly are.'

I must admit here that after my last book was completed in March 2014, I promised myself that I would never write another one.[3] It's a lot of time-consuming work, and just was no longer on my agenda. But then the APS attack happened on 16 December 2014.[4] I was sitting at a friend's house in Islamabad when then Prime Minister Nawaz Sharif appeared on television to announce the attack. Using his commonly-seen somber face, he stated '*afsos hai*,' which can be translated as sad but most often means 'too bad.' I threw a cushion at the television (careful not to break my friend's TV) decrying this attitude, that it was not enough, not sufficient for the prime minister of my adopted country to say this was 'too bad.' This deplorable act that killed over 140 people in a children's school was beyond the scope of saying 'too bad.' It had to be called out for being horrific, monstrous, and that everything about it was against Pakistan. But in my horror, I also realized that this was not an act of the Pakistan I knew, that Pakistanis were also mortified and were standing up all over the country for what was right, just, and authentic.

Hence the idea to write this book was born. I spoke with friends and colleagues who directed me to others and my eyes were opened to what could be deemed 'acts of subversion' occurring throughout the country but what are, in actuality, acts of reclaiming identity and authenticity. This is nationalism in its truest form. I needed to do this research for my own soul, to see what Pakistanis have been doing to right the wrongs that have plagued our home these past thirty odd years. My greatest wish is that I do justice to their efforts.

Notes

1. It took me a few years to return to revise it into a book that was finally published as *Culture, Class and Development in Pakistan: The Emergence of an Industrial Bourgeoisie in Punjab*, Westview Press, 1991.
2. This resulted in *Walls Within Walls: Life Histories of Working Women in the Old City of Lahore*, Westview Press, 1992; republished in Pakistan by Pak Books, 1992. A second edition was published by Oxford University Press with a new Preface, 2002.
3. This book is *Interpreting Islam, Modernity and Women's Rights in Pakistan*, Palgrave Macmillan, 2014; South Asian edition by Orient BlackSwan, 2015.
4. The Tehrik-e-Taliban Pakistan (TTP) has claimed responsibility for this attack on the Army Public School in Peshawar resulting in the deaths of 132 students and 17 others, including teachers. The militants had scaled the school's walls and set off a bomb at the outset of the attack.

Acknowledgements

Where to begin thanking everyone who has provided support, guidance, camaraderie, and hope throughout the process of researching and writing this book? I must start with the most important person in the world to me, my son Sulman Raza, for without his unflagging encouragement and enthusiasm that I continue with this project, and his awareness that he could do just fine when his mom was away, it would have been impossible for me to continue. I also want to thank my two most special friends, Saba Gul Khattak and Chaudhry Shahid Nadeem, who indeed comprise my family in Pakistan and always ensure I have a place to live, a car at my disposal, and good food to eat. I also want to acknowledge my other dear Islamabad friends Zaman Malik, Erum and family, Salma Malik, my former student Shahid Habib, and Adnan Aurangzeb's family. I greatly appreciate the help of his wife, Zenab Adnan, and his daughter Aneela Sulaiman, who became my graduate student at the University of Oregon, in translating Pashto poetry for me. Thanks also to Haya and Hina, who with good heart said they'd create the index for this book so I'd thank them here; I'll thank them anyhow. Finally, a very big thank you to Adnan *bhai* who was so kind to sell me his wonderful Toyota Corolla that I used to travel throughout Pakistan, and his wonderful hospitality in Islamabad and Saidu Sharif.

In Karachi, I am thankful for the hospitality of Zubair and Tehmina Parekh, my old Berkeley friends, and the numerous Careem drivers who unflaggingly brought me everywhere throughout the city, even to places where 'Careem doesn't go.' I have long appreciated the advice of Arif Hasan and Karamat Ali who also facilitated my research in Karachi. Elsewhere in Sindh, thanks goes to my former dissertation workshop student, Rafique Wassan, who helped me with my initial contacts in places I had never traveled to before. Once there, thanks to everyone who not only assisted my research but extended their hands in friendship and helped me with translations of Sindhi poetry; special mention must go to Dr Nadia Agha in Khairpur, Zakia Aijaz and Razaque Channa in Hyderabad, and Saif Samejo in Jamshoro.

I spent quite a bit of time in Lahore, and many thanks to old friends who were always there for me: Mansoor Rana and family, Saif *Bhai* (Faqir Saifuddin), Martin Lau (nice coincidence our timings overlapped!), Sadaf Ahmed, and also to Gauher Aftab for providing so many stimulating, provocative ideas. Elsewhere in Punjab, many thanks to the faculty at Bahauddin Zakariya University (BZU) for all your wonderful help, warmth, and hospitality, Gul Khori and family for providing me with a familial respite in Multan, Sher Muhammad for all his help in Sargodha, and Dr Mussarat Shah and family in Jhang for extending yourselves, as always.

In Khyber Pakhtunkhwa, my dear friends Dr Noreen Naseer and Dr Faiz Jan and Aasya in Peshawar and Azizullah Khan in Mardan ensured that my temporary homes there were warm and convivial; I truly felt 'at home.' Thanks so much to Asim, Mehwish, and their children for welcoming me into their family in Mardan. Khadim Hussain, Bushra Goher, and Afrasiab Khattak provided invaluable guidance for my work in Peshawar.

Special thanks goes to Husnain Rasheed, who went far and beyond the responsibilities of a driver, spending a total of nearly nine months with me on the backroads of Pakistan and always helping me find a gym where I could work out. I look forward to the day when I finally move to Pakistan and can employ him fulltime.

Back in Oregon, University of Oregon graduate students Aneela Sulaiman, Shehram Mukhtar, and Sarah Ahmed provided invaluable research support. I greatly appreciate that Mike Moresi and Geoffrey Marcus, part of the UO IT team, graciously digitized the photographs used herein. I am deeply grateful to Patrick Jones for his help with the book's index, the third that he's worked on with me.

I greatly appreciate the financial support I received that has enabled me to carry out this research. My greatest appreciation goes to the Harry Frank Guggenheim Foundation which provided me with a Fellowship for six months in Pakistan, September 2017–March 2018. Karen Colvard was incredibly approachable and gracious and I greatly appreciate the encouragement and guidance she always offered. At the University of Oregon, Bruce Blonigan was helpful in brainstorming how I could get away to conduct the research. I appreciate the travel grant support from the College of Arts & Sciences and from the Office of International Affairs.

Finally, Nadeem Akbar and the staff and drivers at the American Institute of Pakistan Studies (AIPS) in Pakistan were always available to assist me with logistics, lodging, and whatever would come up. It was great to know they always 'had my back!'

Many thanks to Salman Tarik Kureshi at Oxford University Press, Pakistan for his enthusiasm for this project and to Ghousia Ali, Gulrukhsar Mujahid, and OUP Pakistan's new Managing Director, Arshad Saeed Husain, for all their encouragement and support in helping to bring this book to fruition.

My final acknowledgement is to all the wonderful people within Pakistan who invited me into their homes, sang with me at their *melas*, and continue to celebrate our shared dream of a collective future without violence in Pakistan.

1 | Introduction

The world will not be destroyed by those who do evil,
But by those who watch them without doing anything.

Albert Einstein

Pakistan has been undergoing profound political, economic, and social turmoil for decades. Too frequently, this has resulted in violence and local people in Pakistan are left questioning the causes behind it. This violence often emerges from religious extremism, which both causes and reflects cataclysmic chasms amongst different constituencies. Violence fatigue also sets in, and people are frustrated with the incessant fear that they must live with on a daily basis. It is difficult to move forward with reconciliation when violence remains a constant occurrence.

Violent extremism has manifested in myriad ways over the past decades in Pakistan. In response, the Pakistani state and military have sought to counter this extremism through different strategies that have been fraught with problems. On the other hand, non-state actors—individuals along with local NGOs—are engaging in various kinds of social negotiations and actions to lessen the violence and recapture indigenous cultural identity, often in very inventive ways.

In the past decade, the number of violent acts of religious extremism has mushroomed; most people are at a loss to explain who is behind these acts or how to stop them. Abdul Basit[1] argues that there are many dimensions to violent extremism in Pakistan,

> Violent extremism in Pakistan is a multifaceted and multi-layered phenomenon. It exists in the form of sectarianism, shariah (Islamization) movements, Talibanization, and a multitude of jihadist organizations. Other forms of extremism manifest in the general opposition to American or western policies, in nationalist-separatist insurgency in Balochistan and ethno-political violence in Karachi and parts of interior Sindh.

We must clarify that the sectarianism he refers to tends to focus on non-Muslim minorities, although it is directed towards other Muslim groups, such as Shias or non-Salafis, as well.

The attack on the Army Public School (APS) in Peshawar on 16 December 2014 was a pivotal moment in the Pakistani public's consciousness about terrorism: when 132 children were killed in their school (along with 17 staff members), there was an overwhelming outcry that something must be done. It seems that the violence escalated after the APS attack: 2017 broke records for terrorist attacks in Pakistan, particularly in February with major incidents occurring in Lahore, Sehwan (Sindh), and Balochistan.

Indeed, it appears that many of these acts of violence have been perpetrated by 'accidental guerrillas,' to use David Kilcullen's term. He proposes that many people on the ground, locally, aren't insurgents themselves but circumstances have made them take up action against the state.[2] This would, in part, explain attacks on toll booths, on the nation's motorway, on police stations, and on schools—all symbols of the state. Pape and Feldman[3] argue that the trajectory of suicide bombings closely parallels the changing military and political alliance between the US and Pakistan, especially the escalation of drone attacks that went unopposed by the Pakistani state. They contend that the 'US-inspired crackdown on militant Islamist organizations provided the impetus for local citizens to take up arms against the Pakistan government'.[4] Extremists have also been emboldened by the Salafi rhetoric often used by the state, acting on this to attack mosques and Sufi shrines,[5] laying bare the reality of a sectarian vision held by extremists that some Muslims don't practice the religion acceptably or appropriately.

The focus of this book, however, is not about why some people have become extremists and engaged in violence. It is not addressing the foundations of this extremism: how it began, what forces encouraged it, nor the roles distinct groups have played in encouraging, promoting or joining the violence. There are many conspiracy theories in Pakistan about this, and while one could spend a lifetime to get to the bottom of it, even then, much of what is unknown would remain unknown. Many people in Pakistan have tried to push me to explore this further, but I refuse: to do so valorises these acts.[6] Instead, what we will explore in the remainder of the book are the laudatory efforts of Pakistanis who want their culture back, their lives back and wish to live collectively in a future without violence. These are not 'weapons of the weak,' to use James Scott's terminology[7] of everyday forms of resistance that the disempowered have always used in a culture to resist oppression, but are rather new, innovative acts, used either to recapture local identity or to contribute to creating a new, syncretic one.

Yet Pakistan has been in a quagmire because of the violence. The idea for this research emerged from my frustration of seeing an irresolute state do little to counter violent extremism that has plagued the country since the 1979 Soviet invasion of Afghanistan let loose a barrage of violence. Tensions became further aggravated when the Pakistani state joined US efforts in its 'war on terror' campaign after 11 September 2001. The Pakistan National Counter Terrorism Authority (NACTA) recorded an uptick in violence between 2006 and 2014 (with a significant decline in 2012), as seen in Chart 1.1, and a consistent decline in significant incidents of terrorism since 2015.[8]

Terrorist acts resulting in deaths escalated in the years following the US attack on Afghanistan and jumped precipitously in 2006. As a result

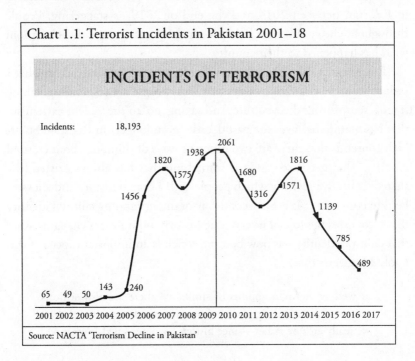

Chart 1.1: Terrorist Incidents in Pakistan 2001–18

INCIDENTS OF TERRORISM

Incidents: 18,193

2061
1938
1820
1680 1816
1575
1456 1316 1571
1139
785
489
65 49 50 143 240

2001 2002 2003 2004 2005 2006 2007 2008 2009 2010 2011 2012 2013 2014 2015 2016 2017

Source: NACTA 'Terrorism Decline in Pakistan'

of the 3,504 violent incidents since 2014, a total of 3,685 civilians, 1,514 security personnel, 7,276 extremists, and 499 'unspecified individuals,' for a total of 12,974 persons, have died in terrorist attacks as shown in Table 1.1.[9] The Islamabad-based Institute for Peace Studies calculates that 2018 experienced a 29 per cent decline in terrorist attacks.[10]

Table 1.1: Deaths from Terrorist Attacks 2014–19						
Year	Incidents of Killing	Civilians	Security Forces	Terrorists/ Insurgents/ Extremists	Not Specified	Total
2014	1570	1476	512	3,268	263	5,519
2015	950	866	341	2,408	73	3,688
2016	522	543	279	897	68	1,787
2017	295	440	215	533	81	1,269
2018	163	359	163	161	14	697
2019	136	142	141	86	0	369
Total	3,636	3,826	1,651	7,353	499	13,329
Source: South Asia Terrorism Portal						

This figure, of 13,329 individuals who have died in terrorist attacks in Pakistan between 2014 and the end of 2019, is staggering. People throughout the country are fed up with the devastation and can't fathom what has happened to their country.

This research does not focus on the devastation but instead on what I seek to valorize: the various ways that local people are responding, taking stands, recapturing their culture, and saying 'no' to the violent extremism that has manifested over the past decade (even longer) in Pakistan. Stuart Hall contends that there are two different ways of thinking about cultural identity. The first is seeing it as something that has always existed, the shared, collective identity which people with a shared history and ancestry hold in common.[11] It is his second way of understanding cultural identity that recognizes the role of intervening history and how it is changing what that cultural identity has now become which is an important focus of this book. He asserts that,

> as well as the many points of similarity, there are also critical points of deep and significant difference which constitute 'what we really are'; or rather—since history has intervened—'what we

have become.' We cannot speak for very long, with any exactness, about 'one experience, one identity', without acknowledging its other side—the ruptures and discontinuities...Cultural identity, in this second sense, is a matter of 'becoming' as well as of 'being.' It belongs to the future as much as to the past...Far from being eternally fixed in some essentialized past, they are subject to the continuous 'play' of history, culture, and power.[12]

Local groups throughout Pakistan are engaging in various kinds of social negotiations and actions to lessen the violence that has plagued the country. They are grasping what has been indigenous cultural identity and then through distinct actions that are reinterpreting it as a product of history, culture, and power, are transformatively affecting the dynamism of contemporary society. In this book, we are exploring a representative sample of what local people are engaged in, the sparks of hope that local people are creating to counter violent extremism, as we analyze why they are engaging in such actions and what they hope to accomplish. In doing so, we observe not only what people are doing but also how they are creating alternative narratives about culture and identity in Pakistan.

This book is also designed to celebrate what is flourishing in cultural performances, music, social activism, and the like in Pakistan today because of people's commitment to take stands against extremism. Much of this book's subject matter is hardly known, even within Pakistan. Each chapter seeks to demonstrate those actions and voices that best characterize these efforts; many more had to be omitted for the sake of brevity, and for that it was a judgement call.

BACKDROP TO EXTREMISM AND STATE ACTOR RESPONSES

This section provides a brief overview of what state entities are doing in their respective efforts to counter violent extremism. The Government of Pakistan did not have any distinct laws to address terrorism until 1974 when it created the Suppression of Terrorist Activities (Special Courts) Act. No special anti-terrorist legislation existed until the Anti-Terrorist Act of 1997, which was subsequently amended fourteen times in the ensuing sixteen years to expand its scope to respond to new kinds of terrorist activities. The state then created NACTA, in 2013, to be the 'focal institution' to unify the state's response to 'the menace of terrorism and extremism (that is) becoming an existential threat to the state.'[13] However, despite NACTA's existence, the political government has had limited success in responding to extremism and terrorism.

The long-delayed National Action Plan (NAP), formulated to combat violent extremism, was launched by the Government of Pakistan a week after the APS attack, on 24 December 2014. The plan focused on cracking down on madrassas (religious schools) that support religious militancy and extremism but includes nothing that addresses what is occurring in the wider society. It addresses penalties for perpetrators of violence by, for instance, lifting the moratorium on the death penalty for those convicted in terrorism cases; allowed military courts for two years to adjudicate terrorism cases; stated that purportedly strict action would be taken against those disseminating hate literature, intolerance, and terrorism; vowed to 'choke' funding of terrorism; stop religious persecution; etc. NAP is housed within NACTA with the intent to strengthen NACTA. However, as with many other initiatives in Pakistan, whether the state embarks on them with the intention to achieve something or not, political infighting and posturing has played a big role in preventing NAP to achieve most—if any—of its ambitions. Hardly any of its twenty stated goals have been implemented.[14]

This became painfully obvious in the release of the Qazi Faez Isa Commission Report in December 2016. This one-person inquiry, under the auspices of the Supreme Court of Pakistan, makes a straightforward indictment of the failure of the state to act and respond to countering terrorism and violent extremism.[15] Supreme Court Justice Qazi Faez Isa had been tasked to inquire into culpability following a deadly terrorist attack in Quetta which killed 70 and injured 112 people which followed the targeted killing of Balochistan Bar Association President, Bilal Kasi, earlier that same day, on 8 August 2016. For that attack, Isa directly blames the Federal Interior Minister, the Balochistan Chief Minister, and the Balochistan Home Minister for providing misleading information that led to significant delays in apprehending the terrorists. But the report goes on to criticize the government, overall, for its 'monumental failure to combat terrorism and perform basic protocols.'[16] In particular, it criticizes the Federal Interior Minister for lacking a 'sense of ministerial responsibility,' for meeting with the head of a proscribed organization and then denying doing so, and for not proscribing a well-known terrorist organization.[17] The report's stinging criticism of the state noted that it has ignored its own National Action Plan[18] to counter terrorism which NACTA was to have coordinated in the following words,

> The NACTA Act is not being implemented and NACTA has categorically failed: NACTA is not fulfilling its statutory mandate, NACTA's law is also not implemented by the members of its Board of Governors, which has never met, and its Executive Committee, which has met only once in three and a half years.

The report criticizes the state's lack of response to violent extremism as 'deplorable, lamentable, and totally tragic' and that it is a 'monumental failure' that the state has been unable to silence extremist speech, literature, and propaganda or in producing and then disseminating a counter narrative.[19] The report concludes by noting that Pakistan,

> was created by those who wanted to ameliorate the condition of the Muslims of the subcontinent, and to uphold the freedoms of those of every faith. The message of Unity, Faith, and Discipline was unfortunately sabotaged by hypocrites and extremists and needs to be rejected.[20]

The political government has often stepped aside to let Pakistan's military take action against extremism, but fighting violence with violence always has its consequences. The military is an institution that most Pakistanis believe will protect them from violent harm, whether the adversary is India, other external aggressors or internal actors promoting internal instability. The military has stepped in four times over Pakistan's history to seize control of the state, often quelling much (though not all) of the population's fears of instability and chaos.[21] But with the military staying on far longer during its last two times, there is a widespread consensus within the country for democratic governance over military rule.

The most crucial acts the military has taken to quell extremism have usually been through distinct military operations—each with Arabic names, not commonly understood in Pakistan—occurring in set periods of time and locales, as seen in their activities in Table 1.2 since 11 September 2001:

Table 1.2: Military Operations against Extremism in Pakistan since 11 September 2001

Military Operation	Year	Locale
Al-Mizan	2002–6	Deployed roughly 80,000 troops within FATA[22]
Rah-e-Haq	2007–9	Against the Tehreek-e-Nafaz-e-Shariat-e-Mohammadi (TNSM) and later the Tehrik-e-Taliban Pakistan (TTP) in the Swat Valley
Sher-e-Dil	2008	Bajaur Agency in FATA
Zalzala	2008–9	'Operation Earthquake', in South Waziristan Agency in FATA
Sirat-e-Mustaqeem	2008	'The Straight Path', a short-lived operation after capturing control of Bara Tehsil in Khyber Agency in FATA
Raah-e-Raast	May 2009	Second operation in Swat, to regain control over the city of Mingora in the Swat Valley
Rah-e-Nijat	October 2009	The 'Path to Salvation', again in South Waziristan Agency in FATA
Koh-e-Sufaid	July 2011	The 'White Mountain', in Kurram Agency, FATA, to gain control of the Thall–Parachinar road
Zarb-e-Azb	2013–14	The 'Strike of the Prophet Muhammad's Sword', conducted in North Waziristan Agency in FATA against the TTP, Islamic Movement of Uzbekistan, East Turkestan Islamic Movement, Lashkar-e-Jhangvi, Al-Qaeda, Jundallah, and the Haqqani Network
Radd-ul-Fasaad	2017	The 'Elimination of Discord' has been the most ambitious effort yet as 17,685 operations were launched throughout the country between February–December

There was a great deal of contention within the military leadership about launching 'Zarb-e-Azb', as the popular sentiment was that most Pakistanis were no longer supportive of these military operations. With the ascent of General Raheel Sharif as Army Chief in November 2013, he gave the final order to commence with the operation in June 2014, which became the largest and the most expansive of the nine operations conducted until then, apart from being the most deathly for extremists and military forces. Indeed, many of the TTP communications after the December 2014 attack on the Army Public School (APS) in Peshawar, said that the attack was a response to the 'savagery' unleashed during the 'Zarb-e-Azb' operations by the army.

The APS attack in Peshawar on 16 December 2014 entirely changed the military's optic on how it would confront violent extremism. This time, it was their *own* children who were killed in their school: 149 victims in total, 132 of them being children.[23] Jon Boone of *The Guardian* wrote on the first anniversary of the APS Attack that it 'spurred Pakistan into tackling domestic terrorism like never before' and that,

> Many say Pakistan itself has changed. After the attack all schools were ordered to rapidly build walls and extra defences. To the consternation of some of Pakistan's European donors the country abandoned an informal moratorium on the death penalty and has so far executed more than 300 death row prisoners.[24]

Many people consider that the 'dance' the military has engaged in for many years with different extremist groups—threatening to destroy them while giving some safe harbour, ostensibly, because they were fighting groups that the army also opposed and because of the political pressure from the highest levels within the government—stopped with that attack. Some survivor accounts revealed that the attackers asked children what their fathers do, and those who said they were in the army were shot. In the wake of the attack, which the Tehrik-e-Taliban Pakistan (TTP) claimed was revenge for the merciless 'Zarb-e-Azb' operation, the army launched massive air strikes in FATA's Khyber Agency. The army is now, constitutionally, empowered to try civilians in military courts, and many have been executed. In 2018, the army launched its first nationwide anti-terrorism operation to 'indiscriminately' eliminate terrorism from Pakistan, even in the PML-N government's bastion of Punjab, a province home to a wide range of violent groups with varying agendas where the government has long appeased these extremists. General Amjad Shoaib (retd.) commented on this announcement,

> In Punjab, particularly in southern Punjab, there are sanctuaries of hard-core militants which have not been targeted before. This time they will be taken to task, and that will help a lot in eliminating terrorism not only from Punjab but other parts of (the) country.

While the army had continued manhunts targeting extremists throughout the country, essentially political reasons had placed the Punjab off-limits for military intervention. Pamela Constable of *The Washington Post* writes that,

> Critics have been protesting this flirtation for years, warning that it could encourage the 'Talibanization' of Pakistani society and arguing that despite their different agendas, the extremist groups share common beliefs, can easily form alliances of convenience, and can be difficult to put back into a box once they gather strength and support.[25]

The army was finally able to get the Government of Pakistan's support for the latest all-inclusive assault, 'Radd-ul-Fasaad', deemed 'Reject Disorder' or 'Eliminating Discord,' which is said to be using force, intelligence gathering, and 'de-weaponizing' extremist groups throughout the country, even in Punjab. Launched on 22 February 2017, of the 17,685 operations the military conducted across Pakistan, there were 13,011 in Punjab, 2,015 in Sindh, 1,410 in Balochistan, and 1,249 in Khyber Pakhtunkhwa and FATA.[26]

In early 2019, Pakistan-based extremists purportedly encouraged a local young man, Adil Ahmad Dar, to launch a suicide attack in the Pulwama area of Indian-held Kashmir. The 14 February 2019 attack killed forty-four Indian paramilitary troops when he rammed an explosive-laden car into the Indian convoy. The Pakistan-based extremist group Jaish-e-Mohammad (JeM) immediately claimed responsibility. The Indian government soon claimed the attackers had links to the Pakistani state and retaliated by sending Indian fighter pilots who crossed the Line of Control (LoC) by Muzaffarabad into Pakistan's Azad Kashmir on 25 February, precipitating the Pakistan Air Force to shoot down one of the jets. The resultant fallout from that action allegedly brought the two countries to the brink of a military encounter and the Government of Pakistan unprecedently closed its airspace to all traffic, including domestic and international commercial flights. Prime Minister Imran Khan released the captured Indian Air Force pilot, Abhinandan Varthaman, on 1 March 2019 in a 'gesture of peace' to diffuse tensions between the two countries. While the Government of Pakistan has stood by its contention that the state played no part in the Pulwama attack, Prime Minister Khan quickly declared that he would revisit the National Action Plan to make it an effective tool to thwart extremism, and would launch 'a decisive crackdown on extremist and militant organizations'[27] in the country, revealing an awareness that the actions of extremist groups within Pakistan could prompt untoward havoc with Pakistan's neighbours, even bringing it to the brink of war—or further.

My concern about the actions of the relatively well-funded state actors in Pakistan—the political government and the military—is that the focus has been entirely on targeting people committing violent acts, to hunt them down, and kill them. As the removal of one small tumour does not eliminate cancer, although it may slow it down in the short-term, the state actors' strategy has not halted incidents of violent extremism in the long-term. In addition, fine lines—some people decry that no lines—exist between some state agents and some extremist actors. Each death evokes multiple people to seek revenge, and the growing deterioration of trust in the state provoked in part by the politically rooted Good Taliban/Bad Taliban rhetoric further diminishes the long-term results of these sweeping attacks. Extremist groups in Pakistan seem to rebound quickly, and many retain a public presence (e.g., Facebook, Twitter, Instagram), especially attractive to disaffected young idealists.[28]

Most foreign official donors operating in Pakistan have also developed formal, explicit CVE policies—to Counter Violent Extremism—but these either provide services (e.g., education opportunities, healthcare access, and job training) or opportunities *they* think up, rather than building on local initiatives. When the latter does occur, local initiatives are often appropriated to suit the intent of the donors. Some have been ill-conceived, based on stereotypes about people rather than actual local values. For example, the USAID-funded animated cartoon *The Burka Avenger*, whose protagonist wears a veil and 'fights evil', conveyed the message to young people that only with super powers could they stand up to injustice. Most have essentially had little impact on supporting local communities and have not led to greater social cohesion, solidarity, or a communal identity.[29]

I argue that what is occurring today is a concerted effort by Pakistanis themselves to bring people together at the public level to reject extremism, to recapture their cultural values and identity, and to celebrate their society. The reality is that a great number of individuals and groups in Pakistan, as we will see in this book, are engaged in doing just this.

ORGANIZATION OF THE BOOK

Local people indeed are responding to violent extremism in unprecedented ways. Many have given up on relying on a state that, by and large, has abrogated or at least hasn't fulfilled its responsibility to provide for the safety and security of its citizens. I have found that people's own experiences with violence have produced a deep resolve to change things. Individuals, local community groups, and community-based Non-Governmental Organizations (NGOs) are increasingly organizing themselves to counter violent extremism in inventive and diverse ways, completely separate from the actions of the state, the military, or global donors. The NGO, Khudi, considers that 'arguably the most powerful—and ultimately the most credible—response has come from ordinary citizens' to counter violent extremism.[30]

No scholarly research exists on what local people in Pakistan are trying to do to stop the spread of violent extremism, which is the focus of this book. Most research has instead focused either on the rise of militant extremism in Pakistan,[31] on how militant extremism is transforming Pakistan,[32] or else contestations within Pakistan between different ideas about Islam and its role in the country.[33] Instead, as with much of my earlier research, this project is based on close ethnographic study of ground realities of people's actions.

I use a representative sample of the myriad kinds of activities in which people are engaged. Based on that, I have created a typology comprised of six categories into which these various activities can be placed: poetry as resistance to violence and extremism; music and performance; art reclaiming identity and meaning; how religious leaders are mobilizing to counter extremism; innovative educational curriculum that promotes critical thinking and emphasizes peace; and other communal actions including groups standing together, other small-group and individual initiatives and activities to 'take back cultural spaces' occurring at public forums. These categories provide the substance of the ensuing chapters, all based on my meetings, interviews, and participant observation with many people and groups in various parts of the country, from Islamabad and Lahore to remote areas of Punjab, from Khairpur to Hyderabad and Karachi in Sindh, throughout Khyber Pakhtunkhwa, and discussions with

Balochis wherever I could meet with them outside of Balochistan. I did not venture to Balochistan out of my concern for the safety of anyone I would meet with there who might be viewed with suspicion for meeting with a foreign woman; such is the fragile situation existing today for activists in that province.

Throughout the country, I found local people responding quite powerfully, standing up to counter violent extremism through music, art, writing, or whatever means inspires them; the APS attack has had a huge influence on getting people to stand up and act. We find a new generation of Pashto poets who have grown up directly opposing violence: when GEO television reports on bombings in Peshawar, crowds are often heard singing Pashto anti-war and resistance poetry in the background that speaks out against hypocrisy, unrestrained power, and oppression. Their Sindhi counterparts hold on strongly to traditions of interfaith harmony laid out in the poetry of Sachal Sarmast and Shah Abdul Latif Bhittai and celebrated today in the poetry of Hafiz Nizamani, Khalil Kumbar, Saif Samejo, and Ishaq Samejo. Writing poetry that enables people to process the violence occurring around them and empowering these same people to stand up in opposition to that violence is formidable. So too is reminding people through art that local culture has value and peace is possible. These kinds of actions affect people's mindsets, enabling them to make choices to stand up for their society and against violent extremism.

Interactive theatre enables audiences to finish the dialogues of plays that address timely and compelling social issues while children are empowered to choose the endings of the online *Pasbaan* comic book stories. The Laal band travels throughout Punjab, encouraging children to stay in school so they can build Pakistan's future while Karan Khan, in his 'Peshawar Zalmi' cricket-team anthem, inspires Peshawar's youth to stand up and celebrate not only cricket but themselves and their communities. Saif Samejo created the annual two-day Lahooti Melo in interior Sindh as an opportunity to 'talk, talk, talk about peace during the day' and celebrate peace, unity, and harmony through music at night.[34] Sheema Kirmani and activists from the Hyderabad Women's Action Forum defiantly danced the *dhamaal* at Lal Shahbaz Qalandar's shrine in Sehwan in February 2017, four days after violent extremists sought to destroy it and killed nearly eighty-five people in the attack.[35] The 'Walls of Karachi' evoke powerful images that speak to cultural cohesiveness in a way similar to the artwork on the walls of Bahawalpur in southern Punjab, and the bus-stops created by the Lahore Biennale provides workers traveling under the harsh summer sun or bitter winter rains with the sense that someone in their community cares to give them shelter. Religious leaders are actively engaged in creating communities to talk with each other and bring messages of interfaith harmony to their constituencies and revisit what is the true message of Pakistan, while Pakhtuns organize for rights under the banner of the Pashtun Tahaffuz Movement (PTM) and minorities mobilize through numerous other forums. We see the long-term investments in promoting peace through innovative curricula at the Bacha Khan schools in Khyber Pakhtunkhwa and the Zoya Science Schools in southern Punjab which result in working-class children imagining themselves as actors helping build the country's future as opposed to ignored bystanders, a common sentiment among their parents today. Entities like Karachi's The Second Floor (T2F), Lahore's Books 'n Beans as well as The Last Word, and Hyderabad's Khana Badosh provide a venue for local people to have a voice and add to the requiem of activities that promote harmony and cohesiveness, while Peshawar's Khwendo Kor and Karachi's Orangi Pilot Project champion long-term incentives to promote participation, self-reliance, and unity. Importantly, they are all doing so with no expectation of support or assistance from either the Government of Pakistan or from the military.

State actors could learn important lessons from these non-state actors' playbooks. It's not about wiping out opposition, but rather about transforming how people think about their own society. Perhaps violent extremists are too caught up in the trope they believe in, but people surrounding them can envision an alternative future and not support the extremists' rants.

Notes

1. A. Basit, 'Countering Violent Extremism: Evaluating Pakistan's Counter-Radicalization and De-radicalization Initiatives', *IPRI Journal* XV, no. 2, Summer 2015, p. 47.
2. D. Kilcullen, *The Accidental Guerilla: Fighting Small Wars in the Midst of a Big One*, 2009.
3. R. Pape and J. Feldman, *Cutting the Fuse: The Explosion of Global Suicide Terrorism and How to Stop it*, 2010, p. 139.

4. Ibid., p. 163.

5. Attacks on Muslim shrines include Pir Rakhel Shah, Fatehpur 2005; Bari Imam, Islamabad 2005; Rahman Baba, Peshawar 2009; Data Darbar, Lahore 2010; Abdullah Shah Ghazi, Karachi 2010; Baba Farid, Pakpattan 2010; Sakhi Sarwar, Dera Ghazi Khan 2011; Dargah Ghulam Shah Ghazi, Maari 2013; Baba Nangay Shah, Islamabad 2014; Shah Norani, Khuzdar 2016; and Lal Shahbaz Qalandar, Sehwan 2017.

6. Some people have already criticized this, saying that I must first unearth the forces behind the violence. Those who think it is important to do that first, should set out to do so. I surmise it as an impossible task and that it takes away from where I want to place my focus: on the extraordinary acts in which people are engaged all over the country to take positions against violence and extremism and to recapture their culture and identity. Tariq Rahman makes a great effort to understand the discourses used by some Pakistani extremists in his chapter 'Pakistani Radicals' in his recent book *Interpretation of Jihad in South Asia: An Intellectual History*, 2019, pp. 216–35.

7. James C. Scott, *Weapons of the Weak: Everyday Forms of Peasant Resistance*, Yale University Press, 1985.

8. These official figures are likely far lower than the actual number of terrorist incidents. Source: https://nacta.gov.pk/terrorism-decline-in-pakistan/.

9. The South Asia Terrorism Portal (SATP), a project of the Institute for Conflict Management, a New Delhi-based NGO, lists the total number of fatalities from terrorist violence between 2002–2018, including deaths of security personnel and 'terrorists/insurgents', as 63,174, accessible at: http://www.satp.org/datasheet-terrorist-attack/fatalities/pakistan.

10. Institute for Peace Studies, *Pakistan Security Report 2018*, 6 January 2019, accessible at: https://www.pakpips.com/article/book/pakistan-security-report-2018.

11. S. Hall, 'Cultural Identity and Cinematic Representation', *Framework: The Journal of Cinema and Media*, no. 36, 1989, p. 69.

12. Ibid., p. 70.

13. NACTA's Preamble. Full details about the goals, structure, and function of NACTA are on its website accessible at: https://nacta.gov.pk/.

14. Saad Ahmed Dogar provides a comprehensive, item-by-item critique of efforts to implement NAP's twenty points in 'What has NAP achieved so far?' *The Express Tribune*, 30 January 2017, accessible at: https://tribune.com.pk/story/1307640/nap-achieved-far/.

15. The Report was released on 13 December 2016 and is accessible at: www.supremecourt.gov.pk/web/user_files/File/QuettaInquiryCommissionReport.pdf.

16. Qazi Faez Isa Commission Report, 2016, p. 85, accessible at: www.supremecourt.gov.pk/web/user_files/File/QuettaInquiryCommissionReport.pdf.

17. Ibid., p. 78.

18. NACTA's National Action Plan has twenty points, some of the most important being that militant outfits and armed gangs will not be allowed to operate in the country; there will be strict action against literature, newspapers, and magazines promoting hatred, extremism, sectarianism, and intolerance; choking financing for terrorists and terrorist organizations; establishing and deploying a dedicated counter-terrorism force;

ban on glorification of terrorists and terrorist organizations through print and electronic media; Balochistan government to be fully empowered for political reconciliation with complete ownership by all stakeholders; and dealing firmly with sectarian terrorists. The list is accessible at: https://nacta.gov.pk/nap-2014/.

19. Qazi Faez Isa Commission Report, 2016, p. 85.

20. Ibid.

21. A plethora of literature exists on the Pakistan military, its motivations for taking state power, and its capricious role in providing domestic security within the country. The best analyses include Hasan Askari Rizvi, *The Military & Politics in Pakistan, 1947–1986*, Sang-e-Meel Publications, 2000 and Aqil Shah, *The Army and Democracy: Military Politics in Pakistan*, Harvard University Press, 2014.

22. FATA was the Federally Administered Tribal Agencies, created by the British, that was comprised of seven tribal agencies and six frontier regions. They had been governed by the 1901 Frontier Crimes Regulations Act and, after Pakistan's independence in 1947, came under the direct executive authority of the President of Pakistan. On 31 May 2018, FATA was merged into the Khyber Pakhtunkhwa province of Pakistan.

23. *Dawn* newspaper has compiled a powerful, evocative memorial for each of the victims of the attack, '144 Stories: Remembering Lives Lost in the Peshawar School Attack', accessible at: https://www.dawn.com/news/1223313.

24. Jon Boone, 'Peshawar school attack: one year on "the country is changed completely",' *The Guardian*, 15 December 2015, accessible at: https://www.theguardian.com/world/2015/dec/16/peshawar-school-attack-one-year-on-the-country-is-changed-completely.

25. Pamela Constable, 'Pakistan army launches first nationwide anti-terrorism operation,' *The Washington Post*, 23 February 2017, accessible at: https://www.washingtonpost.com/world/europe/pakistan-army-launches-first-nationwide-anti-terrorism-operation/2017/02/23/36765c3e-f9cc-11e6-aa1e-5f735ee31334_story.html?utm_term=.cdc039455f49.

26. SATP has compiled these figures. *See*: http://www.satp.org/terrorism-assessment/pakistan.

27. This was declared on 4 March 2019 but as of this writing, no specific new policies have been announced. For further information on what was said *see* Baqir Sajjad Syed, 'Govt plans decisive crackdown on militant outfits,' *Dawn*, 4 March 2019, accessible at: https://www.dawn.com/news/1467524/govt-plans-decisive-crackdown-on-militant-outfits.

28. Jahanzaib Haque and Omer Bashir report on *Dawn*'s April 2017 study that found 41 of the 64 banned extremist groups have a presence on Facebook in Pakistan, as well as on many characteristics of activity surrounding their postings. *See* Jahanzaib Haque and Omer Bashir, 'Banned Outfits in Pakistan operate openly on Facebook,' *Dawn*, 5 June 2017, accessible at: https://www.dawn.com/news/1335561.

29. A different kind of insight for countering violent extremism through de-radicalization programmes, generally supported by governments and/or international donors that focus on job generation/reintegration, changing attitudes, or strengthening social bonds is found in John Horgan, 'What makes a terrorist stop being a terrorist?', *Journal for*

Deradicalization, no. 1, Winter 2014/15, pp. 1–4. For another view on how states and external actors can motivate communities and their leaders to become active in countering extremism *see* Douglas Johnston, Andrew McDonnell, Henry Burbridge, and James Patton, 'Countering Violent Religious Extremism in Pakistan: Strategies for Engaging Conservative Muslims', International Center for Religion & Diplomacy, March 2016, p. 37.

30. Published in quarterly magazine *Laaltain* in 2015. Khudi, now mostly defunct while its principals have moved on to work with other organizations, maintains a Facebook presence, accessible at: https://www.facebook.com/khudipakistan/.

31. Zahid Hussain, *The Scorpion's Tail: The Relentless Rise of Islamic Militants in Pakistan and How It Threatens America,* Free Press, 2013; Arif Jamal, *A History of Islamist Militancy in Pakistani Punjab,* Jamestown Foundation, 2011; and Ahmed Rashid, *Descent into Chaos: The U.S. and the Disaster in Pakistan, Afghanistan, and Central Asia,* Penguin Books, 2008.

32. Mentioned in A. Lieven, *Pakistan: A Hard Country,* New York, PublicAffairs, 2012 and P. Constable, *Playing with Fire: Pakistan at War with Itself,* Random House, 2011.

33. Mentioned in F. Devji, *Muslim Zion: Pakistan as a Political Idea,* Cambridge, Harvard University Press, 2013 and N. Khan, *Muslim Becoming: Aspiration and Skepticism in Pakistan,* Duke University Press, 2012.

34. Conveyed to me in discussions with Saif Samejo in January and March 2018.

35. *Dhamaal* is a trance-like dance often performed at Sufi shrines. Women Action Forum activists in Hyderabad shared their experiences with me in January 2018. The full story is recounted in 'Sheema Kirmani defies act of terrorism, performs at Lal Shahbaz Qalandar's shrine', *Dawn,* 21 February 2017, accessible at: https://images.dawn.com/news/1177132.

2 | Poetry as Resistance to Violence and Extremism

> *Sow flowers that your surroundings become a garden.*
> *Don't sow thorns for they will prick your own feet.*
>
> Rahman Baba (Pashto Sufi poet)

> *My heart doesn't agree with the discourse of priests.*
>
> Sachal Sarmast (Sindhi Sufi poet)

Formidable expressions countering violent extremism can be found in the written word throughout Pakistan. The Sufi tradition is particularly important whether in the Pashto poetry of Rahman Baba in Pakhtun areas and in Sindh where Sachal Sarmast and Shah Abdul Latif Bhittai remain revered, and each of these traditions have powerful contemporary manifestations. Importantly, the Pashto and Sindhi traditions give voice to those standing against established power, against domination, and represent a social heritage that is often hidden in mainstream Pakistan. The choice of language used in poetry is itself a political statement on the part of the writer,[1] and we see this manifest in Pashto and Sindhi resistance poetry as both Pakhtuns and Sindhis are very proud of the language in which the poetry is written as being their own. The fiery passion emanating within the Pashto tradition belies the stereotyped warrior trope while the Sindhi poetic tradition also conveys the syncretic values within this multicultural society and the inherent audacity of its cultural distinctiveness.

This chapter, therefore, focuses on the two main strands of resistance poetry in Pakistan—Pashto and Sindhi—that have their roots in countering oppression and subjugation and are today being availed to reassert authentic local identity. Influential poets writing in Pakistan's national language, Urdu, such as Faiz Ahmed Faiz, Habib Jalib, and Ahmad Faraz, have opposed the excesses of the state in their poetry but unlike Pashto and Sindhi resistance poets, they were not mobilizing large communities through their verses. So, too, is the case of notable contemporary Punjabi poets (e.g., Kishwar Naheed and Harris Khalique), whose poetry is either opposed to the excesses of the state, celebrates their cultural influence on local society, or searches out their own contemporary cultural identity.[2] Instead, the Pashto and Sindhi poetic traditions not only resist subjugation and oppression, they also manifest as 'arenas of struggle' as Barbara Harlow explains,

> Poetry is capable not only as serving as a means for the expression of personal identity or even nationalist sentiment. Poetry, as a part of the cultural institutions and historical existence of a people, is itself an arena of struggle.[3]

Writing resistance poetry is part of an historical process which requires a writer to 'take sides' and oppose injustice and oppression.[4] Aamer Raza[5] considers Pashto poetry to be an ideological tool that retains an important place in society and has been a 'representation of resistance through the ages.' Indeed, what makes Pashto poetry a distinct form of resistance is its relentlessness to uphold Pashtunwali (i.e., Pakhtun values and mores) as a means to restore the honour and glory of Pakhtuns. It is within this moral code that the pride and loyalty of a Pakhtun is evoked to resist the Taliban and other extremist groups. It is not based on allegiance either to a country (Pakistan or Afghanistan) or even to a religion, but rather evokes culture and identity, especially the reinforcement of one's identity as a Pakhtun. Yet this poetry also has a complex, dialectical relationship with Pakhtun identity, which appears in the classical poetry of Khushal Khan Khattak as honour-bound warriors and that of Rahman Baba as tolerant and peaceful. Today, however, we can consider these two categories of identity as progressive/non-violent (being discussed in this chapter) and radical/violent (the poetry of the Taliban and other extremists). This portrayal of Pakhtuns in Pashto poetry, too, is in stark contrast to how Pakhtuns have been portrayed by others. In effect, local poetry can emerge as resistance simply by putting forth one's own account rather than being portrayed by someone else as an anti-colonial, anti-imperialist endeavour.

Harlow[6] finds Baloch poetry to be even more extreme as an arena of struggle to capture identity as there is 'a sadness engendered by an ongoing struggle, a struggle not yet consummated.' There is a long history of Baloch struggling for greater autonomy and agitating for their rights, and the active the nationalist resistance, especially for a greater voice, continues. In Pakistan today, many poets from Balochistan, such as Khan Zaman Kakar and Arif Tabassum, are writing in Pashto as they are ethnic Pakhtuns and identify with the Pakhtun resistance.

Poetry is also easily accessible in areas that have a strong oral tradition, such as Pakistan. Poetry recitations, *mushairas*, have a long tradition in this area and as Qaisar Abbas notes,[7] *mushairas* and musical renderings of poems have provided a popular public voice and tend to transcend social and class boundaries. The popularity of mobile smartphones has enabled fast transmission of poetry—and notifications about upcoming *mushairas*—widely.

PASHTO POETRY

Much can be understood about the power and influence of contemporary poetry by first examining the legacy of what came before it. Rahman Baba, in his poetry, captures the essence of the historical resistance to injustice and domination that characterizes Pakhtun society. He is widely considered to be the most popular Pashto poet of all time, baring the zeitgeist of Pakhtun values. Robert Sampson,[8] a translator of Rahman Baba's poetry, considers that his *Diwan* captures 'the essence of what it means to be a Pakhtun Muslim.' Khadim Hussain[9] writes that Rahman Baba is a symbol of 'humanity, pluralism, non-violence, and the collective aesthetics of the Pashtuns.' Given the tremendous importance of Rahman Baba for Pakhtuns, it was overwhelmingly devastating when violent extremists blew up his *mazar* (tomb) in Hazarkhani, south of Peshawar, on 6 March 2009. One reporter writing about the bombing called it 'a rude awakening for many on how the militants have started attacking sites that are considered holy by many.'[10] Khadim Hussain[11] sees the attack on the shrine as an effort 'to destroy the collective cultural symbols of the Pashtuns.' The attack by these extremists who consider themselves to be 'orthodox Muslims,' or salafis, is in marked contrast to Rahman Baba's message of love, peace, and selfless sacrifice for one's community.

Said to have been born in 1650, Rahman Baba has been described by storytellers as a reclusive Sufi, often strumming a rabab. While much of his poetry addresses love or God, there is also an important component that addresses society and serving humanity. This can be seen in a short poem in his *Diwan*,

> Sow flowers so your surroundings become a garden,
> Don't sow thorns, for they will prick your feet.
> If you shoot arrows at others,
> Know that the same arrow will come back to hit you.
> Don't dig a well in another's path,
> In case you come to the well's edge.
> You look at everyone with hungry eyes,
> But you will be first to become mere dirt.
> Humans are all one body,
> Whoever tortures another, wounds himself.

Rahman Baba is known for having once said that he is 'not made for violence,' a stance far different—and more accurate—than that of the stereotyped martial Pakhtuns. His opposition to violence and preference for harmony, as well as his cognition of the impermanence of life, emerges in another poem from his *Diwan*,

> Come on! Don't be cruel to anyone.
> This brief life is wasted without love.
> None remain in the world;
> All are to leave, whether today or tomorrow.
> Those friends who are seen today;
> All will be gone in a day or two.
> If you like their looks, gaze at them!
> For once they are gone they will never come again.
> Once autumn leaves are detached from the branch;
> The scientist can never graft them back by wisdom.
> When a raindrop falls to the earth from the sky,
> It can never go back up to the sky.
> Don't imagine they will come back to your eyes,
> The tears that your eyes have shed.
> Each day the rising sun is different;
> The one that sets never rises again…
> If there is life in the world it is this:
> That it is spent with others in laughter.[12]

Rahman Baba's message reverberates in the new generation of Pashto poets who have grown up directly opposing violence; when GEO television reports on bombings in Peshawar, crowds are often heard singing Pashto anti-war poetry in the background. Poetry traditionally plays an important role in Pakhtun society but until recent times when recited at a *mushaira* (poetry recital), it has often either glorified God, romance, or recounted the military exploits of Pakhtuns in history. Today, however, with violence and suicide bombings surrounding them, poets in Khyber Pakhtunkhwa are speaking out about hypocrisy, power, and oppression. A study conducted by the FATA Research Centre on the impact of the 'war on terror' on Pashto poetry and art found that their messages often mirror changes taking place in the society,

> The ongoing conflict…brought about significant changes to the institutions as well as to the values, traditions and cultural norms of the region. The values and traditions of a society are captured and represented by the literature of its time…society and literature feed into each other and thus cannot be separated. The war on terror and the violence that it transported to Pashtun society resulted in literary elements of violence and resistance to begin appearing in the region.[13]

Literature and poetry, therefore, can be used both as a tool for domination or as an instrument to raise a voice against injustice and exploitation. After Pakistan joined the US in its 'war on terror' in mid-2012, Pashto poetry was transformed,

> The bloodshed, bomb blasts, drone attacks, and aerial firing compelled writers to forget evergreen topics of love, romance, and nature. The violent circumstances that rose from the ashes of 9/11 compelled Pashto literati to write about broken families, severed limbs, war-torn infrastructure (mosques and schools), and displaced people rather than silky curls and rosy cheeks of their beloved.[14]

Khadim Hussain of the Bacha Khan Trust Education Foundation argues that religious extremists—'fanatics'—in Khyber Pakhtunkhwa have sought, deliberately, to deprive people of secular outlets to accelerate the spread of extremism. Shaheen Buneri notes that Pashto poets are responding powerfully,

> using some of the very arts that religious fundamentalists seek to destroy—poems adapted to traditional Pashto music. In Taliban-heavy areas such as Kurram, Orakzai, Waziristan, Bajaur, Mohmand, Khyber, and Dir, literary gatherings, including *mushairas* (poetry recitals), have become a refuge for traumatized communities.[15]

Sher Alam Shinwari adds that 'every poem created by a poet challenges the Taliban mindset' which many Pashto poets consider to be a foreign import. Talimand Khan argues that 'traditionally, the Pakhtuns have used poetry as an effective weapon of resistance against foreign occupation, the deprivation of their rights, and subsequently, against what is seen as state-sponsored religious radicalization.'[16] Khadim Hussain agrees with that sentiment and contends that Pashto poetry today connects youth 'to a national identity increasingly jeopardized by sectarian violence and conflict.'[17] Its target audience, symbols, and metaphors are shifting as the socio-political conditions are changing, especially given the proliferation of violence in Pakhtun areas. Rahmat Shah Sail contends that while poetry can be cathartic for people, in Khyber Pakhtunkhwa 'it is being suffocated by the continuous fear of terrorism and threats.'[18] He said that whenever he wants a change from the spectacular mountains and beautiful flowers in his village outside of Dargai in Swat, then he loves to go to Peshawar and enjoy the dust and crowds of the city.[19] Sail's well-known poem, 'Peshawar', captures the grief of Pakhtuns who mourn the violence that has overcome the historic 'city of flowers' and in effect, their lives in general,

> I always called you a city of flowers; how can I see you ripped
> apart by bombs!
> I keep your picture forever inside of my shattered heart.
> Oh Peshawar! How can I just let you be blasted by bombs!
>
> Whenever anyone has praised the beauty of London to me,
> Your picture in my heart mocks them with a thin smile.
> Whenever someone has sung in praise of Paris' evenings, your
> Saddar[20] awakens my heart.

When I hear those who praise the mansions of Washington, then
  your beloved Qissa Khwani[21] embraces me.
When I hear those talking about the evenings of Delhi, then I
  recall wandering in the evenings in every street of Peshawar.
Your dust is dearer to me than the colours of spring!
How can I see you be destroyed by bombs?!

When I would get tired of enjoying the mountains, beauty and
  nature,
I would come to experience your frantic pace and I would feel
  relaxed.
When I recollect my sleepless nights, if you would just keep me
  awake, then I would feel I have had a sound sleep.

I would feel thirsty by the side of rivers and ponds,
But when I come back to you, Oh Peshawar, my thirst is gone.
When my brain becomes fatigued in the presence of mountains
  and flowers,
Then I would think about your dust, and it would come to my
  senses like the fragrance of flowers.
You have always been in love with me, so how can I see you be
  destroyed by bombs?

I ran away from seeing the glory of heaven with my soul,
Instead I smiled inside your smoke and kissed your dust.
Listen Peshawar, when the flesh of your dearest people is flying in
  the air like the petals of a flower, I watch in silence, because I
  have no power.
When your beautiful blood turns into drizzling rain,
I perform your funeral rituals with tears in my eyes, for I have no
  power.
O my beloved Peshawar! I am not mute but what can I do?
I cannot say anything because my tongue is wounded.

Nowadays, I am standing on the line between life and death.
Who is going to give me a voice when all the cries of Pakhtuns
  are wounded?
Until you realize who is bombing us, the mud houses will continue
  to be set on fire.

Until we are not united, our collective honour will be torn into
    pieces.
The poor will be killed and the leaders will just discuss what is
    happening.
O Peshawar! Our fate is soaked in blood.

In another poem, he bemoans the state and the agony that Pakhtuns find
themselves in, today,

PAKHTUN

Oh time, if yesterday you displaced or killed a Pakhtun,
Today, whether you accept it or not, the Pakhtuns have awakened.
The whole world will get tired but it won't be able to drown the
    Pakhtuns.
We are spread across the plains and mountains,
There is a tablet that has been carved with the names of the nations
    of the world;
Pakhtuns have forcibly written their names on it with blood.
I accept that we haven't yet arrived at the summit,
But we have climbed many rungs up the ladder.
Maybe he is illiterate, but those literate people also have not read
    about Pakhtuns.
Though time has made scratches all over his face, but still the
    Pakhtun is so beautiful.
His own land has not devoured the Pakhtun, but some of its own
    people have been devoured by others.
Different ages have highly praised Pakhtuns but the present day
    world underestimates his worth.
Behind the veil with his hand on his mouth, Oh Sail,
He is lost in his own land, he has not gone anywhere else.[22]

Rahmat Shah Sail has published fifteen books of poetry and is about to
publish his fourth prose book. He is passionate about how the West ignores
what is actually happening to Pakhtuns and how their culture is being
tragically destroyed. He is frustrated with this neglect,

If I can listen to the cry of each and every Western child,
Why can't they listen to the cries of our children?

Children, whether they belong to the West or the East,
Their style of smiling and crying is just the same.[23]

In this vein, he is deeply concerned about how the West misunderstands Pakhtuns and their culture,

The world hasn't learned how to be friends with us,
The world has always misinterpreted us.[24]

Akbar Sial is even more direct in his admonishment of the violence in Pakhtun areas and its perpetrators,

Don't snatch the pen from our hand with which we make the
    picture of our dreams.
Don't create violence in our village.
Don't bring mayhem to our village.
Don't turn this ancient playground into a blood-red ammo dump.[25]

Talimand Khan cites the deteriorating situation in Swat and the initial vague role of the state to counter the Taliban with the proliferation of resistance poetry there in the past decade. Hanif Qais cites this contradiction when he writes,

It is not only you burning,
My heart is also roasting.
O Swat! They have set you ablaze—
Whether boots or turban.[26]

Shaheen Buneri states that the contest between secular and religious values in Amjad Shehzad's poetry could not be starker,

Even now some people in my village say,
All destinies are shaped in the skies.
Tell the mullah we are not the people who follow his chants,
Our hearts are pacified only with the sounds of singing.[27]

Khan Zaman Kakar, a Pashto poet from Balochistan working towards a doctoral degree in anthropology at Quaid-i-Azam University in Islamabad, an Awami National Party (ANP) member and leading PTM activist, contends that Pashto poetry is primarily resistance poetry, 'fighting, encountering the invaders, in one way or another,' as the history of the region is the history of resistance. He belongs to a progressive literary circle where they believe that literature should take a side—it cannot be neutral— and should resist oppression, terrorism, and war and reclaim the land which is their own. He says it doesn't belong to the terrorists and they must side with people who are fighting against the terrorists. He has never seen an influential poet who appreciates war, terrorism, or *mujahids*. Pashto poets generally resent the way their society has been represented. They are secular and non-violent and believe in political solutions to political problems as they criticize the policies of the state and the global community, at large. It emerged during the colonial era when the British wrongly associated Pakhtuns with violence and guns. Pashto poets have to challenge these stereotypes that Pakhtuns are savage, tribal people,[28]

> Every house has the *diwan* [poetry] of Rahman Baba,
> But still the homeland is being burned in the fire of war.
> Ideas of destruction are not current only in the minds of the
>   congregation of mosques,
> We can see a mullah [symbol of religious conservatism] and a devil
>   in every person.

> The rope that strangled our Najeeb's[29] neck yesterday,
> Today, that same rope wraps itself around his killer.
> Those who had the hand of Bacha Khan placed on their heads,
> They don't need the gold medals of the state.[30]

In his poetry, Kakar seeks to speak truth to power, declaring that not only have Pakhtun lands been devastated but the privacy of their lives has also been taken away from them, as seen in the following couplet of a longer *ghazal*,

> I am sending you the picture of the demolished bazaar of
>   Miramshah,
> I am telling you nothing more about the decline of our honour.
> I want to block the ways of mullahs' thoughts in our homeland,
> That's why I am writing poems in praise of girls' beauty.
> A nationalist is one who wants his/her homeland's freedom,

A nationalist is not someone who just carries a red flag.

If you're writing our private stories in Punjab's newspapers,
Would you think I would not call you a traitor?[31]

Sher Alam Shinwari has assessed that since 2014, there has been an unusually large number of Pashto books and poems published, mostly on topics related to militancy, suffering of people, and restoration of lasting peace in the region. Most poetry written after 9/11 is laden with grief and frustration, but also love and yearning for a bygone way of life. Pashto poets have openly condemned extremism in general and in Khyber Pakhtunkhwa and FATA in particular, often focusing on various aspects of the ongoing militancy.

This 'raised voice' can be heard in the poetry of Abdul Rahim Roghani of Swat, whose poetry has become renowned over the past forty years.[32] The spread of Taliban influence in Swat during the Muttahida Majlis-e-Amal's (MMA) government in Khyber Pakhtunkhwa (2003–8) served as an impetus for him to fight back fervently through his poetry which he regards as fighting against backwardness, corruption, and terrorism; he considers corruption as the seed of terrorism. He criticizes the current state of education in Pakistan, noting that it has failed its people in that while education can teach technology, it is not teaching respectability, honesty, or civilized behaviour. So too, while it can help with skill-development, it cannot improve the justice system and laws. He stands up to corruption, hypocrisy, and injustice with his poetry, which now commands a huge following through cultural performances, often transmitted on television and YouTube. He feels that many people understand the cruelty perpetrated by the upper-class and the religious elite, and now the public is using some stanzas from his verses in their conversations. He asserts that the impact his poetry has on people is like *jaadu* (magic)—they suddenly begin to hate the religious extremists. He sees the mullahs as saying 'don't worry about this world, don't pay attention to work in this world' but that's wrong. His poetry is the opposite of this; he tells people that those who say this are our enemies, preventing us from experiencing development.[33]

Roghani's poetry speaks to how terrorism and political corruption have embroiled Pakhtuns in a conflict not of their making, ultimately transforming their society,

> They take your conscience, they take your faith, and they take your belief.
> They gave the peace-loving Pakhtuns a bad name for no real reason and made them fight *jihad*.
> What is tragic is that they have taken away Pakhtuns' love for the things of this world.
> Oh Lord, shield your Satan, for these people are so satanic that they will take away the Pakhtuns' fear of Satan.[34]

He frequently criticizes political and religious leaders, as in the following six short poems,

> When the Imam [religious leader] has become Satan and the person who delivers the sermon is his son,
> Oh leader, the moment you gain political power, you become a looter and a plunderer and we are cursed.
> When the *pir* presents something to you in the darkness, it loses its essence because Muslims are divided into countless groups,
> When the scholar remains silent, then that nation, oh Roghani, will always suffer destruction.[35]

> We need him, a minister,
> We the people did this good deed.
> Here in this world, when you do good, you do not get good in return.
> Now for the next five years, as minister, he will eat the flesh of our bodies.[36]

> The minister sits before the television and watches televised dramas all night long,
> His conscience remains asleep.
> His people will wake in the morning yearning for his service,
> Yet he will not stir.[37]

> We have to leave our narrow-mindedness behind,
> Without doing this, one cannot expect to progress.

> Come, let us [Pakhtuns, collectively] together get rid of the person
> who preaches,
>
> This preacher brings no good to anyone, so let us get rid of him
> for good.[38]
>
> These slogans of Islam that you hear all over your land and
> mountains,
> This slogan of *jihad, jihad,* and *Allahu Akbar* that you hear,
> If you look into their hearts and you really listen,
> Then instead of *Allahu Akbar,* you will see the dollars that are
> behind this.[39]
>
> Who is behind the division of this land?
> Who captured power and became the king [the person holding
> power]?
> God made this land but it is being controlled by someone else.
> Neither does God have a portion nor does Roghani.[40]

He also has a universal vision, that Pakistanis are part of the global
community and have much in common with the rest of the world, as
comes through in the following poem,

> Whether he is from the West or the East, he is a human being.
> We share the same feelings, the same assets, and we share the world.
> We live in different geographic regions.
> The reason there are so many different languages is for us to express
> our feelings effectively.
> A way of communication.
> If a Pakhtun wears a shalwar with two *panchas* [legs],
> A Westerner also wears trousers with two *panchas.*[41]

A close colleague of Abdul Rahim Roghani's is Usman Olasyar, founder of
the Suastu Cultural Centre in Mingora, Swat. In addition to organizing and
popularizing *mushairas* in the area, the organization also mobilizes people
to advocate for peace and human rights. This commitment can be seen in
one of Olasyar's poems,

The Khan [political leader] is seated on one shoulder, the mullah
[religious leader] sits on the other,
And the *pir* [religious saint] is seated on my back and refuses to
move.
The three of them torment me; I don't earn as much for myself as
I do for them.
I feel battered by them, just as I batter my sitar.[42]

Dr Abaseen Yousafzai, a celebrated Pashto poet and Chairperson of the
Department of Pashto at Islamia College University in Peshawar, perceives
that the fallout from 11 September has impacted every aspect of life in
Pakistan, including Pashto poetry and literature. He claims that contrary to
the ideas that many outsiders hold about Pakhtuns, as history has witnessed,
they have never fought against anyone deliberately.[43] Instead, they have only
fought to protect their people, to protect women, or even to protect their
animals; this has only been done for self-defence, never as offense. Pakhtuns
say that peace is *sach* (truth) and violence is bad. He pointed out,

> Pakhtuns have a rich culture, and there is tolerance, love, love of
> peace; Pakhtuns never want to kill anyone. What has happened
> is against our culture. They don't choose to hurt children, elderly
> or women—they won't fire against those three groups for *any*
> reason. If they're in a *jirga* [meeting] or *hujra* [meeting place],
> they question why have you troubled women or children or
> elderly. This is not Pakhtun culture to blow up a mosque or a
> funeral procession.

He reflects that in Pakhtun culture, people always talk about humanity. As
Pakhtuns love their religion (Islam), it requires them to love others. But
people now, in his area, have no rights,

> Here, people are killed, sacrificed, parents are afraid that when their
> children go to the university, will they return? It's barbarism if you
> don't like what someone says and you kill them.

This prompts him and others to be worried about the future, hoping that
Pakhtun children will be well-educated, whether in government schools
or *madrassas* (religious schools). He thinks that Pakhtun children should

study in Pashto-medium schools, although they should also learn English and Urdu and other languages like Arabic and Chinese. While they should learn other languages, they should not forget their own language, so at least Pashto should be a compulsory subject. He became involved and worked with the Khyber Pakhtunkhwa Textbook Board when it was redesigning curriculum for K-12 grades to try to ensure this. In his poetry, he hopes to convey to the world that Pakhtuns love peace, to show who they really are, and that Pakhtuns are not what those who are spreading propaganda and a bad image of them are purporting. In his poem 'Angai' (Echo)—a powerful, difficult, and violent poem—he writes about Pakhtun children in camps who aren't being educated, and that they will be afraid of the world and become dangerous for the world,

ANGAI (Echo)

I am Gulab Khan, nine-year old
While my sister Palwasha is five
We are from Kabal in Swat, but now sitting in a tent far from our
    village.
My elder brother was stabbed to death far away on a hill,
Until now nobody knows about the murderer.
My uncle was shot dead over violation of curfew,
His clothes burnt while his chest riddled with bullets.
My dad ran a sweetshop in the village,
He lost his life in a nearby explosion.
His charred dead body was taken to our home
Only five persons showed up at his funeral.
None appeared over his mourning ceremony because of war and
    armed conflict.
Similar was the fate of our mom,
We couldn't have a chance to have a glimpse of her face
No pre-burial ceremony was held, a missile hit our living room
In a moment our home was reduced to rubble
Before long, our neighbours reached for rescue,
Our mom and grandma had perished.
There was fire all around, everything was reduced to ashes.
Some bigots exploded our school too,

A part of the mosque wall broke down.
We hurriedly walked to our aunt
She took us along to this tent.
Have a look at the tattered mat,
For us this tent is village, *hujra* and mosque.
O! Black and White people of the world, listen!
These are grandkids of your grandparents
Come over and guide them to a right track
If you remain silent and don't do anything
And if they grow up violent,
Then you won't ever have a sound sleep.

Abaseen wrote 'Best Painting' right after 9/11, and used up four pens while writing it because of his emotions,

BEST PAINTING[44]

At a world paintings exhibition are people from every country,
A din of whites and blacks prevail.

Painters from all countries are stunned with masterpieces and the
    works of mountains and rivers,
Pretty, rosy, charming damsels,
Deserts, rocks, plants and flowers painted with blood.
Art expressing the soul of the artist; amazed, they scan the shades.

In the meantime, I note a painting attracting a thick mob.
I too gaze with curiosity, to find out what is so unusual.
An infant lies, drenched in blood, green smoke hides the
    background.
In a bookstand beside the infant, there's a book wrapped in a green
    piece of cloth.[45] A muslin scarf lies in dust.

He holds fast a nipple in his left hand.
A talisman, in red and white thread, around his neck, lies on her
    chest, a cheek plastered with dust, the eyes bulging out, and
    mouth open.
Died of fear!
Having thrown open his hands as if yearning for the lap of mother.

Under his shoulders and back, some curls of the lace.
Beside the sandy bed, under his thigh and hip, a corner of wrapper
    is also seen.

Lie a few curdled red drops, on the lower line of ribs,
A bullet has pierced, dissecting the chest and hip,
Of which drips out barbarism, blood oozing from the torso,
Having soaked the small delicate penis, which was seen but dimly.
Freshly circumcised, a shell-ring adorning a foot.

Over the frame of the painting, by a thin thread, a paper dangles,
Which reads: 'USA. Best Painting of the Century.'

Another poem, simply titled 'Ghazal' (Poem) also speaks to how life for Pakhtuns was transformed by violence following 9/11,

GHAZAL[46]

Why are the streets of Bagram deserted, the ever-chanting city
    silent?
Why are Malakand and Tatara lying still?
Why doesn't the shepherd's flute play in the hill?
Many a sweet-throated nightingale sang here.

Why are your musical lips pressed today?
They did not let me speak a word.
Why are Eids and the market days dull,
Not a sound rises from the festive green?

Why are the streams of every village so desolate,
The clanking bowls of cheerful girls heard no more?

He prefers to recite poetry in a large hall so that everyone at the *mushaira* are involved and respond to him while he's reciting the poetry. He delivered the following poem, 'Ihtijaj' (Protest), in front of a huge audience in Wadudia Hall in Saidu Sharif, Swat, in 2011 after people had returned following the Taliban takeover of the area and the subsequent military attack to rout them out. When he recounted the poem to me for this book, he requested I leave intact the audience's responses which, for clarity, I have inserted in italics below,

IHTIJAJ (PROTEST)

I am in search of a doctor for the political and spiritual diseases
    of the nation.
Where are the youth who can sacrifice for their nation?
Your funerals have been exploded? (*Yes!*)
Have your mosques been exploded? (*Yes!*)
Your religion and your business were damaged and exploded. Did
    you protest? (*No!*)
How you can speak truth—this is the reason for the explosion and
    the destruction.

You are not like your forefathers. You have lost the glory of your
    forefathers.
Young children were killed in front of thousands of your mothers,
Then your sisters are weeping a lot for their brothers.
The widows are waiting for food, they are begging for food in the
    streets.
So did you protest against this misery, or not? (*No!*)
There is no Gaju Khan nor Bhakoo Khan,[47] and so what happened
    has happened.
You do not have the qualities of your forefathers.

Now you also cannot enjoy your celebrations, no gathering is
    possible, and why?[48]
There is bloodshed at your *jirgas*; *hujras* were disgraced;[49] did you
    protest? (*No!*)
Where is Multan Khan and Ajab Khan[50] so they can come forward
    and save you from the enemy?
You do not have the qualities of your forefathers.

Have your enemies entered your house or not? (*Yes!*)
Have they put the barrel of the rifle to your head? (*Yes!*)
You can't sleep because you are afraid of your enemies and you are
    worried about your future.
Did you protest? (*No!*)
Where is the Afghan Napolean, Omra Khan Jandool?
Did you protest? (*No!*)
You do not have the qualities of your forefathers.

Your blood has become worthless, you change houses at midnight
  due to these enemies and your fears of terrorism.
The schools for your children were destroyed. Did you protest?
  (No!)
Where is Darya Khan Afridi and Emal Khan Mohmand who
  fought against the Mughals at Khyber?
You do not have the qualities of your forefathers.

Was your history destroyed or not?[51] (Yes!)
I am just asking if your history was destroyed or not. (Yes!)
Were your heroes and values destroyed in front of you? (Yes!)
Is hate, hate and hate everywhere? (Yes!)
Did you protest? (No!)
Where is Pir Rohan and Bacha Khan?[52]
You do not have the qualities of your forefathers.

Is the nation fed up with people like the Mughals? (Yes!)
Has every black face become our master or not?[53] (Yes!)
Are the blue-eyed (the British) ruling over us or not? (No!)
Did you protest? (No!)
Where is Sartor Faqir Mastaan, shot repeatedly by the British in
  Malakand?
You do not have the qualities of your forefathers.

Are people stuck in their own troubles?
Are people looking forward to the Day of Judgement?
Our lions have become jackals; did you protest? (No!)
Where is Khushal Khan to awaken the Pashtun nation?
You do not have the qualities of your forefathers.

Where is that person who will cure the diseases of the nation?
I know my careless and proud nation; I know about these people
  who use Islam for their own purposes.
I know about the prize and reward of truth.
I also know what caused the end of Mansoor[54] and of Socrates.

After completing the poem and reciting it to his brother, his brother
became upset, questioning why he is writing poems like this, and that he
shouldn't do so because it's risky. His brother didn't call him for a month.

But Yousafzai considers that this is the power of poetry, and he always tries to speak it.

Hasina Gul of Mardan also uses poetry as a way to counter violent extremism. She has broken social barriers by becoming a famous poet as this is a domain, especially in Pakhtun society, dominated by men. She sees herself as a symbol of resistance today. When she began writing poetry, it was about love and romance but that was short-lived. As tragic events unfurled in her area, the inspiration for her poetry became war and conflict; the attacks on the Army Public School (APS) in Peshawar in December 2014, and the terrorist attack at Bacha Khan University in Charsadda in January 2016 motivated her further to speak out. She also draws inspiration for her poetry from the oppression women face in her society, and how they are not given a decision-making role in their lives.[55]

After the APS attack, Hasina went to Swat to recite her poetry and said that the people in the audience were crying because they were overcome with emotion,

> They said that we are peace-loving too, and they have had it with war and conflict. They said we don't just want this for Swat, but we want this for the whole world. Ultimately, we want to do away with the concept of war altogether. A great number of people are upset these days, and this was their reaction. These people have to die for a war they didn't start… The casualties of war aren't just our lives, it's also our dignity, our children. We are right in the storm's eye, the centre of war. We are the ones who are made to fight; we are the ones who perish. Yet they are the ones who win the war. It is their fate to win, as it is ours to lose.
>
> Pakhtuns are very innocent, trusting people. If someone speaks to them nicely, they are willing to give them anything, even their guns. This is why we fight their wars. This is the problem we face.

Her poetry expresses these sentiments, very powerfully, to her listeners,

> I will not tolerate any wrongful power, I cannot call something
>   that is wrong, right.

But when I look around me, all these oppressive walls, all these suppressive shackles, my lips are sealed and they have deafened my ears.

The oppressive society's eyes bore into me and they swipe at my neck with their claws, trying to silence me, so that no one may find out about my plight.

They want me to listen to them and obey them, but never complain or question.

I wish I could gouge their [oppressive society's] eyes out and break their suppressing claws.

But to no avail, they keep coming for me, tormenting me.

They bind my hands and my feet, and they justify it by telling me where I'll go and to who I'll go.

I look around me, and there's no one I can turn to.

I haven't a home so I bow my head and poison myself, because I refuse to call what is wrong, right.

Sometimes I resist, sometimes I bite my tongue.

Another poem speaks to her frustration of not seeing an end in sight to the violence that is decimating life around her,

Murderers! Tyrants! Enough!

This land has turned scarlet with all the innocent blood that you have spilled.

Eyes have run out of tears to cry at the cemeteries.

Form a *jirga* to bring love to everyone.

Peshawar will be young again.

Nangarhar [in Afghanistan] will have spring again.

Kabul will smile again.

Even death is appalled by what you have done.

Death was something to look forward to when the time was right, but you take people away before their time.

We would look forward to being on our deathbeds and being surrounded by loved ones who would give us a peaceful send-off.

People would go to schools; they would live in harmony and unity, and strangers were treated with utmost respect.

I would have been content that I lived a long, happy life.

But murderers, tyrants! You have showered us with bullets of hate and sorrow.

Please listen to me for a bit; please rest your arms for a lot of blood
has been spilt.

She considers that her poetry recitations affect her audiences' thoughts and actions. She recounts that people have come up to her after a *mushaira* and said we don't want anything to do with this, 'We don't want to engage in war, we want to educate our children, and we want to empower our women. We want to be able to bring about progress.' But the rampant terrorism she sees, such as suicide bombings are impeding all the efforts that people are taking to progress,

> This is our biggest problem. The reason they attack us in the first place is they don't want us to develop, to bring about progress. This is what impedes our efforts. I have a son, and I want him to get an education, to have a bright future, and I don't want him to be exposed to any sort of danger. But unfortunately, that is not the case. When he goes to college, I wonder whether I'll ever see him alive again or not. I get a lot of threatening hate mail but I'm resilient; I feel if something is to happen, then it will happen. I consider myself to be a symbol for the women in my community. If I resign myself to the house, what will become of those women? What will become of the girls? I play with danger. I'm not always accompanied by the men in my family, and I can't just sit at home. All this time that I've struggled, I can't just throw it away by sitting at home. I will make sure my voice reaches the powers that I address through my poetry.

Pakistan bestowed upon her its highest civilian award—the Tamgha-i-Imtiaz—on Republic Day, 23 March 2017, in recognition of her poetry. But while the Pakistan government recognizes her efforts, she doesn't think they will do anything else to cultivate awareness and spread the message she is trying to make among the masses. Through her poetry, she hopes that the feelings she is able to evoke will help people to spread this message among their community. A final poem here captures this sentiment,

> If a house could be built like this, the dream that you have seen I
> have seen as well.
> But alas, our current circumstances have taken our dreams away
> from us.

But I still dream of that house where I will live with you, where all
  our desires will be fulfilled.
Full of love, I shall wear clothes and jewellery of flowers.
Our whole community will break into song, and peace shall prevail
  everywhere.
We shall help solve one another's problems together and the face
  of hatred will be destroyed.
Everyone shall dance and engage in merrymaking at local carnivals.
It will be the season of adorning yourself in henna, dupattas, and
  chadors.
It is the dream of Bacha Khan, it is the vision of Samad Khan, it
  is Greater Afghanistan.

Arif Tabassum, an ethnic Pakhtun, also writes in Pashto albeit from Loralai,
in the northeast corner of Balochistan. He started writing poetry and
engaging in 'literary activism' when he was in tenth grade in Loralai.[56] He
went on to complete an MA in English Literature as well as in International
Relations at the University of Balochistan. A formative experience for him
was during the five years (1999–2004) when he worked at the Institute for
Development Studies and Practices in Quetta. This was a small initiative, in
a small province, where most of his colleagues were young and idealistic. He
engaged youth from all over the country in short six-month courses covering
'critical pedagogy, culture, spirituality and social change, and colonial and
imperialist roots of development in Pakistan.' He has continued working
in the development sector for much of his career but notes that poetry is
his passion, while development is his profession.

He recalls that when he was growing up, there was a *mela* (fair) on
Eid, with music and dancing (*attan*). But suddenly after the 1980s, the
Taliban came and people were inside their own *hujras*, afraid to play
music. "We felt even then that the public space available for people was
shrinking." On the next Eid, people tried to dance without music, since
there was an unannounced ban on *attan* (Pashtun folk dance performed
with music). Some years later, in 2007 or 2008 (when the Taliban were
making incursions into Swat), he and his friends decided that since Eid
was coming they would play music; they wanted to play the *dhol* (drums)
with the *attan*. Local people warned them that there might be problems,
but they had decided to reclaim their cultural space by doing this. So

they gathered the *dhol* players, they started to play, and he and his friends started to perform *attan*. This was an important act for him, reclaiming this cultural space. It was a mind-set that they were standing against—people were afraid the Taliban would do something—and they tried to break the silence. It was through this act that the idea to hold a peace conference in Loralai in 2008 on 'Pashto Literature and Peace' developed. Pakhtun writers mostly from KP and Balochistan came and talked about how the Pakhtun region had been the first area to be targeted, became the most severely affected by violent extremism, and that Pashto literature and poetry can play a role in peace. The book that came out of the conference, eventually, was published in Pashto.

Though based now in Islamabad, Arif Tabassum returns often to Loralai, Quetta, and elsewhere in Balochistan to organize literary events and intercultural activities, the most recent (as of this writing) in September 2017 in Quetta. The intercultural dialogue they held with Hazaras, Balochis, and Pakhtuns was important, so they could discuss the direct conflict Balochis have been having with the federal government. They discussed that Balochis are often kept passive by their *sardars* (feudal landlords); he said that if you see them, 'you'll think they still live in the slavery period.' They criticized Baloch leaders for getting billions of rupees from the federal government, including those for the gas that is taken from Sui, but the funds are not distributed at the district level nor shared with local people. He pointed out that in Dera Bugti, the female literacy rate is less than 2 per cent, comparing it with FATA which is higher at a dismal 3 per cent.

He writes poetry in Pashto as he feels he is making a contribution to his own language and culture by doing so. His poetry is not just literature for pleasure, but is mainly about his language, his identity, and his *watan*—his country, the Pakhtun *watan*. It contains elements of anti-extremism, often against dogmatic religion. He considers that the conflict which the area has been enduring since the Soviet occupation of Afghanistan in the 1980s has changed Pashto literary trends from elaborations of love to life,

> Where poems once focused on *ghairat*—the marshal image of
> Pashtuns as a nation—now Pashto poetry talks about peace,
> tolerance, coexistence, and, in particular, changing nations' image
> of terrorists.[57]

Although Tabassum is a Pakhtun, he is not so focused on religion, a subconscious choice from seeing what has been happening with his language, culture, and land. These sentiments are evident in the following five short poems, especially in how he plays with piety and Pakhtun sentiments,[58]

> Leave me to enjoy the good things in this life,
> If you want to do some accountability, do it in some other life.

> I worship my beloved, and I talk more about my beloved,
> So can I expect to receive a divine message now?

> I can lay down my life on each and every piece of my *watan* [land]
> I don't want to see Pakhtuns divided into different parts.

> A Pashtun-like enemy is living within me,
> That's why I am always fighting with myself.[59]

> Go to the graveyards of my land,
> Bring back Pakhtuns' lives.

In 2003, he was in Europe on the anniversary of the 11 September attacks, and we can see his mixed emotions of what has emanated from Pakhtun areas since then in the following poem,

SEPTEMBER 11 IN EUROPE

> I don't feel safe here in Europe on this day,
> Because I am Afghan, I am young, and I am Muslim.
> Whenever a white person looks at me,
> I feel frightened whether he or she thinks of me as a terrorist.

He sees poetry as having a powerful effect on its audience as it is a genre of literature that enables the writer to express very complex things in an easy manner. Pashto poetry talks about peace, tolerance, coexistence and, in particular, changing nations' image of terrorists; he wants the rest of the world to know about the secular values pervasive in his culture.[60] Tabassum also enjoys reciting his poetry at a *mushaira* because 'whenever you talk about your *watan*, your identity, in your poetry, there will be a lot of applause from the listeners.' He regrets that while his poetry has that impact on listeners, he doesn't have that many opportunities to share it with them. So instead, he recites his poetry 'maybe at a *mushaira* in an isolated place, once a year. But people are not so literate, so the poetry in books isn't read. But people at *mushairas* give me a very good reception.' He is enthusiastic about social media trying to make people more literate in Pashto, and sees more youth trying to write poetry in Pashto and read Pashto. He hopes his poetry is inspiring people. This certainly comes across in the following longer poem,

> We will not buy pistols and canons any more,
> We are fighting the last battle of the century.
> It is not the period of Khushal Khan,[61]
> Why do we still hate Aurangzeb?[62]
> Let us be united and develop ourselves with the world's other
>   nations,
> We will get rusty if we live in such isolation
> O Pashtuns! Know yourself and your worth
> Do not waste yourself in the name of so-called honour
> Our struggle has become much older
> We must start a new movement to find our destiny.

SINDHI POETRY

Switching our focus to nearby Sindh, we see a long legacy of Sufis who have stood up to 'the establishment' and encouraged positive relations between Muslims and members of other religions which has been foundational to Sindhi syncretic culture. In writing about three Sufis of Matiari, Sindh—Sakhi Syed Ruknuddin, Sakhi Hashim Shah, and Syed Hyder Shah (sixteenth and seventeenth centuries' writers)—Zulfiqar Ali Kalhoro contends that they won the hearts of the populace 'by discarding opulence, hatred, intolerance, and bigotry and promoted through their teachings the message of simplicity, tolerance, love, and progressive attitudes in Sindhi society, paving the way for development of syncretic culture in Sindh.'[63] No poetry exemplifies this tradition more than that of Sachal Sarmast (1739–1827), the iconic poet who lived in Khairpur.[64] His real name was Abdul Wahab but he adopted the name Sachal Sarmast, 'truthful mystic,' for his poetry. He wrote on themes of unity, the importance of all groups in society, and the overall power of people and not dogma. A well-known poem of his captures these themes,

> Abandoning the mosque, we get drunk in the Tavern;
> All this beauty and splendour that encircles us is ours;
> Exempt from righteousness and unrighteousness,'
> We, O Sachal, became Truth.[65]

He urged people to seek out truth directly. He died in 1827 at the age of ninety and is buried in his *dargah* (tomb) in the village of Daraza, near Ranipur, in Khairpur district of Sindh. The *dargah* is the epitome of what Sachal Sarmast stood for: graves of Hindu and Muslim followers, both male and female, are interwoven throughout, celebrating the area's syncretic and inclusive heritage. The essence of Sachal Sarmast's poetry can be found in the following excerpt of a poem that is popularly recited throughout Sindh today,

> All religions are confusing people and their clergy are making them
>   even more so,
> How sad it is that conscious, intelligent people are silent and don't
>   resist them.[66]

Opposing characteristics permeate Sachal Sarmast's poetry,

> You by yourself, know what is in your form!
> Why chant 'Allah Allah'? Find Allah within you.
> You listen, you see, Allah's word is witness,
> There is no doubt, O Sachal! That the Lord is One!
>
> We are, what are we?
> We know not, what we are!
> For a moment we are blessed
> For a moment we are accursed
> Some moment we pray and fast
> Some moment we are free spirits
> Now we declare, 'Only we exist'
> Now we declare, 'We don't exist'
> For a bit, our heart is calm

In a bit, we weep rivers
Now we say, 'We are self-realized'
Now we ask, 'Who are we?'
'Sachal' we are only That eternally
What other contracts can we make here?[67]

The syncretism is espoused even more clearly in the next two poems,

Religions got the people confused in the country
The mullahs, the Pundits, the Sheikhs misled the masses
Some bowed themselves in prayers and some settled in the temples,
People of mind never got closer to love even.[68]

and

Neither am I a judge nor an Islamic scholar
I am an ordinary being; neither am I a person of faith nor a
      Muslim,
Appearance-wise I am an insightful person; a *fakir* is what I am,
When it comes to defending the truth, I am a sultan—I am a
      sultan.

I care not for religiosity; I cannot satisfy you in these matters—I
      cannot satisfy
I am not Godless; I am compassionate and full of praise.
Sachal is not my name for I am cleansed of a name
I am a lover who loves with wild abandon.[69]

During his lifetime, some ulema issued *fatwas* (religious decisions) against Sachal Sarmast, that he was a *kafir* (infidel). He was threatened and criticized for his unconventional views on piety, interfaith interactions, and communal harmony,

Qazi burn thy books.
The Master has instructed me:
'Know thyself,' He said.
He taught me the path of heresy.
Some go to Ka'bah, others to *qiblah*,
All these things are mere pretexts.

Why should I turn to Ka'bah?
When my Master in tavern dwells?
Be thou [divinely] mad,
Drink deep the wine of madness.[70]

We can see the interplay of syncretism and secularism in Sachal Sarmast's poetry, as well as his emphasis on the value of thinking for oneself, making one's own choices, and not blindly following tradition,

Tis not in religion I believe
'Tis love I live in.
When love comes to you.
Say Amen!

Friend, this is the only way
To learn the secret way:
Ignore the paths of others,
Even the saints' steep trails.
Don't follow.
Don't journey at all.
Rip the veil from your face.

Neither did I roll a *tasbih* [prayer beads], nor did I ponder and
     pray,
I went to no mosque or temple, nor bow in adoration to any,
Sachal is lucky every day, love is all around him.[71]

His poetry captures the distinctiveness of Sindh where conventional beliefs can be modified and acted upon differently, something unparalleled elsewhere in the region. His *dargah* is not the only shrine that celebrates interfaith harmony; Muslims and Hindus also pray together at Odero Laal (near Tando Adam Khan; Hindus call the saint there Jhulelal).

The same can be said of the poetry of Shah Abdul Latif Bhittai—that he captures the distinctiveness of Sindh —but he does so through getting his strength from the land itself,

When the world was still to be born
When Adam was still to receive his form
Then my relationship began

Fig.2.1: Abdul Rahim Roghani.

Fig. 2.2: Usman Olasyar (far right) with children protesting in Swat.

Fig. 2.3: Professor Abaseen Yousafzai.

Fig. 2.4: Hasina Gul in her
house in Mardan.

Fig. 2.5: Khalil Kumbar with the indomitable Hafiz Nizamani at the 2018
Lahooti Melo in Hyderabad, Sindh.

Fig. 2.6: Saif Samejo.

> When I heard the Lord's voice
> A voice sweet and clear
> I said 'YES' with my heart
> And formed a bond with the land (Sindh) I love
> When all of us were one, my bond then began.[72]

No one exemplifies the social and cultural history of Sindh more than Shah Latif (1689–1752). While Sachal Sarmast has his distinct niche as discussed above, and Lal Shahbaz Qalandar is nationally known (especially by the popularity of the late Nusrat Fateh Ali's song about him), it is the stories and poetry of Shah Latif that Sindhis look to for their collective character. His poetry is based on Sindhi folk stories and places great emphasis on ties to the land and its people and remains a great inspiration for contemporary Sindhi poets. He gives women dominant and active roles in the stories. Durre-Shahwar Sayed[73] observes that, 'In many of his verses it could be argued that he expresses the hopes and fears of the suppressed classes, comforting them in their miseries and encouraging them to struggle for their rights.' Fahmida Hussain,[74] a compiler of his *Risalo* (Message), identifies how he took positions in his poetry to counter oppression, exploitation, and extremism,

> Shah Latif had seen women of his times as weak, helpless subjects in a male-dominated society. Every woman was exploited. He stressed on her emancipation, gave her strength to speak out and face tyrants with courage…he gave them a message to have a strong will against the difficult obstacles of the society. He wanted these weak and oppressed people of the country to smash the idols of artificial and false social values through their will power. He hoped that individual efforts would give rise to a collective ethos.

She finds Shah Latif's poetry saying that change is opposed by 'fundamentalists, orthodox clergy, and other reactionary forces,' and he instead used examples of weak and helpless characters in the form of women. Through their actions, his poetry offers the inspiration 'of struggle, revolt, awareness, bravery, and perseverance, so that one could build his future on these lines.'[75] The following two poems capture these sentiments well,

Look at the birds, O men,
They fly in flocks, in unison.
Bound by their exemplary love
They present for you, a lesson,
An example of co-existence.[76]

Sincerity is bartered away with brutality,
And viciousness feeds on human flesh.
What shall remain in this world,
Is the fragrance of love and kindness,
In a multitude of duplicity and deceit.[77]

A general inspiration to stand for what an individual believes in, is captured here,

Struggle in all sorts of circumstances,
There is no time to sit idle.
If night falls, you may not find,
The footprints of the beloved,
And may get lost in the wilderness.[78]

Then he takes that sentiment and intermixes it with his attachment and love for Sindh,

Craving for the homeland I may die
O king! Don't bind and bury me here.
Do not lay my body in this alien land,
Away from my folks and friend.
If I breathe here last,
Send my body to Malir fast,
To cover my coffin with its scented soil.[79]

A final group of three of Shah Latif's poems judiciously reveal his disdain for 'ill-wishers' of all ilk, the need to stand for justice and to counter oppression,

I pray for the ill-wishers,
Let them live long,
So that they can see our love and unity,
Thereafter may they die of anger and agony.[80]

No greater honour than to lay down life for one's honour and
     truth.
Never negotiate, never return,
There is no greater shame than the blame to compromise with
     untruth.[81]

The poison kills not, mistrust does,
The toxin doesn't harm as do the words, mistrust,
Bitter words and disbelief all contribute in killing your friends.[82]

Sachal Sarmast's poetry is a strong foundation for political resistance in the
contemporary poetry of Hafiz Nizamani. When meeting Hafiz Nizamani
for the first time, one is immediately struck by both his whimsical nature
and seriousness of purpose, not an oxymoron in his case.[83] Sitting on the
floor of his village home, his friend begins singing his poetry,

We are *qaim* [the real thing] in Sufism!
A lot of people run after wealth, but we are not for sale.
We can't steal as our arms are empty.

Another friend takes over with another poem,

You can see how we are; we are there, standing tall. We are not
     changed.
We are workers, whatever we do, we don't see the differences.
We're happy, our prize is for you to look at us with love and
     compassion.
Yet sight is missing, the world is not seeing us as we are.

Hafiz Nizamani himself then joins in,

When the lord is asking through angels to ask for the *hisaab kitab*
     [bill for goods or services], why are you asking me?
Why didn't you give it to me there?
I'm not liable to be questioned—God should be questioned.

He explains that in this verse, he is anticipating what will happen upon
his death. He's telling the people who are there in the other world—'look,
when I was alive there were only punishments, disasters, police officers,

in the name of rulers'— so is heaven now a place to live? There are still punishments and disasters. He says that when he had been alive, he lived his entire life being honest to himself, and he was never bad to women. But look at the name they gave him, *harami* (bastard), although he was the opposite of it. He continues the story, that he will tell those in the other world that, for this reason, he has left the world of the living and is now in their world. He was punished there for being good. He is now here, standing in front of God, but he is still only hearing about punishments. So what is the difference between both? He concludes by reflecting that here on earth, we don't see any of the good of God when we engage with mullahs, so what value is it to be on earth?

Born in the remote village where he still lives, Sohrab Nizamani—just past the better-known ancient town of Matli—Hafiz Nizamani claims to be sixty-five but appears far older. He spent his life as a farmer, raising two sons and three daughters. Smiling and teasing, he states that his two sons, both teachers, are his greatest achievements because neither is a terrorist. His poetic allegiance, however, is not to Shah Abdul Latif Bhittai but rather to Sachal Sarmast, evident in the verse he enjoys reciting of his,

> Do something that reflects you or your inner God.
> Live in a way that you prove to be God yourself.
> God is within you, you only have to bring him out.

A *pesh imam* who leads village prayers and is highly regarded for his knowledge of the Quran and shariah, he too has been the target of *fatwas*. When questioned by mullahs about what he believes in, he said he responded to them by saying that they have all been talking and admiring and dreaming about heaven, but no one has been talking about hell. He was sarcastically criticizing them, that they shouldn't worry about where they'll go when they die. They have created so many hurdles on earth for good people, and he's certain they'll even be able to create obstacles for honest people in heaven,

> First heaven was stolen from us, and now they are preventing us
>   from living the lives we want.
> We used to think that everything horrible that was happening to
>   us was because of Satan, but I can't see Satan here anywhere.

When I came to this earth, I tried my best to do something good
    for my people.
I was very enthusiastic in all of my efforts.
But when I see the so-called cruel Godfathers of this earth
I became sad and hopeless that they have brought havoc to this
    earth, yet I was watching helplessly.
I was sad I couldn't do anything.

I first heard that when I will die I would be honoured on the Day
    of Judgement and I will see beautiful *houris*[84] walking with men
    in an ideal society in heaven,
Alas, I realize that even there the curtains will not be opened
    without paying a bribe to heaven's guard.
They say that this will be our reward, but remaining in heaven with
    these *houris* is not our goal in life.

My body is in so many pieces just like a broken pot that gets
    reassembled but is never whole again,
I am trying my best to get to my destination.
Am I merely a paper flower empty of fragrance?
Am I like that flower who has no fragrance to attract people to a
    path to follow?[85]

He counters the mullahs and their *fatwas* with his knowledge of the
Quran. He recounted how he had been invited to a programme with
mullahs (because he's a *pesh imam*), and when he arrived he announced
that 'We have now unpacked our musical instruments. Now you should
pack up your Kalashnikovs!' He disdains the official funding given to
mullahs, and how madrassas also support them, but they work against the
best interests of the people. Similar to Sachal Sarmast's view, he considers
religious practitioners as part of the core of the problem, as seen in the
following verse,

My wine is ancient, and your *shariah* [religious law] is new.
You only have a prayer rug and a book, and I only have a humble
    heart.
I will drink openly despite sitting beside the *qazi*,
In front of all the other drunkards, I am throwing away all the
    qazi's religious books.

Before the preacher arrives to give his sermon, I am going to foil
his game.
As I am already drunk, the mosque is no place for me.
Oh pious man! You have your piety; I don't have any.
You are afraid of drinking, and I have no fear of it.
I don't have any new pot for ablution as my ablution is with wine,
not with water.
I have an idea who is a human, oh Lord of religion, though it will
take you some time to figure it out.
You are moving in the old ways though the world has changed
phenomenally, and you are reluctant to accept it.[86]

He says that he has been writing poetry his whole life, trying to get people
who have a connection with mullahs—with established religion—to
reject them. When queried about the thousands of people who listen to
his poetry, he added that while they listen to it, most don't believe in it.
However, he sees his true character emerge in his poetry; he believes that
when youth hear him recite his poetry they become energized and begin to
think the mullahs are wrong and the extremists are not strong, as we can
see in this poem that best encapsulates his ideology,

Not Christian, Jew or Muslim, not Hindu, Buddhist or any
religion
I am a human being and bow down my head only to humanity.

Tell the historians I am not afraid of anything
I demand neither *houris* [celestial virgins] nor *gilmaan* [young
servant boys]

Looking at your ways of living, my soul cringes
If it's your religion, then I am with the devil.

We have our own colours of guidance and faith,
Hafiz will always be on the side of vice and dishonesty.[87]

His poetry also harkens back to the love of place—of Sindh—that we find
in Shah Latif's verses,

Look! For our determination, we still stand our ground,
Believe in our words, so we can stand our ground.

There was a lot deception but we were not diverted,
Appreciate us a bit, so we can stand our ground.

O friend! if it had been somebody else, he would have sold him,
There is no other influence over us, so we can stand our ground.

I have gone through every line of history, that
Truth cannot be tainted, so we can stand our ground.

You can live in your world, we would love to be in Sindh, Hafiz,
That is all, so we can stand our ground.[88]

Important to Hafiz Nizamani is that a believer must relate directly to God and not go through any intermediary such as a *maulvi* or *pir*. The latter seek to be gatekeepers, are often corrupt, and prevent people from caring for each other in society due to the specious promise of a reward of virgins after death,

Oh my Love! I am yours, but if I have done anything wrong now
    pardon me,
As I am very ordinary, but I still demand your full love.
Your love is so boundless that you cannot abandon even those who
    are discourteous, careless, and ignorant.
Oh my love! This is who you are.

Neither I demand any account from you nor see any limitation,
It's from your grace that I can overcome any obstacles and
    hardships that I encounter.
When I will kiss the dust [die] with your approval, I need no
    reward except your love.
When my boat crosses to the other side, you will steer it.
You are with me, hand-in-hand, until I reach my destination
    peacefully.
Oh greatness! You are always the supporter of Hafiz
With you by my side, I need not bow before anyone else.[89]

Through his poetry, he seeks to celebrate the need for *insaaf* (justice). People joined together is what can achieve this, being serious with the right character. He says, 'When we unite, the system will change and justice will come.' His message to the world to counter extremism which he seeks to deliver through his poetry is that people are good; humanity is greatest. Each person should be accountable to themselves for all they do, good and bad. In our society, we should pay attention to our children and the dreams that the extremists are selling to our children. We have to live our lives here, and for this, we have to provide awareness to all.

In Tharparkar, eastern Sindh, Khalil Kumbar has become well-known for capturing the struggles and sentiments of people in this Hindu-majority area of Pakistan. Both a poet and an environmental activist, his poetry reflects how people are speaking out to reclaim identity and creating new narratives against violence, deeply tied to the land and natural environment of the desert. When he recited the following poem, it was important to him that the translator first shared the background of the poem with me: his friend, Piaro, had migrated from Pakistan and went to India three years earlier, out of fear of the violence that was spreading in this area. Sindh's inclusive, multicultural foundation remains intact somewhat—more so than elsewhere in Pakistan—but Hindus and Christians often feel under threat there from extremists as well. Kumbar's poem resonates with Sachal Sarmast's secular values and vision,

IF ONLY YOU COULD HAVE STAYED FOR A WHILE

If you could stay for a while, you and I can build such a beautiful land.
Where the sun would light the *bazaars* of Ketti Bandar [historical place of Sindh],
Where the fishermen would drop their nets into the salty River Indus,
Everyone would come back and get good fortune from the earth.
If you could stay, everything can be achieved. You and I will be one forever,
If you had stayed for a while.

In my land, a girl will dance like she danced during Mohenjo Daro's time,
She would blink her eyes like this, and she would move her feet in dance,

Chum chum, chum chum, chum, the bells sound [the sound of
  bells on dancing feet]
Then we will breathe deeply about the very rich traditions of our
  land,
We will remember how our civilization in the past was at the peak,
If only you had stayed for a while.

All these wild murderers will die from the fire of their own ideology
  of hate,
When they see both of us joyfully together,
We can build our own paradise, and we could live by whatever
  way we want to live,
We can go to temples and light candles, we can go to mosques and
  we can recite whatever we want,
If only you had stayed for a while.

Our rivers will return back to us, and our local people who love
  this land will be happy,
We will hear their songs once again on our land,
Sweet fragrances will come from the water returning to our wells
  and peacocks will dance on the roads,
Women will carry water in vessels on their heads from long
  distances,
Every tree will have such a beautiful fragrance,
If only you had stayed for a while.

Our heroes who gave their lives for this land,
Come, you and I will meet to celebrate their sacrifices, their
  heroism, and tell their tales to the world,
If only you had stayed for a while.[90]

Both Hafiz Nizamani and Khalil Kumbar are known for their resistance
poetry, standing up against perpetrators of injustice and domination. They
both hold *mushairas* with Hindus and Muslims in their audiences. Khalil
Kumbar remarked that in Mithi, Tharparkar's district capital, that kind of
social environment where Hindus and Muslims intermix is common; there's
no segregation whatsoever. As an example, he said it was evident during the
2015 funeral procession of Sadiq Fakir, a musician who had lived in Mithi,
when there were pallbearers from temples, mosques, and gurdwaras. There

was no noticeable distinction amongst people who were present there over what religion he belonged to, 'except that he had been a great singer from that land. Hindus were crying, Sikhs were crying, just like Muslims were crying. He gave importance to the land, not to any religion or to any class. In Thar, everyone is equal, we all are happy and sad together.'[91]

There is a third Sindhi figure whose work must be addressed here as well, as it not only captures similar forms of resistance poetry, but Saif Samejo also 'packages' it through cutting-edge channels (e.g., Instagram, YouTube, rock performances) to broaden exposure to a younger audience. Based in Jamshoro, which abuts Hyderabad and is nearly two hours from Karachi by road, Saif Samejo can most aptly be characterized as a Sufi, Sindhi, folk, rock, poet, and singer. He regards himself not as a poet but a lyricist. He founded the band, Sketches, as a medium to celebrate the messages of tolerance and hope and is inspired by Shah Latif virtually 'every step of the way.'[92]

In this chapter, our focus is not on how he uses music as a way to counter extremism (that is included in the following chapter on music, especially his work in establishing the annual 'Lahooti Melo') but rather on his efforts in bringing Sindhi poets together and disseminating their work, and the poetic messages found within his music. For example, in his song '*Darawar* (The Dravidians): Say No to Religious Extremism,' he took the words of Sindhi poet Bakhshan Mehranvi that addresses the role played by religious extremists in Sindh while celebrating its cultural values and in his own phenomenal way set them to music, conveying this powerful message,

DARAWAR (THE DRAVIDIANS): SAY NO TO RELIGIOUS EXTREMISM

I never knew that…in the name of religion, our land would have
    to see such days!
The earth will have its religion too,
The earth will be Hindu or Muslim too,
Enemies of enlightenment and awakening,
Enemies of music and melody,
Enemies of the beauties of the world,
Enemies of humanity, I don't know what they want!
Suppressing laughter's opening respite of sects,
Want to inflict new wounds,

Want to destroy fragrances,
Pains and pains will be seen through religious dogmas.
The dead will have religion too,
The dead will be dug out and dragged down,
The dead will be black or white too.
I never knew that shadows of trees will be Hindu or Muslim too.
Souring birds will be Shia and Sunni too.
I never knew that our land would have to see such days too!
I never knew…

From a young age, Saif was influenced by Sufi singers like Abida Parveen and Alam Faqir, and two *faqirs* who sang at Sachal Sarmast's *dargah*, Sohrab and Jamaluddin. He found them rebellious, very much against the orthodoxy that he had been taught. Then he began to learn about Gautama Buddha and Shiva Nataraja and went on to read Sachal Sarmast's poetry and began to sing his poems. When he was a student at the University of Sindh he came to know of G.M. Syed, the secular, popular nationalist, and began to identify, albeit briefly, as a Sindhi nationalist.[93] He said that G.M. Syed's socialist writing took him to a different place, like Shah Latif's poetry does. The message he took away from G.M. Syed reverberated with that of the poetry of Shaikh Ayaz,[94] the message to get away from religious orthodoxy as it is giving birth to the Taliban, and 'these ideas will get into our homes and eat us.'

In effect, Shah Latif has inspired him to realize that everything in the world is a story and the world is ruled by storytellers,

> Armies have stories; Pakistan is a story. As the story gets older, it becomes a myth, and whoever carries it, becomes dangerous. A storyteller can take people in any direction. Sachal's stories are talking about the earth. Sachal is talking about the people of the earth—they were born here, from here. Shah Latif doesn't believe we are coming out of the sky—we are all from here. It is the cognitive stories that are the most powerful.[95]

He regards Sindhi Sufism as not separate from politics but rather it embraces a political element, 'the one who farms the lands has more rights to the land than the feudal.' He points out that Shah Inayat had been killed in this area during the time of Shah Latif because he was spreading that message perhaps 260 years ago. He realizes that he is no longer a Sindhi nationalist but he embraces the Sindhi worldview. He was seeing Sindh's story with his own eyes, from within. If a Hindu temple is burning, his heart is burning. It's not their faith that comes under attack, but rather the political act is to make Hindus insecure in Pakistan (as Khalil Kumbar expresses in his poetry). Saif sees the violence being perpetrated by religious extremists against Hindus, making them feel insecure. These acts prompted his observation that what is being told about the religious extremists, the Taliban, is broadcast on national media in the Urdu language, bringing in hatred. He concluded,

> So, use Sindhi! We were listening to a national story that was based on hate. What you do right now, what you think right now, your direction will be that. If my intention is to use hate language, I can get a lot of people to hate you. But in the Sindhi language—the verses of Sachal and Shah Latif—they don't have this hatred.

In poetry and in music, he is celebrating Sufism.[96] He considers Sindhi Sufism to be very different than what exists in Pakistan's national narrative. Instead in Sindh, the Sufi is against 'the kingdom', against the establishment, and against the mullahs. Sindhi Sufism is a rebellion. He characterizes the foundation of this in Sachal Sarmast's resistance and that Shah Latif is more focused on one's own self and is very calming and meditative. While Sachal can give fire to protests against the mullah and the establishment, Latif is about self-liberation and at the same time talks about nationalism, women, and victims: but for Latif, first the individual must liberate himself. He says,

> To fight specific injustice, like today, that being perpetrated by the mullah, we look at Sachal. But to build a society, there is Latif. Latif is deeper than this.

He adds that Shah Latif talks about having a healthy mind and body. He doesn't only talk about people, he also talks about birds, insects, trees, fish, animals, and other creatures, saying that he is all of these things. He writes in Sindhi and espouses 'Sindhiat,' a humanity where there are morals, goodness in society, and their identity as Sindhis. When he and other poets recite Latif's poetry, Saif Samejo sees them as trying to create a narrative through Latif to fight against terrorism, using him as a shield, as an identity card. He concludes,

> Latif was seeing things beyond Sindhis. He was, of course, in love with the land and the people, as anyone can be in love with anyone else; for him, Sindh was this important. He felt rooted here; he can grow his branches far, but he was grounded here. That's why he returned, he came back. He gave his body to this part of earth.

We find many of these sentiments in the poetry that Saif Samejo often sings, as seen in 'A Person' that he has written,

A PERSON

The mortal I was and you breathed the life in me
Wove the fine threads of attachment around me
Showed me the different shades of truth
And taught me the language of fearless ecstasy.
You showed me the unity, the eternal oneness
And just when I was starting to believe in One
You revealed yourself in a beloved, mirroring yourself in many.
But for all my understanding, I am still far away from the truth
Mistaking shadows for reality
This shadow-hunting revolts my soul, leaving me breathless
And my being howls and weeps in the agony of separation
We all were idols made up of the dust and dirt
Into whom you breathe life
And sowed the seeds of desire and unity
And yet I do not know the art of loving
For all your grace, I seem to have learned to condemn only,
I walk around pretending to be a holy man,
While the vileness of my heart spills all around me, smearing even
    the clothes that I wear
You made me dance in abandon, intoxicating my being with love
You taught me to differentiate the right from the wrong
You taught me unity and you taught me separation
And with this came the abandonment, the myriad differences in
    the name of religion and caste
The mortal I was and you breathed life in me
Wove the fine threads of attachment around me.

The famous poem, 'Mein Sufi Hoon' ('I am a Sufi'), has been sung by the great Sindhi singer Abida Parveen as well as by other *faqirs* (Sufi singers). This version below is slightly different as Saif Samejo uses the first line, but adds innovation in the rest of the poem,

> I am a Sufi, the ecstatic one, I walk the pathless path.
> He and I are one and the same.
> Just as thread is woven out of a cotton ball, I too am woven from
>   His thread.
> He is the one who wills it, He is the one who creates it, He alone is.
> When Bulleh Shah found his beloved, both of them ceased to be.
> When the deepest union happens, how could there still be two?
> He alone is the reason for my agony, He alone is my cure.
> He is my pilgrimage, He is the pilgrim.
> He is Makkah, the holiest of the holy, He is the desert, the vast
>   land of loneliness.
> He is the one who is being worshipped, He is the one who
>   worships, too.
> He is the lord and the servant, He is the paradox that embraces
>   it all.
> And I rejoice in Him.
> I am a Sufi, the ecstatic one.
> I walk the pathless path.

Ishaq Samejo, a Sindhi poet, is an Associate Professor of Sindhi Language and Literature in the Department of Sindhi at the University of Sindh, Jamshoro and the Director of its Institute of Sindhology. He is an editor of the popular Sindhi literary magazine, *Saranga*, published by the Saranga Literary and Cultural Society. He is a member of a number of other editorial boards, literary societies, and is deeply involved in the language and literature field in Sindh. He too is a poet who writes about valuing local culture and resisting the lure of violence, as evident in his poem 'Before the War' that he wrote during the last week of February 2019 when it seemed that war between India and Pakistan was imminent,

BEFORE THE WAR

> 'Before the war, what was here?'
> Before the war, here was a deep green vale,

Orchids of black plums, long queues of golden shower trees,
A waterfall cascading from above, a fine oval-shaped lake,
And a hamlet near the lake.
In the hamlet, there were playgrounds, public parks, a small souk,
    and a vegetable market.

'What else was here before the war?'
Before the war, a mosque, temple, and church existed in the same
    street,
Allah, *Bhagwan*, and God were friends,
Here were hues, lights, birds, and butterflies, roaming together.

'Was there anything else here, before the war?'
Before the war, here was a wine shop owned by a money lender,
A shop of indigo, a hut of a lyricist, a parlor of a sitar-player,
Talk of a pretty lass, and a bunch of young lovers.

What else I can tell you, that before the war, there was no war here.
And more importantly, there was no cemetery around.
And now, there is nothing but the cemetery.[97]

Writing poetry that enables people to process the violence occurring around them and empowering these same people to stand up in opposition to that violence, is formidable. The Pashto and Sindhi poetry presented above has powerful messages of breaking stereotypical tropes, of capturing the essence of identity and culture, and of moving past adversity and tragedy to believe in a better collective future together. Indeed, a *mushaira* can have an extraordinarily powerful impact, in the long-term, more than guns, prison sentences, or other forms of punishment.

Notes

1. B. Harlow, *Resistance Literature*, 1987, p. xviii.
2. Qaisar Abbas (2018) provides an interesting discussion of Saraiki poets in southern Punjab as representing a marginalized group and offering 'multiple voices of resistance' in their quest to create a separate Saraiki province out of southern Punjab. However, it is seeking to establish a distinct identity, not to counter violent extremism, as is the case with Pashto and Sindhi poetry.
3. B. Harlow, *Resistance Literature*, 1987, p. 33.
4. Ibid., p. 40.

5. A. Raza, 'Voices of Resistance: Pashto Poetry as Bulwark against Extremism,' *The Dynamics of Change in Conflict Societies: Pakhtun Region in Perspective,* 2013, pp. 61–2.

6. B. Harlow, *Resistance Literature,* 1987, p. 41.

7. Qaisar Abbas, 'Cultural Identity and State Oppression: Poetic Resistance to Internal Colonialism in Pakistan,' *Pakistaniaat: A Journal of Pakistan Studies* Vol. 6, 2018, accessible at: http://pakistaniaat.org/index.php/pak/article/view/353.

8. Sampson, R. and M. Khan, *The Poetry of Rahman Baba: Poet of the Pukhtuns,* 2010, p. iii.

9. K. Hussain, *The Militant Discourse: Religious Militancy in Pakistan,* 2013, p. 77.

10. Husham Ahmed, 'Attacking shrines and the culture of peace', *Dawn,* 3 November 2010, accessible at: https://www.dawn.com/news/813512.

11. Ibid.

12. R. Sampson and M. Khan, *The Poetry of Rahman Baba: Poet of the Pukhtuns,* 2010, pp. 98–9.

13. FATA Research Centre, 2014, p. 4.

14. Ibid., p. 5.

15. As quoted in Shaheen Buneri, 'Poetry Fights Back,' *Boston Review,* January/February, 2012.

16. Talimand Khan, 'Putting the "verse" back in "subversive",' *The Friday Times,* 12 June 2015, accessible at: http://www.thefridaytimes.com/tft/putting-the-verse-back-in-subversive.

17. As quoted in Shaheen Buneri, 'Poetry Fights Back,' *Boston Review,* January/February, 2012.

18. As quoted in Hidayat Khan, 'Bleeding the Pen Dry: Hundreds of Pashto poets remain unpublished as support for Verse Withers,' *Express Tribune,* 30 June 2013, accessible at: https://tribune.com.pk/story/570197/bleeding-the-pen-dry-hundreds-of-pashto-poets-remain-unpublished-as-support-for-verse-withers/.

19. Rahmat Shah Sail discussed his poetry with me in his village Wartair in Dargai, District Swat, on 7 February 2019. Aasya Rehman and Faizullah Jan helped translate his poetry from Pashto to English. The poem 'Peshawar' is in his Pashto-language book, *The Beauties and the Spring Breeze,* Peshawar, Mangal Kitab Kaur, 2009, pp. 25–8.

20. Saddar is the large market-area of Peshawar.

21. Qissa Khwani bazaar is the large traditional market in the middle of Peshawar where money lenders and others gather.

22. Rahmat Shah Sail, *Za da Khazan da Panrey Panrey Sara Orajedam,* Peshawar, Mangal Kitab Kor, 2018, p. 5. Translation by Aasya Rehman.

23. Recited orally to me at his home in February 2019. Translation by Aasya Rehman.

24. Rahmat Shah Sail hand-wrote this verse and wanted me to include it here. Translation by Faizullah Jan.

25. Ibid.

26. Talimand Khan, 'Putting the "verse" back in "subversive".'

27. Ibid. This is from Amjad Shehzad's poetry collection, *Na* (No), published in 2001.

28. These reflections were shared with me during a meeting in Islamabad on 23 December 2017.

29. This is a reference to Naqeebullah, whose extrajudicial murder in Karachi in January 2018 triggered a massive protest by Pakhtuns that resulted in the Pashtun Tahafuz Movement, discussed in Chapter 7.

30. Khan Zaman Kakar recited this to me in a meeting in Islamabad on 13 February 2019.

31. He recited this. He explained to me that Pakhtuns have a strong storytelling tradition, and stories of their homeland should be told among their own people, not broadcast on global media by outsiders who don't understand them.

32. This is based on interviews with Abdul Rahim Roghani at his home in Butkhela, Swat in August 2016. Most of Roghani's publications are in Pashto, though one has been translated into English titled. *Selfish: a Book of Humour, Fun and Advice, based on the Harsh Realities of Life*, Mingora, Shoaib Sons Publishers & Booksellers, 2017.

33. Communicated to me at a meeting in Swat in August 2016.

34. Ibid.

35. Recited orally to me in Butkhela, Swat. Translation by Aneela Sulaiman.

36. Abdul Rahim Roghani, *Da Ranra Saskey* (Drops of Light), Peshawar, Aamir Print & Publishers, 2014, p. 250. Translation by Zenab Adnan.

37. Recited orally to me in Butkhela, Swat. Translation by Aneela Sulaiman.

38. Abdul Rahim Roghani, *Da Ranra Saskey*, p. 190. Translation by Zenab Adnan.

39. Ibid., p. 191. Translation by Zenab Adnan.

40. Recited orally to me in Butkhela, Swat. Translation by Aneela Sulaiman.

41. Abdul Rahim Roghani, *Da Ranra Saskey*, p. 382. Translation by Zenab Adnan.

42. Recited orally to me in Butkhela, Swat. Translation by Aneela Sulaiman.

43. This all was conveyed to me in an interview at the Pushto Academy, University of Peshawar in January 2017, and follow-up interviews in 2018 and 2019.

44. Abaseen Yousafzai handed me this poem in English that had been translated by Dr Sher Zaman Taizai.

45. This is a common practice for wrapping a Quran.

46. Abaseen Yousafzai handed me this poem in English that had been translated by Alamgir.

47. These were great Pakhtun leaders of the past who focused on helping local people; he is saying we no longer have leaders like them.

48. He is referring to the event when people were celebrating a wedding at Spin Boldak and bombs destroyed the whole town.

49. Normally, all decisions are made in a *jirga*; a *hujra* is a multipurpose place where jirgas are held. Here he is referring to a *jirga* that was being held in Dara Adamkhel when it was bombed and everyone was killed.

50. Multan Khan, an Afridi, began the fight for independence from the British; the mother of Ajab Khan, also an Afridi, hit a British police officer who had attacked their house on the road to Dara Adamkhel.

51. This refers to the destruction of the statue of the Buddha at Bamiyan and how the old history of Gandhara was also destroyed by the Islamist extremists.

52. Pir Rohan was a fifteenth century spiritual leader, reformer, and author of the first prose book in Pashto. Bacha Khan was a twentieth century populist Pakhtun leader who promoted non-violence and raised his voice against the British, saying we want 'our sweet land to be free.'

53. He is claiming that terrorism in the area is the result of bad people who stole Pakhtuns' things and they painted their faces black.

54. Mansoor was a Syrian Sufi stoned by his people for showing a special spiritual attachment with Allah, the peak of mysticism, and was then hung by the local ulema.

55. This section on Hasina Gul and her poetry is based on meetings held with her in Mardan in January 2017, when she recited her poetry from her hand-written notes and some that has been published. All of her poetry is translated either by Zenab Adnan or Aneela Sulaiman.

56. All of this was conveyed to me in a meeting with Arif Tabassum in Islamabad on 9 March 2018.

57. Shaheen Buneri, 'Poetry Fights Back,' *Boston Review*, January/February, 2012.

58. All of these poems were translated into English in my presence by Arif Tabassum.

59. He explained that they say that Pakhtuns are used against Pakhtuns, since 1979 when Russia invaded Afghanistan. So he is focusing here on self-destruction, because when Pakhtuns are fighting with each other, it's really with themselves.

60. As quoted in Buneri, 'Poetry Fights Back,' 2012.

61. Seventeenth century Pakhtun warrior-poet of the Khattak tribe who encouraged revolt against the Mughal Empire and advocated for Pakhtun unity and nationalism through poetry.

62. Seventeenth century controversial Mughal emperor of India who championed orthodoxy, today regarded as Salafi practices in Islam.

63. Zulfiqar Ali Kalhoro, 'The Mystics of Matiari', *The Friday Times*, 26 October 2018, accessible at: https://www.thefridaytimes.com/tft/mystics-of-matiari/.

64. Ayaz Gul, *Mysticism, Sindh and Sachal Sarmast*, Sachal Chair, Shah Abdul Latif University, Khairpur, 2011, p. 7.

65. K.B. Advani, 'Life and Personality' in Ayaz Gul, ibid., p. 36.

66. Recited to me in Sindhi and translated by Zakia Aijaz, 15 February 2019, in Hyderabad.

67. Ahmed H. Makhdoom, 'Sachal Sarmast, Sindhi Secular Sufi Poet: The Philosopher, Mystic & Scholar,' *Indus Asia Online Journal*, 5 July 2010.

68. Ibid.

69. Mehr Khadim, *Sachal Sarmast's Urdu Kalaam*, Bahawalpur, Saraiki Adabi Majlis, 2005, p. 135. Translation by Aneela Sulaiman.

70. Translation by Jethmal Parsram Gulrajani in 'Sindh and Its Sufis', Madras, Theosophical Publishing House, 1924, accessible at: https://iaoj.wordpress.com/tag/sachal-sarmast/.

71. Aulia's World http://www.auliasworld.com/2013/08/sufi-sarmast.html.

72. Indus Asia Online Journal, accessed at: https://iaoj.wordpress.com/baba-bulle-shah/.

73. D. Sayed, *The Poetry of Shah Abd Al-Latif*, 1988, p. 74.

74. F. Hussain, (ed.), *Selection of Verses from Shah Jo Risalo*, trans. S. Haque Memon, F. Hussain, A. Siraj Memon, and N. Siraj Memon, 2018, p. 19.

75. Durre-Shahwar Sayed, *The Poetry of Shah Abd Al-Latif*, Jamshoro/Hyderabad: Sindhi Adabi Board, 1988, p. 17.

76. This verse is from the 'Sur Dahar' chapter of Shah Latif's *Risalo*, in Sayed 1988, p. 40.

77. This verse is from the 'Sur Barvo' Sindhi chapter of Shah Latif's *Risalo*, in Sayed 1988, p. 42.

78. This verse is from the 'Sur Sasui' chapter of Shah Latif's *Risalo*, in Sayed 1988, p. 43.

79. Malir was a town during the time of Shah Latif and has merged into Karachi today. This verse is from the 'Sur Marui' chapter of Shah Latif's *Risalo*, in Sayed 1988, p. 49.

80. This verse is from the 'Sur Aasa' chapter of Shah Latif's *Risalo*, in Sayed, 1988, p. 107.

81. This verse is from the 'Sur Kedaro' chapter of Shah Latif's *Risalo*, in Sayed, 1988, p. 110.

82. This verse is from the 'Sur Yaman Kalyan' chapter of Shah Latif's *Risalo*, in Sayed, 1988, p. 113.

83. Hafiz Nizamani discussed his poetry with me in Sohrab Nizamani in January 2018 and in Hyderabad in March 2018.

84. These are said to be mythological beautiful celestial virgins who will accompany pious Muslim men in heaven, after death.

85. Translation by Zakia Aijaz and Aijaz Mallah in Hyderabad, in February 2019.

86. Translation by Amar Sindhu and Arfana Mallah in Hyderabad, in February 2019.

87. Translation by Saif Samejo in Jamshoro in February 2019.

88. Translation by Imran Khan Bozdar and Arfana Mallah.

89. Translation by Aijaz Mallah in Hyderabad in February 2019.

90. Khalil Kumbar, *The Intense Pain of Broken Bones*, Sarangana Publishers, 2018. Translation by Zakia Aijaz.

91. Told to me in Hyderabad in March 2018.

92. This and all comments herein attributed to Saif Samejo are through personal conversations at various times in 2018 and 2019.

93. G.M. Syed (Ghulam Murtaza Syed, 1904–95), is regarded as one of the prominent founders of modern Sindhi nationalism.

94. Shaikh Ayaz (1923–97) was a major Sindhi progressive political poet known for his translation of Shah Abdul Latif's *Risalo* and other literary works as well as for the social and political influence of his poetry on Sindh.

95. Conveyed to me in Jamshoro in January 2018.

96. More will be discussed about his music in Chapter 3.

97. This poem was given to me by Ishaq Samejo, and translated from Sindhi by Manoj Kumar.

3 | Music and Performance

Music expresses that which cannot be put into words and that which cannot remain silent.

Victor Hugo

Throughout Pakistan, rich traditions of music and performance exist from small hamlets to large cities. Oral histories provide communities with important understandings of heritage while ongoing performances provide identity and social meaning. Villages, historically, would be entertained by singers and performers while rites of passage were always delineated with music, regardless of religious community. This is something inherent within South Asian culture in general and within Pakistan, in particular: each region has its own musical heritage, from Balochistan to Punjab to Baltistan; *ghazals* and *qawwalis* were performed by men with strong voices long before Bollywood popularized these poetic expressions.

The state has periodically sponsored musical and theatrical events and, even less frequently, lent support for institutionalizing the promotion of their legacy and activities. However, it has also found itself criticized for promoting something deemed un-Islamic in certain quarters, especially since the promulgation of Zia ul Haq's Islamization programme began in February 1979. Ever since then, over the past forty years, music and performance have periodically been attacked by those who see them as un-Islamic; the majority of those holding this view are commonly perceived as being extremists. Musical performances have at times been attacked and prevented from occurring.[1] In Khyber Pakhtunkhwa, the provincial government has episodically banned the performance of music.

Music and performance have emerged in the past decade (theatre rather longer than music) as vital ways in which Pakistanis are taking stands to recapture local culture and values and to state definitively that something—their authentic identity—has been taken away from them without their consent. Musicians and actors are declaring that Pakistanis have been mischaracterized and misrepresented, especially as being violent and extremists, and many are using music and performance to rectify what they perceive as these social distortions.

This chapter explores the activities of four musicians from various parts of Pakistan who are using their craft to make social statements to counter violence and extremism: Saif Samejo and his 'Lahooti Melo' in the interior of Sindh, Taimur Rahman and his Laal band in Punjab, and Pakhtun musicians Gulab Khel Afridi and Karan Khan. The list is by no means exhaustive— many, many, more performers could be added to it such as Gulzar Alam whose music is sung in the background whenever protests against violence erupt in Peshawar or Arieb Azhar who founded the 'Art Langar' in Islamabad but is now shifting it to Karachi since he started running The Second Floor (discussed in Chapter 7). But the four musicians discussed here are representative of the kinds of work in which musicians are engaged to celebrate communities and bring them closer together and take a stand against extremism. For example, Saif Samejo created the annual two-day 'Lahooti Melo' in interior Sindh as an opportunity to talk about critical subjects—thus far, peace, women's rights, and the environment— and celebrate culture, peace, unity, and harmony through music at night[2] while the Laal band travels throughout Punjab encouraging children to stay in school so they can build Pakistan's future. Gulab Khel Afridi questions how the Pakhtun has come to be more closely identified with guns than with the rabab, a musical instrument that syncopates their lives throughout Khyber Pakhtunkhwa while Karan Khan, in his 'Peshawar Zalmi' (PSL cricket-team) anthem, inspires Peshawar's youth to stand up and celebrate not only cricket but themselves and their communities.

This is followed by an exploration of five theatrical and dance companies' efforts to do the same: Ajoka in Lahore, Tehrik-e-Niswan in Karachi, the Lahore-based Interactive Resource Centre and all its affiliates in Multan and Khairpur, Da Torsaro Saadar in the greater Peshawar area, and the Pushkalavati Theatre Company in Charsadda. The Ajoka Theatre Company has been questioning political and social change since Zia ul Haq's regime and has skirted being charged with subversion by performing plays that are seemingly historical; Sheema Kirmani and her Tehrik-e-Niswan has done the same through dance performances. Interactive theatre enables audiences to finish the dialogues of plays that address timely and compelling social issues, empowering them to see the myriad choices that they can make, and offshoots from the Interactive Resource Centre are now found throughout Pakistan. While Da Torsaro Saadar and the Pushkalavati Theatre Company are far smaller in scope, they are also having an impact on how both their performers and their audiences view extremism and the act of reclaiming culture. Indeed, each of these groups are proving to be exciting ways of raising a voice and affirming local values, sentiments, and cultural identity as they take stands to counter extremism.

MUSIC AS A MEDIUM FOR COUNTERING VIOLENT EXTREMISM

We have seen in Chapter 2 how poetry can be a powerful source of resistance to perceptions of injustice and misrepresentation; music, too, can capture powerful sentiments of identity, ideals, and principles. Drawing comparisons with Palestinian resistance music is useful as ethno-musicologists have researched the latter extensively. Randa Safieh asserts that music is a significant tool through which Palestinians construct, preserve, and assert their identity while also enabling them to resist Israeli occupation.[3] Moslih Kanaaneh argues that Palestinian resistance music does even more than this as it 'incites, provokes, mobilizes, and brings people to action' and plays various political and cultural roles as it,

> generates sentiments; forms national and political identities; and shapes party affiliations, goals, tactics, and ideologies. At the same time, politically and ideologically manipulated folklore songs signify 'a return to the folk', the embodied 'pure' Palestine.[4]

David McDonald, another ethno-musicologist of Palestinian resistance music, sees it as offering a unique opportunity for thinking critically about the nature of Palestinian nationalism, identity, and resistance. He argues that music becomes a performative resistance process,

> a means of intervention, of subversion, of agency, that enables new (or consolidates old) meanings of self and other. This intervention is not one of power, per se, but one of perception. For within each moment of performance lies the opportunity to re-signify what it *means* to be Palestinian and what it *means* to fight for Palestine's recognition.[5]

In Pakistan, there are numerous instances of music as a 'performative resistance process' despite the extremist trope that secular music is un-Islamic. Aside from the popularity (especially among the young) of Coke Studio and the existence of local music awards (e.g., Hum, Lux Style, Nigar, Pakistan Media, and ARY Film), most musicians' voices singing about social life and political transformation have been silenced, especially since the time of Zia ul Haq. Songs about love and religion can be aired and performed on Pakistan television, though ballads of conflict, trauma, and even recapturing of indigenous cultural sentiments are incongruously missing. Of course, this has been rectified somewhat with the rise of YouTube and online streaming services, but it has taken the emergence of 'Patari'—a home-grown streaming and production company launched in February 2015—to provide a popular platform where Pakistani musicians from all genres can have their music broadcast and available.[6] It has provided a venue for Abid Brohi, a rapper from remote Sibi in southwestern Balochistan, thirteen-year-old tea vendor Jahangir Saleem, Peshawar-based Pashto singer, Malala Gul, the enormously popular rap group Lyari Underground, and many of the musicians who will be discussed in this chapter.

Saif Samejo and the Sketches (Interior Sindh)

We became familiar with the poetry of Saif Samejo in the previous chapter, but where he has made his name as a Sindhi, Sufi, folk, rock star is with his band, the Sketches, based in Jamshoro, Sindh. The Sketches, which he began in 2003, has aired their music on Patari since the platform's founding, and they now use it as their near-exclusive outlet for songs, soundtracks, and their 'Lahooti Live' sessions. Saif Samejo draws his inspiration from Sachal Sarmast and Shah Abdul Latif Bhittai's poetry as well as from Sindhi culture itself.

When Saif Samejo was young—he was born in 1984—he was influenced by Sufi singers like Abida Parveen (she sang exclusively in Sindhi then), Alam Faqir (was an actual *faqir* himself), Sohrab Faqir, and Jamaluddin Faqir, the latter being singers/*faqirs* at the shrine of Sachal Sarmast in upper Sindh, outside of Khairpur.[7] His maternal uncles used to take him to the shrine where the singers were reciting Sachal Sarmast's poetry whose message, as we saw in Chapter 2, was very different from mainstream Islam and certainly from the orthodoxy that was permeating Pakistan during the regime of Zia ul Haq. He began to explore the works of various religious leaders and thinkers and started to realize what Abida Parveen and other Sufi singers were singing about, and he began to sing Sachal Sarmast's poetry. He sees Sindhi Sufism as having an important political element, whose foundation goes back to the late seventeenth century and the time of Shah Abdul Latif Bhittai, when Shah Inayat is said to have claimed that 'the one who farms the lands has more rights to the land than the feudal.' Saif considers that Mughal Emperor Farrukh Siyar had Shah Inayat executed because he was talking about communism 260 years ago, but his message has become a foundation of Sindhi society.

Saif credits the poetry of Sachal Sarmast as teaching him resistance; his spiritual searches as teaching him a different side, that God is within you, that you don't have to search for him; and Shah Latif Bhittai as inspiring him that when you close your eyes holding a musical instrument, 'when you pull the string, the music goes on.' He came to understand that human belief is grounded in objective as well as cognitive realities, and it is the cognitive stories that are most powerful. As a story gets old, it becomes a myth and whoever carries it, becomes dangerous. A storyteller can take people in any direction. Saif said that Sachal Sarmast is talking about the people of the earth, of Sindh: they were born here, they are from here, and Shah Latif's poetry continues to tell their story. The story of 'Sindhiat' became Saif's story, the story he sees with his own eyes, from within. He credits this with how he came to start performing music. He said that while it was easy to sing in Urdu, the national language, he felt that at that time he needed to sing in Sindhi. Inspired by the poetry of Shaikh Ayaz, he turned to singing music in Sindhi,

> I have an art that has strings, and it will fight your swords.
> Your huge empires are shaking now against music, art, and poetry,
> You are so weak, having bombs in your hands.[8]

This is what inspired him and others to pick up their guitars while they were students at the University of Sindh. He said they didn't need 'invaders' as their heroes, but instead needed people who had lived here, felt this land.

He said, 'Sachal felt us closely, Latif felt it even more. None of our Sufis gave us weapons. The people with the weapons wanted them killed.'

They began playing concerts in schools and colleges, singing Sindhi and Sufi poetry. He says,

> We started to sing against *mullahs*; Sufism here does not just mean to sit in a cave, being a Sufi here is different. The Sufi is against the kingdom, against the establishment. When you believe in God who is unlimited and omnipotent, then why do you need so many people to have control about God? When you are talking against the mullah, you are rebelling. Sufism is a rebellion. We were the only band singing in Sindhi, Saraiki, Punjabi, and Urdu. We wanted to communicate with students. We were also students at that time.

Saif said he knew that he should take it to a musical battlefield—he doesn't like the word, but feels it's appropriate to get people to know about it. He says, 'We were fighting against extremists, and we didn't want to give them this society.' So he and two other musicians started the Sketches in 2003 and created the band's slogan 'We believe in music' largely inspired from Sachal Sarmast and Shah Latif's poetry. The band's composition changed, the other musicians went onto other ventures as the Sketches was doing 'Lahooti,' a journey. Nomi Ali joined the band on guitar in 2013, then Owais, and a Nepali friend Roshan Sharma joined in 2017, coming to Sindh to do occasional concerts with them. The cover of a DVD that The Sketches released captures the distinctiveness of the band,

> The Sketches is a poetic rebellion. They brought music out from the comfortable, air-conditioned chamber rooms to the open skies of the desert, singing songs in the language of common folks, marinating them in the brine of indigenous melody and retaining their raw, virginal appeal. Saif Samejo, the founder and the lead vocalist of the band…grew up in Sindh when its lands were treaded by the ecstatic Sufis who travelled from places to places singing songs in strange, poetic dialects which made a lasting impression on him. When he founded the Sketches in 2001, he did not have any formal training in music. All he had with him was the memory of those long-forgotten songs and their haunting beauty.

From 2001 to 2007, they travelled all over Pakistan covering underground concerts. During this journey they realized that news media carefully crafted an image of Pakistan which didn't do justice to the essence of his country at all. Yes, there was violence, there was insecurity but alongside there was also enormous resilience and faith in humanity. Their music spontaneously embraced this resilience, this faith and the dialects of the common folks who had preserved the history and essence of the country in their poetry and instruments, which had no room in the projected image of Pakistan carried out by the media.

In 2013, they performed a song of Shah Latif's poetry at Coke Studio. At that moment, it came to him that they should not be doing this kind of music alone and that they needed to bring villagers out to join them, and he decided to start the 'Lahooti Live Sessions'. He took the concept Lahooti—a traveller having no destination, a seeker of the truth—from Shah Latif's poetry.

He brought people together to sing Sindhi poetry from hundreds of years ago. These were not commercial artists, but musicians singing poetry from their hearts, telling the pain of the soil: how a man sitting on the ground feels, and how he feels when the water doesn't come; how a village poet knows about the ecosystem and knows not to kill the trees. They were soon doing two monthly sessions with between a hundred and two hundred people in the audience at night.

They did these sessions for three years, until 2016, recording and preserving the music of Sindhi poets and singers to bring to people everywhere. They recorded about three hundred musicians from Sindh, from elsewhere in Pakistan, and even from outside of Pakistan.

They decided to go all out and put on a musical performance. The first 'Lahooti Melo' was held in April 2016 at the Hyderabad Club with roughly seventy artists performing traditional, rock, fusion, rap, and all sorts of music. Over 30,000 people registered to attend the concert; even more people showed up for it. He recalls that he sold his car to afford the concert. Saif sees the 'Lahooti Melo' as an opportunity,

> to keep our music and art traditions alive. In the world, we have very few but important oral traditions and performances. Through

Lahooti, it is important to keep these traditions alive, the traditions of this land, but we also have music from elsewhere in Pakistan and from around the world. You're listening to another part of Pakistan, listening, learning. We are sharing, it's a collaboration.

They took all the necessary precautions, complete with security. The second 'Lahooti Melo' was held in January 2017, and became 'a journey to bring poets together to tell a story that is not written in Pakistan Studies.' They introduced sessions to discuss politics and to talk about India and Pakistan relations. His motive was to show that Pakistan 'is not a threat to the world. We say, let Pakistan be a country for everyone. Let everyone breathe free here. We try to convey these things in our festival. This is the feeling that keeps me going as a Sindhi.'

The third 'Lahooti Melo', 3–4 March 2018 was billed as 'a festival to talk music, poetry, art, and dance' and largely focused on the theme of peace. They were able to get some major sponsors, including the Sindh Culture Department and the US Consulate in Karachi, which enabled them to pay for transportation costs of some of the artists and speakers. Each day had musical performances and panel sessions during the daytime, many of which addressed important, timely issues about peace and harmony, as seen in Figure 3.1.

Tens of thousands of people attended the musical performances both nights, and joined in dancing and singing. The euphoria throughout the entire event was profound, even when the crowd celebrated Holi—a festival where people throw coloured powder on each other—on the second day. But most importantly, this was being held in Pakistan: no untoward incidents, just tens of thousands of people talking, singing, and dancing until late into the night both days, as can be seen in Figures 3.2 and 3.3.

The fourth 'Lahooti Melo' was held in February 2018. Saif had considered not holding it when some charges were lodged in the Pakistan #MeToo movement at some musicians who had performed in the 'Lahooti Melo' in 2017. He was devastated when he heard that some people he had trusted had taken advantage of other aspiring musicians. But many people pointed out to him that the 'Lahooti Melo' could also be a powerful platform against such actions, and it was decided to dedicate the event to 'the liberated woman.' The fifth event, held in January 2020, was dedicated to global warming and climate change, with scientific discussions as well as sharing of 'indigenous knowledge and wisdom.' Saif said the theme was selected as 'it's our collective responsibility to take care of our environment. We should feel responsible for every act we do to nature.'

In the fall of 2019, the Sketches brought back the 'Lahooti Live Sessions' as an online-only platform featuring music by indigenous artists and occasional collaborations with more mainstream ones.[9] The latest release featured the 'Wandering Ascetics version' of Ram Kali, one of Saif's favourite poems of Shah Latif. It includes a duet between Saif Samejo and Sindhi singer Bhagat Bhooro Laal, and also features the famous Nepali musician Roshan Sharma. In addition to acoustic and electric guitars, the live session includes indigenous instruments including the surhando, frame drum, pakhawaj, mirdangam, ghungro, shakers, tambourine, and the khartaal; they added a few more, including the veena. Saif explained the meaning of the poem,

> The lyrics are about yogis, lahootis, ascetics, and such characters. The kind of people that don't take any burden upon themselves— of thoughts, ideologies, etc. They aren't bound by society's relationships and rules. They are free. They are governed by the laws of nature and they understand better who we are. This is one of the many personas of Shah Latif.[10]

He remarks that he feels the poetry is 'talking about us...I find great pleasure in singing the expressions and the layer-upon-layer of emotions present in indigenous poetry.' This pleasure is evident in Figure 3.4, when Saif was accompanied by other Sindhi musicians to perform on the death anniversary of Shah Latif in Bhittai, Sindh, in October 2019.[11]

The Sketches released their third studio album, 'Saanjhi', on 20 December 2019 on the Rearts record label with the hope of taking it global. Saif Samejo, Nomi Ali, Atif Kalyar, and Roshan Sharma performed on it.

Building on the heritage of Sindhi Sufism, Saif Samejo has taken a powerful stand to assert local proclivities and values. In doing so, he and fellow performers are defying those extremists who try to suppress such actions and transform local culture into something it has never been.

Taimur Rahman and the Laal Band (Lahore)

In Lahore, the provincial capital of Punjab, another musician has started a band defiantly opposed to extremism and against efforts that distort local culture into something it has never been. Taimur Rahman,[12] a child of liberal, socialist activists, grew up believing in a progressive Pakistan and sees music as having a distinct ability to touch people's sentiments and capture their values,

> Pakistani people LOVE music! It's in their blood, in their heart. None of the *maulvis* and all understand how much people love music. It's cathartic, when they can clap, sing, and dance with it.

He had gone to the UK to do his MA at the University of Sussex and then went on to complete his doctorate in Political Science at the School of Oriental and African Studies (SOAS) at the University of London. He returned to Pakistan just as the Lawyers' Movement was inspiring people to believe that a progressive Pakistan was possible. He began teaching and started his band in 2006 with his cousin Haider Rahman and three others, and they were soon joined by Mahvish Vaqar, Taimur Rahman's wife, with the goal to support the lawyers' movement. During demonstrations, they would play music. They received a lot of positive attention and soon released their first album. While they were invited to go abroad for concerts, there were few opportunities to perform in Pakistan because of the violence and bombings that were occurring in the mid-2000s. Live performances had essentially stopped.

Taimur notes that the Laal band has always had a social goal since the days when it started with the lawyers' movement: to make people aware and to get the movement the recognition it deserved. As lead guitarist and vocalist, Taimur kept writing songs to spread the message of peace, tolerance, freedom of expression, and the idea of being secular. He acknowledges that his purpose was to provide a counter-narrative through music and that they wanted to reach out to people at the mainstream level. They sing about responsibility, that Pakistan's future is in children's hands if they stay in school, and also to enjoy life. The message is that we want a progressive Pakistan—and a happy Pakistan. He says that,

In Pakistan, we've started rationing happiness. You can't do Valentine's Day, no *basant*,[13] no dancing…it makes for a very unhappy society. People say 'we are just so happy to see these children singing and happy.'

The band was singing the poetry of Faiz Ahmed Faiz and Habib Jalib, the late Pakistani revolutionary poet and left-wing activist who were known for their opposition to martial law, authoritarianism, and state oppression. Taimur started to write songs but didn't find a lot of support as people were accusing them of following an American agenda, and that it was not their war. In 2012, he wrote 'Death to Terrorism', which few people liked when he first wrote it. It was before the APS attack and before Malala Yousufzai was attacked in Swat. When he sang this initially, he used to feel somewhat defensive. At the time, public opinion was that people speaking about these sorts of issues are working on a western agenda but he realized that they had to focus on extremism,

DEATH TO TERRORISM

Police barricades on every side, bomb blasts at every corner
The ignorant march to 'sacrifice' themselves after having lashed
    women

They take the name of Islam and then blow up market places
Burn down girls' schools and reduce our dignity to dirt

These stooges of imperialism, since when did they become our
    friends?
These puppets of imperialism, since when did they become our
    friends?
Death to Terrorism!

Look at our media anchors, look at those NATO tankers
Look how men have turned into sheep, just look at this circus

These leaders are all worthless, they lie and deceive the people
To imperialism they say ok, ok. Who will step forward and stop
    them?

These stooges of imperialism, since when did they become our
  friends?
These puppets of imperialism, since when did they become our
  friends?

Death to Terrorism!

When the state narrative started to claim that this was Indian, Taimur
and the Laal band responded that this counter narrative is who we are as
Pakistanis. They started a campaign, *Yeh Hum Nahi* (This is Not Who We
Are), and included other Pakistani musical stars in it including Atif Aslam.
But he found it wasn't enough to say 'this isn't us,' but that they had to
answer 'what are we?' and who do we want to be? How could he make the
narrative of the progressive writers a narrative at the grassroots?

Their activities went through various permutations. Now when he
sings 'Death to Terrorism,' the response is an immediate 'absolutely.' He
had already been performing in *katchi abadis* (unregulated slums) for the
Anjaman Muzareen Punjab (a movement of landless tenants and peasants)
between Khanewal and Okara in Punjab. He wanted to build enough
momentum so that at some point in time, in the future, they could mobilize
people in the thousands to stand against terrorism and extremism.[14] He
used that model, but shifted it to schools. In 2013, the Laal band started
playing in colleges and universities and soon expanded to primary schools,
performing at roughly 130 schools a year. They were warmly invited into
many private schools, though getting into government public schools has
been a challenge. They started at small schools, then expanded to larger
ones throughout the province as more people started supporting Laal. But
he wanted to get into government schools as that's where his working-
class audience is, which is often overwhelmed by religious extremism.
He went to the provincial Punjab government, asking for permission to
go into public schools—he even gave them a list of schools—and didn't
ask for anything else aside from permission to perform there. They never
responded other than asking him to do an assessment study, presumably
as he is a political scientist.

When I asked Taimur about how Laal is received at schools, he said,

It's been through the roof, fantastic! These are people who have never seen a concert, a rock concert, at their school. They think it's something only upper-class people can enjoy. There's been a remarkable follow-through by the students—they contact us on social media, they write notes, they stay in touch. They have become a part of the conversation—they like the (Facebook) page, follow the page, but then they become part of the conversation about extremism.

When the band goes to perform at a school, as can be seen in Figure 3.5, students have a transformative experience,

Kids who have never witnessed a live performance before, and they don't know what satisfaction you get from a live performance—and these kids are exposed to all the darkness there is in sexism, religious stuff, etc.—they're forgetting all of that and they're just dancing like crazy people, and they're free.

Their work, though fulfilling, is not without its frustrations. It has been difficult to raise funds to support the band. While Taimur has a steady job as a Professor of Political Science at LUMS, the others in the band are professional musicians and he is concerned about their welfare. He also has to constantly explain and re-explain what they hope to accomplish when they contact schools. He tries to convey the message that they are striving for a more open, secular, democratic, and enlightened society, but some people in Pakistan still don't want to hear that. When they do, they enthusiastically invite the Laal band to perform.

Given his academic position, all of the travel is tiring and it takes time out of academic work and other things he has to attend to. He is also frustrated that they haven't received the kind of media coverage that they would like. The school concerts are small, and except for some coverage in *Dawn*, no one has written much about what they are doing. But then he reflects over what has happened since they began performing in schools and that the response from the students has been amazing, 'so whatever difficulties we have, they seem trivial.'

There were some unexpected things which surprised them that turned out very well. For example, all the teachers at one school were wearing *niqab* (a veil over a woman's face, generally a sign of conservatism), so they were anxious about how they would be received. But when they started singing Punjabi wedding songs, the teachers became so enthusiastic that they started to sing and dance and encouraged the students to get up and sing along with them. This is the goal of how he structures his concerts: Taimur makes a point to jump into the audience and have them participate in the music. Shouting, screaming—that's why live performances are so important for Music for Peace. Everyone becomes an active participant— even I did when I attended a Laal band concert in Lahore in 2017!

Since 2015, they have expanded their Music for Peace campaign. Prior to that, they were playing in schools, colleges, and communities, wherever they could go. But now they are arranging for performances in a more organized way, first focusing on school-going children in poor areas and then expanding to college performances in Khyber Pakhtunkhwa. He sees that province as 'the eye of the storm for extremism in that it has impacted Pakhtun society immensely, especially those forces fighting against extremism.' They were invited to perform at Abdul Wali Khan University in Mardan a year after Mashal Khan, a student falsely accused of blasphemy, had been tortured and killed. Taimur said that the administration was very cautious as they didn't want to have another incident there but they also wanted their campus to be a place of life and music and this is the kind of activity that could help promote that. The university administration asked them not to mention the issue, a painful memory that they don't want to talk about. Taimur did speak about tolerance but didn't take Mashal's name. It was a moving experience for him and the reception there ended up being wonderful.

To him, that was the high point of Music for Peace, because they're all about using music to heal communities. Music for Peace has exposed people to seeing the effects of music and that people need to open up about these things.

In 2019, the Laal band was releasing their third album, 'Rung' (colour), one song at a time. (The first album was released in 2008 followed by the second in 2012.) While there has been a progression from one album to the next, thematically they have been pretty much the same, promoting social change from a progressive point of view. The message in 'Rung' is that life is full of colours and that people are different colours, and all people deserve to be loved. Another song, 'Apna Aap Milay' ('I Hope You Find Yourself') is about self-discovery with the underlying message that we have to connect with who we are as a civilization to find peace,

APNA AAP MILAY (I HOPE YOU FIND YOURSELF)

Under this sun and moon, in the darkness of this night
May my pain find voice, my suffering find speech, may I find my
   own self.

When will the evening to behold begin, when will the morning
   of poetry begin
When will the state of my heart be free, when will the night of
   love begin?

Is there a dawn behind the curtain, is there light beyond the wall?
The colour of my beloved's lips, that's the colour of my banner

Under this sun and moon in the darkness of this night,
May my pain find voice, my suffering find speech, may I find my
   own self

When will the sorrow of my heart abate, when will I make it
   through this night
When will this banner flutter, when will our voices be heard?

When will this garden of flowers bloom, when will the tavern
   resound with laughter?
When will my life be complete, when will the season of love begin?

Under this sun and moon, in the darkness of oppression
May my pain find voice, my suffering find speech, may I find my
   own self

Light a flame of hope, forge your own destiny.
Whichever road you roam, whichever way you go, may you find
   your own self.

May you always find your own self. May I always find my own self.
Whichever road you roam, whichever way you go, may we find
   your own selves.

A final one is a love song he sang with his wife, Mahvish, that promotes public displays of affection and love for each other. He says that when affection is shown for someone, they become very visible.

Taimur says that while Pakistan has 'rationed happiness', there are small ways in which they can break through that, and he thinks they have. His is a private initiative, and if only the state and the wider society could undertake similar kinds of initiatives, 'it would develop a popular culture that could be robust against extremism.' He points out that the Frankfurt School[15] speaks about how popular culture can enable fascism or be a powerful buffer against it; Laal is trying to do just that. It is seeking to change how authority is perceived, lending itself towards a more democratic culture.

Gulab Khel Afridi, rabab master (Peshawar)

> Every musician who adjusts the pegs of the rabab,
> His tuning burns my heart.
>
> Rahman Baba[16]

The above quote from Rahman Baba highlights how pervasive the rabab is in Pakhtun culture and throughout Pakhtun areas. When Gulab Khel Afridi says that he is seeking to revitalize the rabab as a symbol of Pakhtun identity, he doesn't mean that it is no longer being played.[17] Indeed, it is, in every village, district, and city where Pakhtuns live. But instead he seeks it to be revived as a symbol of Pakhtun cultural identity saying,

> Where did the idea come from that the Pakhtun cannot live without his *banduk* (gun)? We can live very well without the *banduk*; we cannot live without music and dancing.

Born in 1977 in Khyber Agency, he studied until 6th grade at the only primary school in his village, but couldn't continue as the higher secondary school was too far away. He instead started to learn to play harmonium with his father's encouragement so he could earn an income playing at *mehndis* (pre-wedding celebrations) and at weddings. He soon switched to learning the rabab as he considers it to be a special instrument in Pakhtun culture, going back over 5,000 years. He claims that it was invented by nomads in two areas of the region, Kosht (in Afghanistan) and Swat. They would roam the area and play it to collect money or tokens from people. The harmonium is not a Pakhtun instrument, and has little history in Pakhtun areas as does the rabab. To amplify the rabab's cultural importance, he said,

> There was a time when three items were always present in a *hujra* (area for male visitors): a rabab, a *janamaz* (prayer mat), and a *chillum* (hookah). If you look at a rabab, you will see that it includes slight etchings of nearly all the prominent animals found in the region.

He repeatedly points out that the rabab captures the soul of Pakhtuns and is crafted from materials native to the region. He owns a number of rababs, each hand crafted from local wood.

He began to perform at weddings and other cultural festivals and made his premier on PTV (Pakistan Television) in 1998 and later played on the radio. At the time, he was giving lessons out of his home to two or three students at a time, much like he had gone to his teacher's house when he was learning how to play the rabab. In 2012, he discussed with various friends that he wanted to launch a music academy but they counselled him to wait for the socio-political turmoil in the region to settle and only then open its doors. Four years later, in 2016, they agreed with him that the socio-political situation had improved and that he had good reason to go ahead with his plan. He was getting requests from people interested in learning the instrument and he didn't want to waste any more time by not teaching them. He especially wanted to start teaching online classes and launched his Gul Rabab Academy via Skype, WhatsApp, Facebook Messenger, and FaceTime in November 2016.[18] He has students from various countries taking online classes with him, and Pakistani students from Lahore, Karachi, Islamabad, and elsewhere who cannot physically come to Peshawar to study with him also register for online classes. In 2019, he was teaching more than fifty students either in person or online.

While he enjoys performing, he also greatly enjoys teaching the rabab, especially to children. He feels he is helping pass on an important aspect of cultural heritage. He sees music as a language in itself, and the rabab is a symbol of Khyber Pakhtunkhwa 'in its entirety.' Many parents have told

him that aside from having their children learn traditional music, they also
learn about Pakhtun artistic expression,

> The rabab is not solely a musical instrument. Kind of like my
> name is Gulab Afridi, my clothing, my shoes are an extension of
> myself, how I choose to reflect my cultural identity. When I teach
> children how to play the rabab, I also tell them that they are not
> to perform in jeans. If you cannot wear a traditional waistcoat or
> turban, at least wear a Chitrali *pakol* (soft woollen cap).

More recently, Gulab has joined with other musicians to promote peace
between India and Pakistan under the 'Aman ki Asha' project. He recorded
a song on Radio Pakistan that his country is now peaceful and that he hopes
this newfound peace will last. He says,

> Yes, I definitely sing about wanting peace in the country.
> Whichever country I visit, I know that since those people are
> foreigners, they have no connection with our language and cannot
> understand it but we can convey messages through music. Music
> is a language in itself.

He joined a multinational delegation of musicians and travelled along the
old Silk Road to promote peace, and represented Pakistan in the CPEC
Culture Caravan in November 2017; he is seen performing during this
in Figure 3.7. He takes being an ambassador for peace by performing his
music very seriously, and is proud that he is able to represent a true cultural
image of Pakistan abroad. Representing Pakistan in more than twenty
countries, Gulab said that 'as a Pakistani, I feel proud when I represent
my beloved country through music in other countries. We are a peaceful
nation and hate terrorism.'[19]

He has become a frequent participant in Pakistan National Council of
the Arts (PNCA) concerts to play a role in conveying the message that the
region's culture needs to be promoted and safeguarded. When he performs
for an international audience, he is using music to show that Pakhtuns are
a peace-loving people, still struggling to come out of that violent period
where they had been trapped and observes,

People now realize that we are a peace-loving people. We love our musical instruments and music. The people who are thinking of Pakhtuns as violent—we are showing, through music, that we are peaceful and peace-loving. We are showing other Pakhtuns, too, that we are peaceful. We don't want violence. Our message goes through music. We play good music so people can see we are peaceful.

While the rabab is an indigenous instrument, he also hopes to take it to new heights by doing fusion with it. He aspires to use it to perform with other international musicians 'so that the whole world will know it, and then the whole world will know what Pakhtun culture really is.'

He also joined a group of noted artists and performers on World Music Freedom Day in March 2019 who were pressing for the provincial government of Khyber Pakhtunkhwa to resolve their various longstanding issues including releasing monthly stipends, provision of security, preservation of fast-disappearing traditional music tools, launching of an endowment fund, creation of an art academy, and advocating for a special package for artists of the merged tribal districts.[20] Notably, they condemned the killing of artists and rising violence against them in Khyber Pakhtunkhwa and demanded the government launch an annual folk music festival and exchange of troupes of artists to promote peace through music in the region.

Karan Khan, Pashto Singer (Peshawar)

Karan Khan is a popular Pashto singer, originally from Mingora in Swat but now based in Peshawar. He began studying music in 2004, has released seventeen albums in a variety of genres, and made his mark as a musician being defiant in the wake of extremism when he became the goodwill ambassador for the 'Peshawar Zalmi,' a Pakistan Super League (PSL) cricket team, in 2018.

Born in 1983, he went to Karachi after 10th grade to work in a textile mill; he didn't know what else to do.[21] He worked for a year, and on Eid in 2001 attended a Pashto variety musical show. He went to the organizer and asked if he could sing there. He began to sing a popular Gulzar Alam song and everyone enjoyed it so much that they asked him to sing another song. Then they asked him to come sing at another function on the second day of Eid. He was so greatly encouraged by the other musicians that he decided to attend a music academy in Karachi. He studied there with A.R. Anwar for four years, did about 150 performances in Karachi during that time, and then returned to Swat. There, he studied with Sher Jan Ustad for three years.

He was already performing a lot in Swat when the violence began in 2007. After the fighting intensified in 2008, he and his family left and became IDPs (Internally Displaced Persons) in Swabi where he cut his first album in 2009 and started a radio programme. The IDPs began to return to Swat in September 2009. He decided to perform at Swat's Saidu Medical College as a way to help his community return to normalcy. The sound technicians were afraid to come from Peshawar, and were charging them three times the usual cost. As there was a curfew, they ended up having to stay there all night, even though the performance had finished. He performed in Swat because it is his home and is important to him, 'It's my *mulk* (country), my *mitti* (ground).' He feels that if he didn't go, the music of Swat would die. He was nervous that this might be his last programme and that it was possible they could be killed by a bomb blast. There were only about six soldiers there during the concert, so if the terrorists wanted to bomb it, they couldn't do anything about it; if they bombed it, the whole building would fall. He also felt that if he, someone from Swat, didn't go there to perform, no other musician from Peshawar would go there.

He did a brief stint in Peshawar and then left to perform in Dubai after his first album had come out. Things were improving in Swat, but he was still worried about his three brothers in the police and his father in the army, as the extremists were targeting such kinds of officials. He started to choose poems to sing about what he had seen and experienced in Swat and more about current affairs in his songs. A Pashto singer in Afghanistan, Shafiullah Babarzai, wrote a poem 'Pray for Khyber Pakhtunkwa,' and he was inspired to sing similar works for Swat. He then wrote about Bacha Khan's philosophy in his song, 'Bacha Khane Pakardah' ('Bacha Khan's Vision'). He said that whenever he sings that song, it makes him cry; it was hard to record it, because he always cries. He sings about his own reality and about human rights and says 'singing is very powerful.' He sings *qawwalis* (Sufi devotional music), *ghazals* (short poems of rhyming couplets), and stories from Pakhtun folklore, often chronicling the angst of Pakhtuns today living amongst violence and separated from their families. When he can't find poetry about issues important to him or that which evokes sentiments he seeks to capture, he writes his own poetry. He now reads a lot, which is why he's doing his PhD in new genres in Pashto poetry at the University of Peshawar.

Aside from performing in Dubai, he has performed in Malaysia and seven other countries. In 2015, he went to the UK and did three concerts for charities.

Pashto poetry is traditionally structured in two lines, *tapas*. There is always a lot of information in these two lines. Karan has become famous for having introduced a new genre of Pashto poetry that has five lines, *tapazey*, which he feels makes the two lines easier to understand. People have liked it a lot and other singers have started to sing in the same style. He later introduced another style with six lines, *takoreza*.

He was asked to become the goodwill ambassador for the Pakistan Super League (PSL) team, Peshawar Zalmi, and travelled to Dubai with them in late February 2018. The song he wrote for 'Peshawar Zalmi' is inspirational, not particularly for the team but for all Pakhtun youth— the *zalmi*, in Pashto. He did this work with no compensation as a message for Pakhtun youth. They have endured the unrelenting abusive stereotype of being terrorists and extremists, and the song is a powerful inspiration for them to 'get to the field' and show the world the character of Pakhtun youth.

PESHAWAR ZALMI ANTHEM

We are moving ahead in getting education and ripening our skills
We share a common vision and a clear goal
Whether we are from the upper or from the lower region[22]
We are thankful to God that people appreciate Peshawar youth,
    Peshawar Zalmi!
Peshawar youth, from the upper and from the lower.

We celebrate our victories together and we share our defeats
Our girls and young boys, we have common victories and common
    losses.

Every Pakhtun who is outside of his home and land, stand firm
    beside us,
Let the world know who we are
Whether from the upper or from the lower region.
Let the Peshawar youth prove to the world that the Peshawar Zalmi
Have the same character as the youth of Peshawar!

Our youth are energized and the world will witness our spirit
That we don't care about victory or loss.
We want to show the world that we're getting to the field;
We don't care about winning or losing
We just have to come out to the field and play the game.[23]
That we are scattered everywhere, that is the pain that we carry
    with us.
The youth is my army whether they are from the upper or the
    lower region.

Peshawar youth seek peace and development, learning skills and
    getting educated
This is your team, oh Pakhtun youth, each one of you are heroes.
When you are together, then every day is a festive day,
Whether you are from the upper or the lower (calling for unity)
Don't hesitate but instead get inspiration from our shared success.
Peshawar youth, Peshawar Zalmi![24]

It is noteworthy that there is no mention of cricket in the song. Its audience is the youth of Peshawar and it is calling upon them to stand up defiantly in the face of adversity which has plagued the region for some years, to 'seek peace and development, learning skills, and getting educated' and to become the heroes of their own lives.

THEATRE AND PERFORMANCE

Theatre and other forms of performance such as dance are generally representations of a social message an artist seeks to convey to an audience. Sometimes they are just stories being told, albeit often imbued with moral, ethical, or political implications. In Pakistan, given the historic lack of support by the state, there has been a resultant stifling of freedom of expression and thought in the arts, which is evident by there being fewer theatres and performance halls in major cities compared to other major metropolitan areas in the world. Many performers have thus been both hesitant and defiant to perform, as Sheema Kirmani writes,

> Arts can only exist in a society that is tolerant of divergent opinions and open to questioning on every conceivable aspect of life… this is made impossible in Pakistan…(where) any divergence from traditionally held beliefs or expression of an idea that goes against the grain of one or the other sect brings with it the threat of physical violence. Dance, or any art form for that matter, if it has to be of any value, must touch upon sensitive issues and not avoid them, as we are unfortunately forced to do.[25]

Out of necessity, theatre and performance in Pakistan—trying to convey a cultural or political message—has often represented it symbolically so as to resist authoritarianism and extremism. This section explores what five of these theatre and dance companies have sought to do to reclaim local culture and take a stand against extremism: the Ajoka Theatre Company in Lahore, Tehrik-e-Niswan in Karachi, the Lahore-based Interactive Resource Center and its affiliates in Multan, Khairpur and elsewhere, Da Torsaro Saadar in the greater Peshawar area, and the Pushkalavati Theatre Company in Charsadda.

Ajoka Theatre Company (Lahore)

The Ajoka Theatre Company has been questioning political and social change since Zia ul Haq's regime and has skirted being charged with subversion by performing plays that are seemingly historical. The late Madeeha Gauhar told me that they have long been talking about the growing intolerance in society, providing,

> an alternative narrative about a culture of non-violence that has existed for generations, a syncretic culture that has always existed here…Ajoka is political theatre: anything that talks about change—change in society, the individual, your mind-set—taking up issues that are controversial, issues that are not easily discussed (e.g., the blasphemy law and gender issues).[26]

She considered that Ajoka's theatre performances were countering extremism since the 'seeds' for extremism were sown during the Zia era, 'long before the Taliban started bringing their violence into Pakistan.' Their vision was to link traditional form with contemporary reality. Ajoka's plays became a space where the audience could gather not only to see the performance, but also to discuss and meet with like-minded people.

Madeeha Gauhar founded Ajoka in 1984 and became its founding director, producer, and principal actress, producing and directing over fifty original plays usually with her main collaborator, Shahid Nadeem. He had previously been imprisoned by the Zia ul Haq government and was adopted as a prisoner of conscience by Amnesty International. He met Madeeha Gauhar in London where he was in exile and went on to become the main scriptwriter for Ajoka.

The Ajoka Theatre Company, whose logo is 'theatre for social change,' states it has three objectives:

1. To perform socially meaningful theatre and thus contribute to the struggle for a secular, democratic, just, and egalitarian Pakistan.
2. To promote quality theatre in Pakistan, blending traditional forms with modern techniques and contemporary awareness, and provide entertainment which has a social purpose.
3. To promote the cause of peace and enlightenment in society through innovative and enriching art, for the masses.[27]

Its emphasis has been either on history or historical figures—e.g., *Hotel Mohenjodaro*, Dara (Shikoh), Bulleh Shah, and Manto—or on social issues such as bonded labour, religious intolerance, female education, partition, gender violence, extremism, and corruption. The very first play they performed, *Jaloos* (Procession) in 1984, captured issues as people came out in public. Other plays explicitly touch on political issues and social conflict including *Yahan Se Shehr Ko Dekho* (See the City from Here, which is about four women in prison), *Dekh Tamasha Chalta Ban* (Watch the Show and Move On, which is about religious intolerance and the blasphemy laws), *Border Border* (on the theme of peace between India and Pakistan) and *Lo Phir Basant Aee* (Basant has Come Again, which is on the curbs on freedom of expression and censorship).[28] They find that even the historical dramas are revelations for people today as they don't know much about these protagonists and that their reinterpretations of historical and cultural heritage are often different from the official narrative. One of their best-known dramas is *Burqavaganza* where the concept of the *burqa* (veil) is used to uncover some of Pakistani society's 'darkest secrets' through ironic satire and subtle humour references to target past and present political parties.[29] The writers, according to Madeeha Gauhar, are actually taunting the society by stating that everyone wears a *burqa* but it's just the privileged perspective that has to be hidden from the world and that gets used for one's personal favour at the expense of Islam and women's rights. The play then goes on,

> to narrate the classic tale of forbidden love, where a young couple is forced into hiding their love by pretending to be hidden in a *burqa* which gives them the freedom to be together in the streets and even to hold hands, something for which they can be hanged if they dared to go in public revealing their true identities. However, the irony takes a tragic turn when the young couple gets married but later after the marriage the families find out of their romantic premarital affair and both of them are hanged to death. At this point, the curtain falls and the writers ask the audience, does the *burqa* actually protect the people or does it expose them?[30]

The play is a metaphor to talk about the process of Talibanization, and was prohibited from being shown in many venues in Pakistan including the National Arts Council (PNCA) in Islamabad but was able to be staged in Ajoka's native Lahore in 2007. Shahid Nadeem, Ajoka's main scriptwriter, thinks that people have raised objections to the performance because of their own political enmities,

> When they said this play has made fun of 'beard and *burqa*' and we cannot let people make fun of it, it became big news. Here, culture is something you can easily sacrifice. The matter was picked up by international media and a debate started on social media. It became a major issue as to whether the *burqa* is a part of Islam or not, and whether theatre has a right to raise it as a subject. The thing is, we had used the *burqa* as a metaphor, a dramatic device to make a social and political point, that why are you trying to cover things. It's not just a woman's face, but beauty, art itself—

they're placing a *burqa* over these things. We pointed this out in the brochure of the play.[31]

He said that all of Ajoka's work is geared towards extending cultural space and to challenge the extremist mindset.

Another major play of Ajoka's is *Dara*, the story of one of Mughal Emperor Shah Jehan's sons, which explores 'the multiplicity of Islam's history.' The programme-note for the play states that the conflict between Dara Shikoh and his brother Aurangzeb was not only over succession but especially over ideals,

> Promoting tolerance and diversity, Prince Dara Shikoh—a liberal Sufi, poet, and scholar of comparative religion—wanted to build on the vision of Akbar the Great to bring the ruling Muslim elite closer to local religions. Prince Aurangzeb, a religious zealot, wanted to impose shariah law on India's predominantly non-Muslim population…the battle between the two princes represents two conflicting interpretations of Islam—a clash that still rages in the Muslim world today with serious international implications.

This play has been banned, then unbanned, and banned again in Pakistan for its obvious political implications.

In 2005, when Shahid Nadeem was also the director of the PTV academy in Islamabad, he produced an Ajoka telefilm, *Mujahid*, that showed two Pakistani men fighting in Afghanistan alongside the Taliban. One wanted to stop and be rehabilitated while the other wanted to continue his fight in Pakistan. The film poses the question, who is the real *mujahid*? A controversy erupted in Parliament between those who thought it insulted the concepts of jihad and martyrdom and those who introduced a counter resolution to say how good the telefilm was and that it was raising awareness. Shahid Nadeem retells that the government agencies demanded to review a copy of the telefilm, and deemed there was nothing wrong with it, so PTV could air it again in the future. However, once Shahid Nadeem left PTV, they never aired that film again.

According to Shahid Nadeem, Ajoka's greatest challenge has been to fight against people who want 'to control the narrative.' He said,

We believe in presenting our version of what Pakistan is meant for in a manner that is inclusive, not offensive, to any section and is entertaining as well. People enjoy the presentation. We don't lecture them, we let them make their own decisions—to have a balance between entertainment and the meaningful content. We have seen that if you address it in the right way, people who are biased, conservative, etc., they open up if you present this in a balanced way.[32]

He considers Ajoka's focus on peace between India and Pakistan fights extremism, because extremism feeds on ignorance and hatred. Their plays instead make reference to the common heritage and culture between the two countries and don't demonize the other.

Ajoka attracts huge audiences wherever they perform in Pakistan, whether in small or large cities. Sometimes people are deliberative in coming to attend the plays, knowing fully that they perform political theatre, though others just come to have a nice time as it's free entertainment. Shahid Nadeem considers that regardless of the reasons why people attend, the plays generally have an impact on the audience.

Ajoka has organized a memorial theatre festival in collaboration with the Lahore Arts Council (27–29 September 2018) to honour and remember Madeeha Gauhar. The dedication notes that she left behind 'a rich and vast legacy of socially meaningful theatre and art-based peace-building' and that the over fifty original plays she directed and produced 'celebrated Pakistan's rich cultural heritage and addressed sensitive, even tabooed subjects with sensitivity, courage, and innovative direction.'[33]

Ajoka will continue on with plays and other new initiatives in the post-Madeeha Gauhar era. They have begun 'Ajoka Evenings' on the lawn beside Ajoka's headquarters in Lahore, where they hold dramatic readings with talented actors and new talent. Shahid Nadeem says that the idea is 'to create cultural space, and reach out to different sections of the society who may not come to theatre, but will come to this kind of event.'[34] They are also engaged with the new Institute for Art & Culture in Lahore which Shahid Nadeem considers to be a progressive school of art, language, and culture as well as of cinematic and digital arts; he is the head of their film and television programme.

Ajoka Theatre Company still performs whenever they have the opportunity. Shahid Nadeem says that the emphasis today is to link the fight against extremism with the fight against climate change and 'the false identity of our background as Arabs, as if we have no indigenous roots with this land. We are a part of South Asia, because of our culture and our literature.'

Tehrik-e-Niswan (Karachi)

Sheema Kirmani and her Tehrik-e-Niswan dance company has often defiantly sought to be a cultural conscience. She began adult literacy and craft classes for women and decided in the early 1970s to try to give women a platform for their creativity by organizing a women's *mushaira*. She continued to perform informally until they performed on the premises of a Meena Bazaar (a *bazaar* for women) in 1979 where only women were present for shopping. She realized that this was a place where women were coming and many had sat down to watch them perform. She realized that all the work they were doing thus far happened at once when the women watched the play and could relate to the stories and that was what they had to do: become a cultural group and use dance and performance as a medium to connect with people to talk about rights. It was totally a volunteer organization for a number of years.[35]

The group began to engage in cultural action more formally in the 1980s. They performed in various schools in Karachi and partnered with the Orangi Pilot Project in Orangi (discussed in Chapter 7). The idea of the performance was to build a rapport and to connect with people's stories and talk about their lives. Sheema says that they saw the greatest change within female teachers themselves who would come up with stories that she would put in her upcoming performances. In the 2010s, their focus has been on performing *natak*—desi theatre—for youth. They create small *nataks*—thirty to forty minutes long—and go to schools in low-income areas all over Karachi and perform there, many being areas where violence is part of people's everyday life. The plays are attacking and subverting ethnic and religious violence.

She began performing Bharatanatyam and Orissi styles of dance as a soloist in 1981 and began teaching dance in 1983. It was an act of defiance to Zia's promulgation stopping all forms of dance, especially by women. She has always had death threats on her since she began dancing. At that time, she says, it was very clear to her that the state, the government, and the establishment was against what she was doing but the public was with her. She asserts that dance has given her power—and that men are threatened by the power that a woman gains through dance—and that this is the inherent message in her work.[36]

One of her first performances was *Aurat* (Woman) in 1980, which has subsequently been performed over a thousand times. In her effort not only to 'represent reality but also try to shape it,' she made a minor change in the original script penned by Indian street theatre activist Safdar Hashmi so that the female lead defines her own place in society. Years later, in 2005, they performed *Aakhir Kyun?* based on true incidents and case studies of women killed in the name of 'honour.' The play was created in workshops with community members who had been in direct contact with or themselves had been victims of attacks for 'honour' and was performed over a hundred times.

She wrote *Hum Rokaen Gae (We Will Stop): a Theatre Play for Peace* soon after Salman Taseer, the popular governor of Punjab, was murdered in 2011 for speaking out against the blasphemy law.[37] The performance held in an open-air auditorium at the Arts Council in Karachi in 2012 was very powerful.[38] It opens with men fighting—with choreography—and finally dying. Sheema walks up to the dead bodies and recites Jinnah's declaration on 11 August 1947, 'You are free.' She continues to recite (in Urdu) the entire 11 August speech that people can go to their places of worship as religion is not the concern of the state. She then asks, 'But what is happening in Pakistan today? In the name of religion, people are being killed' and this has become quite common, with blood everywhere. She then portrays her angst in dance, soon joined by the men of her theatre company as they rise up, no longer dead. She walks up to a woman who is collapsed on the ground asking 'Who are you? Who hit you? What is your name?' After declaring her name to be Margaret, she breaks into a ferociously powerful dance resembling a Punjabi *bhangra*, and is then joined by other women and men in the company. They shift to depicting farming and interact with the feudal landlord who makes unreasonable demands on them and refuses a request for a modest loan for medicine for a

Fig. 3.1: Panel sessions on both days at the
Lahooti Melo, 2018.

Fig. 3.2: Saif Samejo and other Sindhi musicians performing at the Urs of
Shah Abdul Latif Bhittai, October 2019.

Fig. 3.3: Taimur Rahman and the Laal Band performing at a
school in a working-class area of Lahore, November 2017.

Fig. 3.4: Gulab Khel Afridi in his studio,
February 2018.

Fig. 3.5: Gulab Khel Afridi playing rubab at the PNCA, Islamabad,
celebrating the earlier CPEC Cultural Caravan, March 2018.

Fig. 3.6: Karan Khan in his studio in Peshawar,
February 2018.

Fig. 3.7: Scriptwriter Shahid Nadeem with Madeeha Gauhar, speaking
with the author at a home in Lahore, 2017.

sick child unless the mother has sex with him. They are joined by a mullah, complete with huge prayer beads, who curses the workers when he finds out that they are Christians. The agricultural labourers argue with the landlord that he is being unjust and unreasonable. The mullah promises the landlord that if it is a *fatwa* against the Christian workers that he wants, he'll get it. We then see the mullah make a claim that they said blasphemous things and that they are *kafirs* (nonbelievers). The workers are beaten amidst cries that they are '*kafirs*' and 'Christians,' and soon a woman is encircled and, through dance, is presumably raped. Sheema then joins the defiant farmer/dance group, proclaiming this must stop. But then she asks, who will stop them? Each one of the farmer/dancers declares 'I will stop them!' They then turn to the audience and scream out, 'Will you stop them?!' and conclude with dance and singing. The audience is clearly moved by what they have seen, clapping and singing along with the troupe.

Sheema said that when shrines are attacked, artists are attacked and freedom of expression is not allowed; that is when dance is important. She said to me,

> Dance is my resistance to fundamentalism, to oppression, to control. To the control of spaces, especially those spaces that are occupied by independent women, especially at Sufi shrines. Art, music, and culture can never be crushed or restricted by either religious fundamentalism or any other kind of borders and boundaries.[39]

She argues that dance and other forms of performance have been taken away from people's lives and 'the only music they hear is *filmi* music, therefore, bringing dance and theatre into people's lives is a very important mission.' She considers that everything that Tehrik-e-Niswan does is standing up to extremism: just that they are performing—men and women together—are singing and dancing, in a troupe that is comprised of people of different religions and different class backgrounds, is a statement of defiance. They select controversial topics such as the right of a woman to own her own body and to own her own mind—the mental independence that most people are reluctant to give to women.[40] We can see this in the opening poem of the play *Aseer Shahzadi* (The Captive Princess),

To live among the stonehearted structures and tyrannical
    institutions of our society,
We are taught to be ashamed of ourselves (as women) and are
    compelled to crumble beneath the weight of oppression.
Our tyrannical institutions are pushing us closer and closer to
    self-destruction.
We are surrounded by walls and ominous partitions,
Here lives the captive princess,
Reared on superstition, in bed with unfair compromise,
The mother of grief and despair,
Tormented by the echo of her sisters' plight,
An intoxicating dance of raw emotion.
These tyrannical structures can be torn down,
This captive princess can also be set free,
This imprisoned princess who has a flame-like body,
With a soul of tempered steel,
Whose tongue can voice her deepest thoughts,
Whose arms have great, easy strength,
Whose fingers craft and create with finesse,
Once this imprisoned princess frees herself,
She will breathe fearlessly,
She will dance with glee,
She will discover her being and purpose in life.[41]

Tehrik-e-Niswan has begun holding youth conventions for cultural
appreciation annually since July 2017. They bring about three hundred
young people together for a seven-day residential convention; they had
met the youth when they had performed at their schools during the year.
Sheema said that all the conventions, all three years, were inspiring and
rejuvenating for her, that there's still hope in the young people. She said
that they reinforced to her that art is the only way to counter extremism and
that 'this is how the arts are so subversive: they make people think about
beauty, harmony, and peace. The extremist narrative that has been pushed
down our throats has to be countered through cultural intervention.'[42]

    She travelled to the tomb of the Sufi saint Lal Shahbaz Qalandar
in Sehwan in the interior of Sindh on 17 February 2019 to dance the
dhamaal to mark the anniversary of the February 2017 bomb blast.[43] There
she danced to a *qawwali* recording of Amir Khusro; she said that some

people consider that dancing to a *qawwali* is blasphemous. She said that by bringing it out in the open, she was powerfully confronting the forces of extremism. She intends to go to other saints' shrines including the *dargah* of Sachal Sarmast and the ashram at Sadu Bela (the island outside of Khairpur) in the future, to perform and reclaim their indigenous cultural heritage.

Interactive Resource Centre (Lahore)

Interactive theatre enables audiences to finish the dialogues of plays that address timely and compelling social issues, empowering them to see the myriad choices that they can make. The 'grandfather' of interactive theatre in Pakistan, Mohammad Waseem, founder of the Interactive Resource Centre (IRC), is working on countering violent extremism through reclaiming creative and cultural spaces and enabling people to participate in it.[44] He sees interactive theatre as a powerful way to do this as,

> You cannot change people by giving sermons, or lectures in classrooms, or trainings. People can only change themselves when they have clarity on issues, and that can only come about through critical dialogue. IRC creates spaces for that dialogue. While others are using culture as entertainment, we are using entertainment to question culture.

Offshoots from the IRC are now found throughout Pakistan as people have come from all over—including Swat, Multan, and Khairpur—to be trained in interactive theatre.

Mohammad Waseem, the head of IRC, was a founding member of Lok Rehas and Ajoka, but broke off from them in 2000 to found IRC. The idea behind it is to impart education through dialogue between all participants, actors and audience alike. He contrasts IRC with Ajoka, which is a more traditional form of theatre—it is a performance, not a dialogue. He makes the distinction that,

> traditional theatre creates a line between performers and the audience. The audience can either like it, dislike it, or leave; they can't change the performance. We (in IRC) have to create a play

that includes social and political errors—that way, people can talk.
Art can help you to bring people together, but the important part
is creating a dialogue.

The main kind of performances that they do are 'forum theatre' where they
work with non-actors, figure out what's important in their community,
what they need to fix, and they put together a play about it. It is not
traditional theatre as the actors and the audience can make a new scene or
add a new character. The plays usually peak at the time of an impending
catastrophe (e.g., about to marry off a young child, or members of different
religions are at the pinnacle about to fight with each other)—and the
play stops there. The actors then ask the audience what they think should
happen and have them act it out.

Mohammad Waseem and others from the IRC have travelled throughout
Pakistan providing trainings in interactive theatre at universities, NGOs,
and occasionally other sites, and have built a very strong network. He
estimates that they have worked with more than 4,000 people in the past
15–20 years, helped create and train at least 300 theatre groups—most
comprised of 8–10 people (although some student groups were far larger)—
and about fifty of those groups remain active today. The other groups work
independently and don't have to be affiliated with IRC afterwards.

The IRC has received funding from USAID, NED (the US-based
National Endowment for Democracy), and from the United States Institute
for Peace (USIP) to support its activities. Waseem says that they accept
the funding because it enables them to expand their efforts, but with
the condition that only they decide what the plays are about. Half of
the funding they take in is from such grants while the other half is from
consultancies and commercial work, including renting out IRC's studio
space. An example of the grant work is the theatre presentation they did as
part of the motorcycle campaign, Women on Wheels, for the Government
of Punjab. The play was about the need for female mobility, to target
a stigma, and was also linked to sexual harassment. They performed it
throughout Lahore, at Liberty Market, in Anarkali, Government College
University, and in the outskirts in Johar Town. Funding from USIP
supported three plays IRC performed on interfaith harmony in Lahore,
Multan, and Bahawalnagar comprised of actors from mixed religious

groups (Muslims, Hindus, and Christians). For example, one of the plays was 'Kalpana to Kirin,' about how members of the Hindu community change their names to avoid discrimination. This eye-opening performance enabled audiences to complete the story in inventive ways which differed everywhere it was performed.

Waseem realized that 'micro-issues should be linked to macro-policies,' and for that purpose he decided they needed to use a variety of media. They set about making documentaries and films on 'CVE'—Countering Violent Extremism—for the US Embassy. Two of the six films were about non-Sunni Muslim Pakistani soldiers who lost their lives in Pakistan: a Shia from Parachinar (from the erstwhile Kurram Agency in FATA) and an Ismaili from Gilgit–Baltistan. The other four were about a Christian soldier from southern Punjab; Nusrat Ara, an activist in Mardan; a tribute to Aitzaz Hassan from Hangu, the boy who sacrificed his life in January 2014 to save other students at his school when terrorists attacked it; and about the security guard who stopped an attacker from entering a church in Youhanabad, in Lahore, who also died in the process.

The IRC also performed plays and developed films focused on interfaith harmony. Waseem developed a three-month course complete with practitioner guidelines for trainers and ran this course at public universities throughout the country. He also engaged twenty-five religious leaders from different sects—and ultimately made a network—and gave them a three-day training in peace building.

Waseem decided to establish residential workshops in Lahore on how to make a script, do the camerawork, and overall how to make a documentary. Selected students were divided into groups of two and were tasked to write a larger documentary story that would be on the themes of peace, tolerance, and interfaith harmony. They wrote stories on Sunni/Shia marriages and Sufism, but occasionally also focused on cultural heritage (including a film on Multani khussas, the ornate, artistic gold-thread shoes from Multan). Some of the films were then turned into talk shows and showcased on local TV stations.

The IRC also trained three hundred students in Bahawalpur in southern Punjab in five different mediums: photography, theatre, citizen journalism, visual arts (drawing and painting), and music. They began with a workshop on human rights and peace-building with the themes of peace, tolerance, and cultural heritage. Those working on visual arts made drawings of their ideas of peace and tolerance, the journalism students made stories on those themes, the music club collaborated with folk singers of the area, and the photography club ended up creating a limited-edition coffee table book.

They have also done a lot of work on campus radios at universities in response to Requests for Proposals (RFPs) from donor organizations. They have trained students at the University of Peshawar and at BZU in Multan on how to make audio documentaries and emphasized the themes of peace, tolerance, and gender equality. They went ahead and designed twenty radio programmes that were broadcast on their own university's radio channels and on the FM stations in their cities.

IRC further expanded their scope and created ten digital stories for the internet version of *Dawn* newspaper. This inspired Waseem to create MAATI TV in 2012 as a venue where their films could be constantly viewed.[45] IRC's information on MAATI TV describes it as 'a web-based interactive video site aimed at creating an alternative narrative of Pakistan, promoting democracy, human rights, and equal citizenship through digital storytelling and social media advocacy.'[46] Towards this end, to develop alternative narratives, they use documentary shorts, interactive theatre, citizen journalism, and online advocacy campaigns on various themes including human rights, culture, and music. Videos highlighted on the MAATI TV's site include all of these themes, which can be seen in the following titles: 'The Story of Blue Pottery', 'Maati Explains Fundamental Rights', 'Understanding the Students Solidarity March, 2019', 'Sounds of South Punjab: Rooman Malick', 'Maati TV | Climate Change in Pakistan', and 'Maati TV | Celebrating Diwali in Pakistan'. Additional videos include 'Maati Explains | The Responsibilities of State and Citizen', 'Hunger Free Pakistan', 'If not Democracy, then What?', and 'Why we should read our Constitution', all of which are forcefully standing up to countering extremism.

We can see other groups elsewhere in Pakistan which have been heavily influenced by the IRC. In Multan, Athar Jahanian created a local branch of the IRC, having learned theatre from Mohammad Waseem and having worked with Ajoka.[47] He had started performing in 2000 when he was fifteen. At the time, Ajoka was training community groups, and he was a community theatre activist and trained with them. He performed for

Ajoka in community festivals in Multan and surrounding theatres as well as in Lahore until 2004, when he started his own group in Multan, The Multan Theatre Group. Comprised of four women and six men, the group was interested in performing 'Theatre of the Oppressed,' based on Paulo Freire's ideology, an interactive forum theatre similar to what Jahanian had learned with the IRC.

The Multan Theatre Group performs community theatre throughout southern Punjab including in its Provincially Administered Tribal Areas (PATA) and elsewhere on Pakistan's southern coastline (e.g., Turbat and Gwadar). Jahanian said that as there is no tradition of theatre in the area, they partner with local NGOs and go wherever they have campaigns. They have performed forum theatre about the local justice (*panchayat*) system, domestic violence, human trafficking, promoting girls' education, against early marriage, child sexual abuse, and child labour. When the Government of Punjab was establishing the Violence Against Women Centre in Multan, they performed plays at local colleges and universities to make people aware of it and also performed at the centre's opening.

Athar Jahanian said that his group starts conceptualizing plays by listening to original stories and then they improvise the script with actors. He does the directing, along with his younger brother Aftab, and often with Waseem from the IRC. He thinks the biggest impact they have had is encouraging awareness,

> Theatre is political action and pushes people towards political awareness. We think that when we perform in front of people, they start thinking about those issues. There is a transformation that happens in people's minds, and when they have to act, they realize what they've learned...We ourselves had to transform before we can promote change. Inside, we have to challenge our acts—what are we doing, right or wrong? So with our performers, we discuss all these issues together in a study circle. We talk about the laws, the UN Declaration of Human Rights, and about current social issues.

In 2008, they began to branch out and perform about peace and interfaith harmony, with support from Norwegian Church Aid. They met with religious leaders from all sects, meeting first with 'ulema separately, then together, and then performed in front of their communities in an area near their *masjid* or madrassa. They sang Sufi poetry—often Bulleh Shah's—conveying messages of peace. They continued the peace and interfaith programme with Community World Service until they ended the programme in 2017.

Athar Jahanian sees important changes in southern Punjab as a result of their forum's theatre performances. He said that the people who didn't understand each other at first, are now reaching out to promote greater understanding and are themselves regularly conducting programmes about peace and interfaith harmony. A number of 'ulema in Multan have joined together to promote peace. He said that his group provides them with regular training to promote peace building by talking about human rights, conflict resolution, transformation of attitudes and behaviour, and how that happens,

> We understand that through performances, you can transmit a message, but we also need to meet with them regularly. Like, we had them read the UN Declaration on Human Rights, and tell us what in this is against Islam. No one found anything.

Taking a cue from the Lahore-based IRC, they have started interactive radio dramas on local FM stations. They have done four hour-long plays, and change the script each time they do a performance. Because they can take live calls on radio, the format is that they perform the play and people call in about what actions the characters might take. He considers that it is the interactions between the actors and non-actors that is important. Even if they are talking about a negative thing, they raise the question of how it can become something positive. He narrated an instance when the audience questions why a man has his young daughter married, and they talk about the laws that exist, that a girl should be educated, and what are the Islamic *farz* (obligations) in getting a girl educated. They don't take disagreements as negative remarks, but as an opportunity to expand the dialogue.

They used to have 8–10 performances per month, but since the National Action Plan was adopted in 2015 which requires an NOC (No Objection Certificate) before they can perform, they now only do 2–3 performances monthly. Most of these are now at private universities and colleges where they are not prevented from performing.

Due west from southern Punjab, in Sindh's Khairpur city, another interactive forum theatre company was established with goals similar to the IRC and the Multan Theatre Group. The Indus Theatre Group[48] began in 2002 as an offshoot of the Indus Resource Centre in Khairpur which was engaged with many development projects, mostly with Action Aid, and wanted to use theatre groups to convey their messages. The first plays focused on encouraging people to vote, for women to get involved in elections, and to promote girls' education.

Mohammad Waseem from the IRC had come to Khairpur in 2006 and trained them in interactive forum theatre to do a performance on violence against women. He later helped them perform a play about child labour and education. These were 'half theatre' plays, that the audience watches and then performs the last part of it. One of the theatre group members, Islam, who has been performing for over fifteen years, voiced his frustration with interactive theatre in that people in the audience just want to watch, and they have to push them to join in and act. So now they put their own person in the audience who steps up when necessary, which encourages others to volunteer as well. He said that he has performed in over a thousand dramas in the past fifteen years, and they have never had a performance that people didn't appreciate.

In July 2011, the Indus Theatre Group formally registered with the Government of Sindh as the Indus Theatre Development Organization. They did this to expand their activities as well as be able to build up support from international donors including from UNICEF, WorldVision, USAID, and others. The group's philosophy as to why they perform now became more clearly articulated,

> In situations where there is profound distrust, fear, and anger, theatre is a useful medium to bring people together to share stories and trigger emotional responses. The model of using participatory learning methods to explore a group's main concerns and then creating a play in order to debate the issues could be used in many situations. Theatre is a liberating and unifying experience as well as fun.[49]

For example, during the build-up to local elections in 2015, the Indus Theatre Group started to do street theatre at the encouragement of Pahel

Pakistan (a local organization) which had received funding from USAID. In fifteen days, they did ninety-seven street theatre performances in Shikarpur and Kambar Shahdadkot promoting people to register to vote and then to go to the polls and vote. Islam relates that,

> There were 'no-go' zones in Shikarpur, but we went there, and they wondered why we had come. We told them we have to perform a play, and they welcomed us. We said that we are not terrorists, though it seemed that some people there thought that we were. Each performance was twenty minutes to a half hour.

They have also done street theatre performances about immunization/vaccinations and good nutrition as well as about child labour and children's rights. He considers that street theatre is a good technique to involve people in *bazaars*, public grounds, and even in the front yards of people's homes. He also observes that it is risky sometimes because the authorities of an area don't want them to perform, fearful that their message will be against them or that they'll be provocateurs.

There are a number of other theatre companies, albeit smaller in reputation than the ones that have been discussed above, who are nonetheless having powerful impacts on their audiences in Pakistan, including Da Torsaro Saadar in the greater Peshawar area which has learned from the Interactive Resource Center directly and the Pushkalavati Theatre Company in Charsadda.

Da Torsaro Saadar (Peshawar)

Momin Khan and Wagma Feroz founded Da Torsaro Saadar (Women's Chador, but here meaning protection) in Peshawar in 2010 for the purpose of promoting women's empowerment, human rights, education, and peace. Both of their families are originally from the erstwhile FATA, though Momin Khan's family shifted to Charsadda about 200 years ago. They registered Da Torsaro Saadar in 2015 as a social welfare organization and they bring volunteers together to foster positive change and help create a tolerant society. Their vision is 'a society where men and women share equal rights and responsibilities and where women are considered human beings and not a commodity.'[50]

Momin Khan told me that he started out concerned about negative comments men often make about women and sees this as a kind of violence. They questioned the psychological and emotional impact of making such comments and decided to use theatre as a tool for education.[51] Khadim Hussain then approached them to put on interactive theatre in each of the Bacha Khan schools (discussed in Chapter 6) to promote the idea of non-violence.[52] They did that as well as performed on the theme of child marriages; indeed, they trained children on how to perform theatre around the topic of early child marriage and it changed many of their thoughts and provoked them to resist being forced into an early marriage.

Da Torsaro Saadar is an all-volunteer initiative and performs interactive community theatre for free in villages wherever people ask them to come. They have done performances with only men, only women, and with both together. When they performed interactive community theatre with women about child marriage, the reaction of the women was powerful as most of them had been married in their childhood. Momin Khan said,

> The women who were sitting there said that our marriage happened when we were young, but we won't let this happen to our daughters. The women vowed that they won't give their daughters in early childhood marriage or force them later on. When you see the reaction of the people to the performance, it's really great.

Over time, they sought to change people's views about women working in a range of professions. For example, they had plays about the harmful effects of negative comments about women nurses, especially how men make comments about them and doctors make comments about them. They asked nurses to write the scripts and do the acting, with a big focus on non-violence. The message they were conveying was about human rights and that people should realize what their rights are.

They started political leadership training using interactive theatre throughout 2016. They were based in Peshawar most of the year though spent October–November in Quetta and did performances in Kabul, Afghanistan, in March and June of 2017. They utilized interactive theatre in all three locales focusing on promoting critical thinking and political engagement amongst youth. The plays looked at their societies' problems and the interactive theatre aspect enabled them to discuss solutions. He said that in some areas, there are often fights over small things so they talked about violence and the consequences of violence for other people, including innocent observers. They thought that to do good work in Pakhtun society it would be best to use indigenous resources, so they rely heavily on the example of Bacha Khan and his philosophy of non-violence.

They have also conducted street theatre in Charsadda, Swat, Malakand, and Hangu to promote voting awareness, democracy and why the vote is important, with the occasional support of UNDP. The UNDP analysed the impact of their street theatre campaign and found that the impact has been significant: the turnout is far greater in areas where they have done these performances.

In mid-2018, Momin Khan met with various friends and cousins in Charsadda and they decided to do more street plays in their local vicinity. He agreed to train six or seven men in their *hujra* and taught them interactive theatre techniques. They are now performing mostly about female education and women's rights. In his 'day job' as a post-polio campaign zonal field monitor, he still sees that people vaccinate daughters, and not their sons, and most cases are boys who get polio. This is because, the local people are worried that their sons might fall sick or become impotent, and they are less concerned about this for their daughters so they agree to inoculate them. They incorporate the need to immunize sons in their performances as well.

These performances are with the community people, in their *hujras*, or in gardens, or in front of mosques. Each play is short, only about 10–15 minutes long, and they can perform two or three plays at a time, taking about an hour. They perform in the early evening after *asr* prayers, when people are free.

Momin Khan perceives there are three stages that their audiences go through when they see them perform. The first stage is that people say this is different and God won't like it. In the second stage, the people make jokes and ask them why they are doing this, that they should leave it and begin to call the actors by their occupational roles ('chaiwala' serving tea or 'sabziwala' selling vegetables). In the third stage, the audience appreciates what they are doing; he feels they haven't reached that stage enough yet. But he knows the more they educate people about their rights, the further they are promoting their goal of taking a powerful stand to counter extremism.

Pushkalavati Theatre Company (Charsadda)

We conclude this chapter by looking at the small (and now defunct) Pushkalavati Theatre Company based in Charsadda (whose ancient name is Pushkalavati), a very conservative part of Khyber Pakhtunkhwa. I am including it here to underscore that theatre is being performed in unanticipated places throughout Pakistan. This troupe was started in 2009 by Hayat Roghanay as a way to encourage local youth to start writing dramas, to bring in young local actors, and to give something new to the local people.[53] People in Charsadda were no longer familiar with theatre as extremism had stopped all such performances. The seven actors in the group would assemble at the now defunct Millat Booksellers in Charsadda and would go rehearse in an open area near the old railway station. They started to perform at weddings as a way to start, and then began to narrate against extremism in their plays.

Two years later, in 2012, Roghanay joined the faculty of Bacha Khan University (BKU) which enabled him to meet more potential actors from other parts of Khyber Pakhtunkhwa such as Bannu and Waziristan, and therefore interject some diversity into the acting cast. They rehearsed and performed at times that didn't interfere with students' class schedules. He also recruited actors from a high school in Charsadda, the Muslim School, to give them an opportunity to act.

From the outset, they focused on resistance subjects such as questioning if they have freedom of speech and freedom to talk in their own language, Pashto. They also performed a play about the terrorist attack at BKU in January 2016 and in a third play, they asked the audience to stand by their fellow community members and recite 'Win while standing united or lose while standing divided.' A final play presented all of its actors as having little in common and being from disparate parts of the country, but a gardener nurtures them and brings them together. It concludes with everyone agreeing that the country will collapse without their efforts and they must find a way to remain unified.

When I queried the students about why they performed, one of them told me that he started off participating in the plays thinking he was only acting but soon grew deeply impressed by Bacha Khan's theories and philosophy. He said, 'I say this because Pakhtuns have become notorious in the world for being a violent people; these plays give us an outlet to prove that we are not violent, that we are good people.' Another student said that they feel 'this is the best and proper way to convey our message to people…theatre is a medium that is enjoyed by many and helps bring people together. Watching a play on Bacha Khan helped me relive what he stood for and advocated in his community.' A third student offered that 'Indeed, Pakhtuns themselves know that they are a peace-loving nation. We are gardeners looking after our garden and it is time to deliver this message to non-Pakhtuns.' Another performer hopes that their eight-minute play about the gardener nurturing his seeds will be screened around the world 'to show people that Charsadda is a small town and all we want is peace and an outlet for artistic expression.'

The theatre troupe remained under Hayat Roghanay's tutelage until he left BKU in 2017 to work at the Bacha Khan Markaz in Peshawar. He believes that he planted a seed in Charsadda, and although it's no longer called the Pushkalavati Theatre Company, student groups still perform theatre that makes their audiences question what is happening in society around them, and encourages them to stand up to violence and extremism.

Notes

1. *See*, for example, Salman Ahmad's powerful description of how his band was prevented from performing in Lahore in 1982 when it was attacked by zealots, including one youth whose 'eyes filled with a madness that has nothing to do with God,' in his book *Rock & Roll Jihad: A Muslim Rock Star's Revolution*, Free Press, 2010, p. 12.
2. Conveyed to me in discussions with Saif Samejo in 2018 and 2019.
3. Randa Safieh, 'Identity, Diaspora and Resistance in Palestinian Hip Hop,' in *Palestinian Music and Song: Expression and Resistance Since 1900*, edited by Moslih Kanaaneh, Stig-Magnus Thorsen, Heather Bursheh, and David A. McDonald, Indiana University Press, 2013.
4. Both citations are from Moslih Kanaaneh, 'Introduction: Do Palestinian Musicians Play Music or Politics?,' in *Palestinian Music and Song: Expression and Resistance Since 1900*, edited by Moslih Kanaaneh, Stig-Magnus Thorsen, Heather Bursheh, and David A. McDonald, Indiana University Press, 2013, p. 10.
5. David A. McDonald, 'Epilogue,' *My Voice is my Weapon: Music, Nationalism, and the Poetics of Palestinian Resistance*, Durham, Duke University Press, 2013, pp. 283–4.
6. For a good detailed review of the role 'Patari' has been playing in the music scene in Pakistan, *see* Saad Sayeed, 'Home-grown streaming app helps Pakistan's musicians find voice,' *Reuters News*, 7 February 2017, accessible at: https://www.reuters.com/article/us-pakistan-music/home-grown-streaming-app-helps-pakistans-musicians-find-voice-idUSKBN15N0MS.

7. This section on Saif Samejo, The Sketches and 'Lahooti Melo' is based on extensive conversations with him and others first in January 2018, then in March 2018, and in February 2019 as well as ongoing communication and interactions. All quotes are from these conversations unless otherwise noted.

8. Saif Samejo recounted this poem of Shaikh Ayaz to me in January 2018.

9. For more about the return of the 'Lahooti Live sessions' in August 2019, *see* an interview with Saif Samejo by BandBaji, 'I Find Indigenous Poetry Liberating,' *Dawn*, 25 August 2019, accessible at: https://www.dawn.com/news/1501584.

10. Ibid.

11. Saif posted this photograph on Instagram; printed here with permission.

12. This section on Taimur Rahman and the Laal band is based on extensive conversations with him and others between 2017 and 2019 as well as ongoing communication and interactions. All quotes are from these conversations unless otherwise noted.

13. This springtime festival celebrating the onset of farming in Punjab is closely associated with Hinduism. The Government of Pakistan periodically bans flying kites on *basant* ostensibly because of the dangers involved (children falling off roofs chasing kites; the glass-laced strings cutting people), but many people think the real reason is its association with Hinduism.

14. A music video that the Laal band posted on Twitter is accessible at: https://twitter.com/jaun_online/status/1104303486865420288.

15. This is a reference to the renowned school of social theory and critical philosophy at Goethe University in Frankfurt, Germany.

16. From, *Sow Flowers: Selections from Rahman Baba, the Poet of the Afghans*, translated by Robert Sampson and Momin Khan, Peshawar, InterLit Foundation, 2008, p. 31.

17. This section is based on numerous conversations I had with Gulab Khel Afridi between 2018 and 2019, as well as listening to him perform, both in his studio and in public.

18. Sher Alam Shinwari covers the launching of Gulab's academy in 'Artist opens academy to teach rabab playing,' *Dawn*, 14 November 2016, accessible at: https://epaper.dawn.com/DetailNews.php?StoryText=14_11_2016_182_010.

19. From Syed Ansar Abbas, 'Rabab academy becomes symbol of peace in Peshawar,' *Pakistan Forward*, 28 December 2016, accessible at: https://pakistan.asia-news.com/en_GB/articles/cnmi_pf/features/2016/12/28/feature-01.

20. Sher Alam Shinwari reports on this in 'On World Music Freedom Day, Peshawar's artistes plead for government support,' *Dawn*, 4 March 2019, accessible at: https://images.dawn.com/news/1181982/on-world-music-freedom-...1.

21. This section about Karan Khan is based on conversations I had with him between February 2018 and March 2019 in Peshawar.

22. The valleys of Khyber Pakhtunkhwa and Pakhtun parts of Balochistan.

23. Here Karan Khan is implying both the game of cricket and the 'game of life.'

24. Translation by Karan Khan, Aasya Rehman, and Professor Faizullah Jan in Peshawar, in February 2019.

25. Sheema Kirmani, 'Tehrik-e-Niswan's *Tilismati Tees Aur Aik Saal* (Magical Thirty and One Years),' in Sheema Kirmani et al., *Gender, Politics, and Performance in South Asia*, Karachi, Oxford University Press, 2015, pp. 24–5.

26. This section on the Ajoka Theatre Company is based on interviews I had with both Madeeha Gauhar and Shahid Nadeem between 2017 and 2019 in Lahore and other parts of Punjab. This particular quote is from a meeting with Madeeha Gauhar on 24 October 2017 at the Ajoka office in Lahore. She passed away soon after that from cancer in April 2018.

27. These objectives are delineated in the programme notes for *Humsaya*: Indo–Pak Theatre for Peace Festival, 15–20 March 2017.

28. Some of Ajoka's plays can be found in Shahid Nadeem, *Selected Plays,* Karachi, Oxford University Press, 2009; the play about the blasphemy laws, *Dekh Tamasha Chalta Ban,* is in Ashis Sengupta (ed.), *Islam in Performance* Bloomsbury Methuen Drama, 2017.

29. This is quoted from unpublished stage notes on *Burqavaganza* that Madeeha Gauhar shared with me.

30. Ibid.

31. Told to me in an interview with Shahid Nadeem at the Ajoka offices in Lahore on 28 October 2017.

32. Ibid.

33. This and other references that follow are from the programme notes from the programme for the Madeeha Gauhar Theatre Festival, 27–9 September 2018 at the Alhamra Art Gallery, Lahore.

34. This was related to me in an interview with Shahid Nadeem on 3 January 2019 at the Ajoka headquarters in Lahore.

35. This was told to me in an interview with Sheema Kirmani in Karachi on 15 February 2017.

36. I interviewed Sheema Kirmani at her home in Karachi in 2017 and 2018; this comment is based on a conversation with her elsewhere in March 2019.

37. This play is in Ashis Sengupta (ed.), *Islam in Performance*, Bloomsbury, Methuen Drama, 2017.

38. Sheema provided me with copies of many of Tehrik-e-Niswan's plays. This is my translation and observation of *Hum Rokaen Gae*.

39. This is from a conversation on 19 October 2019.

40. This is from a conversation held on 27 February 2019 at her home in Karachi.

41. This is my translation from viewing *Aseer Shahzadi,* one of the plays Sheema Kirmani gave to me.

42. This is from the conversation on 27 February 2019.

43. A photo of Sheema Kirmani and members of the Hyderabad Women's Action Forum dancing in defiance at the tomb a few days after the bomb blast in February 2018 appears at the very beginning of Chapter 7.

44. This section on IRC is based on interviews I conducted in Lahore with Mohammad Waseem and his daughter, Risham Waseem, between 2017 and 2018.

45. All of their videos can be viewed at: https://maatitv.com.

46. From IRC's pamphlet on MAATI TV.

47. Information in this section is based on an interview with Athar Jahanian in Multan on 21 November 2017.

48. This section on the Indus Theatre Group is based on interviews I conducted with a number of members of the theatre company at their offices on 8 January 2017.
49. 'Introductory Profile, 2017–18: Indus Theatre Development Organization, Khairpur Mir's Sindh' provided to me by ITDO.
50. From a Da Torsaro Saadar handout on the organization.
51. This section is based on interviews with Momin Khan held in Peshawar on 18 February 2018 and 30 January 2019.
52. The history, philosophy, and impact of the Bacha Khan schools are discussed in Chapter 6.
53. This section is based on discussions I had with Hayat Roghanay and members of the theatre company on 26 January 2017 in Charsadda and with Hayat Roghanay in Peshawar on 30 January 2019.

4 | Using Art to Reclaim Identity and Meaning

Fig. 4.1: *Lizard on the Wall, in Memory of the APS Attack*, Munawar Ali Syed, Karachi.

There are numerous robust, exciting, artistic activities occurring throughout Pakistan where people are using art to reclaim identity and meaning, and hence countering the narratives of violence and extremism. Nearly everywhere one travels, we can see signs of spontaneous street art promoting peace, nature, and love for Pakistan. In this chapter, we will explore a few of these efforts, notably 'Rang dey Karachi' which morphed into the 'Walls of Karachi' project; the wall paintings of peace drawn by Islamia College art students in Bahawalpur; and ways that groups celebrate their communities through art including the activities of the Awami Art Collective in Lahore and the Lahore Biennale and, in particular, its artistic bus-stop project.

Karachi elicits dramatically distinct cultural contours given its history: once a small fishing village transformed into a port city during the British

Raj, it became the destination of choice by non-Punjabi immigrants into Pakistan following the 1947 Partition, overwhelming the indigenous Sindhi population. There is little that culturally holds together this city of migrants; the World Population Review estimates that 90 per cent of the residents are migrants or their descendants. Once Pakistan's national capital (until it was shifted to the newly built city of Islamabad in 1960), Karachi remains the country's 'economic capital.'

Its ethnic make-up has been utterly transformed. At independence in 1947, Sindhis comprised nearly two-third of the city's residents; with migration by *muhajirs* (Muslim immigrants from India) at partition, Pakhtuns in the wake of the ongoing turmoil in Afghanistan, and economic migrants throughout Pakistan's history, that number today is a mere 7 per cent of Karachi's population. In 1998, Pakhtuns were 11 per cent of Karachi's population, and now are 20 per cent. *Muhajirs* and their descendants, numbering 9 million in Karachi, comprise 45 per cent of the city's population today. Roughly 45,000 migrant workers come to Karachi in search of jobs every month.[1] With a metropolitan population of roughly 23 million people—the fastest growing metropolitan area in the world—its density is also among the highest in the world, third to Dhaka and Mumbai.[2]

Many of Karachi's residents live in *katchi abadis* and other slums, lacking basic services. Several parts of the city, especially the poorest areas, suffer from unrelenting infrastructural problems: 12–15 hours of daily energy load-shedding and voltage reductions; security concerns resulting in significant travel delays; and schools, businesses, food delivery systems, and the like all confront myriad obstacles just to maintain current levels. The deterioration of its public transit network and the proliferation of automobiles and private minibuses cause unprecedented traffic congestion, bottlenecks, and pollution.

For a number of years Karachi, despite being Pakistan's largest city, has resembled a lawless frontier. It had come down to ethnic parties frequently being the arbiters of community and family disputes regarding crime, property, marriage, and divorce.[3] Political and religious zealots, gangs and mafia-style criminal organizations had overpowered social and political life in the city as people feared targeted killings and kidnappings, although somehow industrial production kept plodding along.

The opening photograph of an art installation by Munawar Ali Syed, Figure 4.1, captures well the power of art in reflecting social turmoil. Inspired by the APS attack when he crafted this sculpture, the artist depicts a crocodile devouring schoolchildren's books. This powerful work captures the common phobia about lizards, which often fall from ceilings—but then as the terrorists and extremists in Pakistan became so powerful, the lizard grew huge and transformed into a fearful crocodile. He had felt, as an artist, what could be their contribution to help his community heal, and he also became worried about his own children. He realized that when crocodiles cannot control their bloodthirsty hunger, they also eat their own eggs, just like the extremists at the APS School attacked Pakistan's own children and devoured their books.

PAINTING OVER HATE LANGUAGE AND PROMOTING PEACE

In the context of this violence, a group of University of Karachi students and teachers of Visual Studies, from a wide swatch of socio-economic backgrounds, came together and started 'Rang dey Karachi' (The Colours of Karachi) in 2010. Most were directly affected by the violence that was taking over the city. For example, they would travel to the university on buses but if there was a strike, they couldn't get there, or if they were at the university and there was an explosion, their parents would be worried but as the buses were stopped, their parents couldn't travel to the university to ensure they were safe. Munawar Ali Syed recounts that he 'and a group of pals and buckets did stencils on the walls', a reaction when fifteen people were killed daily,

> Every day we heard news, 14 people killed, 15 people killed. Of course, religious and political extremism were the two big factors—there were road jams after *juma* prayers. Everyone was affected.[4]

They questioned what they were doing as artists, and felt it was cathartic to start painting colours on walls in the city. They ventured out to a walled-area near Jinnah's mausoleum, and were immediately encountered by a policeman who tried to stop them. Munawar recounts telling the police that they were not doing something wrong and to the contrary, wanted to do their part to bring about peace in Karachi. While the policeman was sympathetic, he told them to leave his area and not to do anything there. The group then understood they had to devise a strategy whereby they could do something quickly. Munawar reflected on the group's motivations for drawing the walls when he said,

> The walls of Karachi are spreading hatred—we can only see the political or religious slogans plastered on them. Some take these walls to be a marketing hub and use it for cheap business purposes. We had decided to revamp these walls by a Stencil Art Project and aim to paint around 1,500 walls in areas such as Saddar, Numaish, Gora Qabristan (white people's cemetery), and Civic Centre.[5]

Karachi's numerous underpasses, many of which had become defaced by chalking with political and religious messages, in addition to advertisements, immediately came to mind. They created four or five stencils, replete with words and images, and painted them on underpasses. They wrote a counter narrative to violence in Urdu on the stencils *phir bahar ayegi* (lit. spring will come again; like flowers blossom in a season, things will transform like a flower). They understood their audience was the people traveling on the buses, so they tried to convey a simple message at their level, literally and figuratively, as high on the walls as possible, so that people could see them from bus windows. They became a guerrilla art movement—go to a wall, scrape off the existing graffiti, paint over it (either in white or in colours), and then put the stencils on as seen in the three photographs in Figure 4.2.

Soon after the death of Karachi philanthropist and rights activist Abdul Sattar Edhi in July 2016, the 'Rang dey Karachi' artist-activists once again went onto the streets of Karachi with stencils of Edhi's face and applied them to some walls in Karachi, as can be seen in Figure 4.3. They expanded their efforts to three other areas: the Cantonment train and bus station, where people seem to always congregate; the Numaish part of the busy Saddar trading area where there was already a lot of chalking; and the outside wall of Islamia College on the very central Jamshed Road. One of the artists, Veera Rustomji, a student at the Indus Valley School of Arts and Architecture, stated that her feeling at the time was that,

> It's time we rescued Karachi's long-standing walls from those who pollute it and reclaim it back. Half the city is drowning in garbage

and the other half in religious, political, lewd, and intolerant text that can be seen at every nook and corner. If you look around, you will only see dirty walls full of opinionated content and slogans. We want to repaint those walls.[6]

They did this sporadically for four years, and police often caught up with them. When Munawar's group questioned why the police didn't stop those who were chalking the violent political and religious graffiti, the police responded that since the other miscreants come in the middle of the night and they don't witness them, the police couldn't stop them as they were stopping Munawar's group, who they could see!

Noor Jehan Bilgrami began the Purskoon Karachi (Peaceful Karachi) initiative in August 2013 and invited the 'Rang dey Karachi' group to draw stencils and paint on the outside walls near the Karachi Arts Council. She had been feeling frustrated and helpless with the violence and gloom that had descended on Karachi at that time. One day, she went to Sohrab Goth in the aftermath of a devastating fight between *muhajirs* and Pakhtuns and afterwards the army had bulldozed the shelters that the Pakhtuns had built there. She saw women going through the rubble the next day to salvage whatever remained of their homes, and she was overwhelmed by this. She began to draw a series of paintings in her studio, but also felt she couldn't close herself in a studio to paint what was happening in Karachi. She reached out to artists, architects, sculptors, and writers,

> This has to be beyond the confines of my studio and beyond a gallery space into the city itself. I wanted to connect and bring about positivity to the city.

They held a lot of discussions and agreed that they wanted to celebrate themselves and the city, hence the idea of Purskoon Karachi came into being. They started it with the firm belief 'that art and culture are the only ways of uplifting society and addressing the issues of strife.'[7] They put big posters from stencils—much larger than the ones originally used in 'Rang dey Karachi'—supporting *aman* (peace) on the walls, and Munawar Ali Syed noted that,

> We realized that size matters in Karachi. To work on a big wall,
> you need a big stencil. In Purskoon Karachi, we used six feet big
> stencils. We understand people can't see small sizes.

Figure 4.4 is a Purskoon Karachi stencil, particularly noteworthy as we can see the faint writing of an extremist group not fully covered by the whitewash, over which images to deweaponize Karachi were drawn.

Three months after its founding, Purskoon Karachi organized the three-day 'Purskoon Mela', one of the largest creative festivals ever held in Karachi, which drew thousands of people to its art and installation shows, talks, plays, theatrical productions, and to hear a *mushaira* (poetry recitation) and Sufi music. These were held at the Karachi Arts Council, the National Academy of Performing Arts (NAPA) (renamed from the old Hindu Gymkhana) and the Cantonment Station, where they had begun to extend their efforts to renovate the nineteenth century building 'that was crumbling with neglect.' Renovating the Cantonment Station was seen as a long-term plan for people to feel proud of who they are and their cultural heritage. It's the entry, the gateway, to Karachi, and Noor Jehan Bilgrami feels that when one enters the city, it's important that they become transformed by engaging with something beautiful. They discovered there were so many layers to the old station: by scraping away over twenty layers of paint from the fabulous cast-iron columns they opened up the arches, discovered a beautiful marble floor in one area, the original woodwork was revealed, and the whole station was revived. She said that this was her project that she had taken up,

> To bring peace and harmony to the entry into the city, rather than
> be pushed back into madness. How do we show this is a peaceful
> city? By rediscovering what had been there before…Peeling off the
> layers, which represented the layers of violence that had happened
> to Karachi, was a very therapeutic experience for the artists.

The group held an award ceremony for the porters to celebrate the station's completion, and honoured the oldest porter there. All along, train passengers were sitting on the benches, using the works of art. Where once a site of violence, Karachi was now responding to its residents in an expressive way and providing them with comfort and meaning.

A year later, in December 2014, the group organized 'Purskoon Baithak', which created a small park—'an environmental oasis with a grove of trees'—at the entrance to the Cantonment Station. Beneath these trees, twenty-nine groups of architects, designers, and artists created permanent inventive and ergonomic benches, each of which 'is an artistic piece, which helps to create an environment of a sculpture-garden, the first of its kind in Karachi.' She said that while the benches were being installed, travellers, porters, and other people just began to sit on them!

'I am Karachi' partially emerged out of these efforts. Adeela Suleman, an artist who heads the Fine Art department at Karachi's Indus Valley School of Art & Architecture, had been engaged in public activities to counter violence in Pakistan for a long time. She recalls that 'I am Karachi' became a consortium when it adopted the Karachi Youth Initiative (KYI). They approached her about the need for a wall-painting project in Karachi to counter the hateful religious graffiti and the military symbols, and she appreciated that there was money involved so they could pay the artists.

She resisted the initial terminology they were using, 'Reclaiming the Walls of Karachi,' because while one can 'reimagine,' the question arises, who is reclaiming the walls from whom? She thought it generates feelings that are harmful and hateful. The entire approach changes when you reclaim something that *is* yours, but the walls of Karachi were never theirs. Hence she started the first phase of 'Reimagining the Walls of Karachi' with the KYI. Small groups of university students, such as 'Rang dey Karachi,' were already painting walls, but the new project was also to paint over negative graffiti. She and her students removed all the graffiti they saw at a given location so they couldn't be targeted as supporting one group over another as seen in Figures 4.5 and 4.6. She recounts that not one negative incident occurred.

Indeed, 'Reimagining the Walls of Karachi' has been a phenomenal artistic effort. They reached out to some of Karachi's most blemished urban slums, Nazimabad and New Karachi (near Mangophir, past Orangi), as well as the busy M.T. Khan Road, Gulistan-e-Johar, and the tower on M.A. Jinnah Road, among other sites. A total of sixteen artists participated, drawing 6 feet by 4 feet stencils on 1,700 walls in Karachi, repeating each stencil a hundred times between April and June 2015. While two-third of the stencils have since been covered over by other chalking, the paintings that were drawn still exist.

'Reimagining the Walls of Karachi' had three phases. The first included students in primary and secondary schools in Lyari, Shireen Jinnah Colony, and other slum areas of the city. They encouraged the children to paint their walls and draw maps of their area, promoting the idea of inclusiveness and knowing their city. The second was incorporating people like Munawar to remove hate graffiti and do stencilling. Finally, she sent out a call for people to send in their designs. They selected most of the designs, and had the artisans and signboard painters make sketches on the walls, as shown in the six photographs comprising Figure 4.7, that were then filled in by Pakistan's infamous truck art and cinema billboard painters. She recalls,

> Once these artists were out on the road, they were the heroes. The best part is, there was not a single incident from the public; nothing was negative. People stopped and asked, can we paint with you? Do you want water? People were whistling and clapping.

'Reimagining the Walls of Karachi' was then transformed into 'Walls of Peace', a second phase of the larger project. A total of 2,300, 8 feet by 10 feet walls were painted in the first phase, and an additional 350 walls of better quality were painted in the second phase. In June 2016, an open competition call went out to art schools throughout the city, and artists from a wide range of backgrounds were selected to share their visions of a unified, peaceful Pakistan. One of those selected, Madiha Sarwar, understood the initiative as being about removing and whitewashing negative graffiti, and have something instead on the walls that is colourful, attractive, and can have an impact on society, celebrating pride, heritage and culture.[8] Her wall, 'Joyous Melodies' (Figure 4.8) depicts the musical instruments of Pakistan and the positive values of peace and tolerance that music helps to nurture. When asked how she feels to be a part of the 'Walls of Peace' project, she said,

> I feel super proud about it, how people are responding to my mural. My mural is impacting society—people are stopping and looking at it, to figure out what it is about. An artist is always conscious when they present their work to an audience. You never

know how people will receive it. I've been very satisfied about the
response. This is something really good and it should be promoted
in Pakistan.

Madiha considers that many people in Pakistan are so impressed by the
west and want to be like that. But they also need to learn about traditional
and cultural values and then pass them on to their children and the 'Walls
of Peace' initiative is conveying this to a wide audience in the city.

Another painting that epitomizes the 'Walls of Peace' initiative in
Karachi is 'Sowing Seeds of Peace' (Figure 4.9). Just down the large wall
where 'Joyous Melodies' is painted we see a young boy in a field ostensibly
sowing vegetable seeds, but then we realize he is spreading roses, a sign of
peace, for all to enjoy.[9]

Adeela Suleman has mixed feelings about the impact that the Walls
projects have had on promoting peace and countering extremism. She
thinks that some people look at them and don't think about it. Karachi is
so big that the walls are just a drop in the ocean. But at least it counters
the negative thoughts that may otherwise be there,

> For a child to see something against Shias, or something ISIS has
> written, that's negative. It has diverted the attention for that very
> moment you're passing by, and not thinking of something negative.

'I am Karachi' has now largely taken up supporting 'The Walls of Karachi'
initiative, and intends to expand it into other areas of the city. A former
president of 'I am Karachi,' Jamil Yusuf, said it is comprised of 16–20
NGOs that are members, though 60–70 NGOs from many areas are
participating in all their functions.[10] The current head of 'I am Karachi',
Amin Hashwani, said he intends to channel the group's efforts in three
directions: reclaiming public spaces (including expanding 'The Walls of
Karachi' initiative); changing public discourse; and bringing together civil
society and giving them a platform. He wants it to stand *for* something,
not against something; he doesn't want to polarize society.[11] He hopes to
create a viable institution that will be there beyond his lifetime, and create
a movement that penetrates into society. He acknowledges that such efforts
are hard to measure, so 'you sprinkle things around so it sprouts over a
period of time. It's about *inspiring*. Whatever you do in Karachi can never

be enough for its population of 20 million people.' Yusuf intends for 'I am Karachi' to keep painting walls as this is one thing that has become more visible and has a sense of permanency, 'but it's not about painting the walls—but what activities we do around the walls that get painted.' By February 2019, 3,500 walls had been reclaimed and painted because of this initiative. His long view of the obligations of leaders like himself in 'I am Karachi' is that,

> We need to be co-authors and co-creators of a good society. No politician will give up their power. Poor people don't have the luxury for compassion. Underserved communities respond positively. We provide them with opportunity.

> Pakistan has come all the way around. We've been through all this violence; while there will always be people on the fringes who support violence, but that's changed. Fifteen years ago, the majority of people supported having shariah—now, we don't want this Islamization of the Taliban, that whole illusion is gone. Pakistan went through that dire experience at a very heavy price.

There are numerous other grassroots aspects to the 'I am Karachi' initiative, including holding music and film festivals, mentorship programmes (musical talent hunts), sports (they are looking at various sports clubs to increase capacity in underserved clubs), and they may even collaborate with the horticultural society. What I heard from everyone involved with 'I am Karachi', when I spoke with them, is that its goal is to be inclusive, positive, and celebrate Karachi and its diversity.

A similar initiative has been sparked in Bahawalpur in southern Punjab. Dr Nasrullah Khan Nasser, Principal of the College of Art & Design at Bahawalpur Islamia University, observes that Sufism's values dominate the area and that 'people love harmony here.'[12] Muslims, Hindus, and Christians have long lived amicably together. He was brainstorming with his students about how to capture that harmony in the much beloved city of Bahawalpur when they observed there were wall-chalkings throughout the city bringing a sense of disarray and violence. The Islamia University art students took to the streets of Bahawalpur and began to paint symbols of peace on its walls, as seen in the three photographs comprising Figure

4.10. This is not simply painting walls—we see this a lot in the major cities of Lahore, Rawalpindi, and Islamabad—that have no intentional theme. These walls are instead a deliberate attempt to spread a message of harmony and peace. Some people from civil society donated the paint, and the Nestle Corp. gave the students water.

Dr Nasrullah Khan Nasser notes that in the three years since they painted the walls, no one has put posters or chalking on them or defaced them in any way. He and his students erected a panaflex near Farid Gate, one of the seven gates to the old city of Bahawalpur that he helped renovate in a classical heritage manner using the simple colours of nearby Dilawar Fort.

This gate was named in honour of the nineteenth century Sufi poet of the area, Khwaja Farid. He selected a stanza of one of Khwaja Farid's poems that look towards a positive future to be depicted on the panaflex, as seen in Figure 4.11, the English translation of which is,

Farid, you should be happy that disappointments are not forever.
A day will come when everything will blossom.
Time will change and things will be better.

Dr Nasrullah Khan Nasser said that Bahawalpur used to be full of numerous military monuments, complete with missiles and warplanes. Many of those missiles and other martial artefacts, however, have been taken down and replaced with other things, like vases and cultural artifacts that encourage traditional values of this area such as harmony and peace.

There is a monument that his college designed not far from the painted walls at the university's entrance that celebrates learning, knowledge, and peace. Two books provide the monument's foundation, and a pen nib, used for writing, adorns the top, as seen in Figure 4.12. Thirty students—most were females—were involved in designing and building the sculpture.

Building on this budding trend of public art being drawn with peace themes, ten local artists joined with fifteen international artists to create a 24-yard long painting entitled 'Pearls of Peace' at the five-day Second International Watercolour Biennale in Jamshoro, Sindh in February 2018 held at the Mehran University of Engineering & Technology (MUET) Figure 4.13.[13] The long mural celebrates local culture, especially focused on the impoverished Hindu-dominated area of Tharparkar.

CELEBRATING COMMUNITIES THROUGH ART

Artists and social activists have been collaborating in recent years on ways to use art to celebrate their communities and hence recapture cultural identity, one that has nothing to do with extremism or violence. A very deliberative process has been employed in Lahore by members of the Awami Art Collective (AAC). In discussing the reasons behind the AAC's determination to use art in creative public ways, one of its founders, Raheem ul Haque, a professor of Public Policy at Forman Christian College in Lahore, writes,

> Public space is thus an important medium, attested by the fact that it's termed the 'geography of the public sphere' as it invites interactions among the public which could lead to a deliberated and informed position. However, being socially produced, it is not a neutral space because it encompasses differentials in power among the interacting publics...Thus, public space can be categorized as a site of struggle, control, and domination because the public's interpretation of space and corresponding behaviour generates culturally bound discursive resources which, when taken as a whole, would echo broad ideological processes.[14]

After the APS attack in Peshawar in December 2014, various artists, academics, and political activists held a meeting in Lahore along with various members of theatre groups, cartoonists, and various progressive activists to try to figure out that now that the state was no longer chasing after them—it was finally chasing after the extremists behind the bombing—how best they could use the space that had been created. Raheem recalls that they perceived that 'for the first time the state seemed to allow space to progressive voices and peace activists against the extremist voices which had dominated the media and thus discourse over the last few decades.' The meeting concluded with three shared observations:

1. It was too early to take extremist forces head on as they remained quite powerful.
2. There was a need to engage citizens rather than sloganeering against the state and extremists to capitalize on the change in state policy which was allowing more space to progressive forces.

3. Protests needed to be more innovative and creative to grab people's attention.[15]

The artists and activists associated with AAC told me that, basically, they wanted to do public art. They chart their lineage from the Indus Valley civilization and their heritage from centuries of amalgamation of various civilizations that have enriched Pakistan. But they acknowledge that this cultural richness is not appreciated because of a lack of respect and recognition for the arts and artists. They argue that culture, heritage, and development are all important and are the issues that drive them. They began to mobilize around the need for freedom of expression especially in the light that the state does not provide the necessary tools, including curricular options in government schools, to appreciate art. They see that art education is constrained through self-censorship and bans and that its expression within private spaces of studios and art galleries precludes its reach beyond the existing networks.

The AAC's first art performance was at Racecourse Park during the Spring Festival in Lahore on 15 March 2015, and revolved around the concept of a *takhti*, a traditional writing board that was shared as a symbol to devise a response to the massacre. The *takhtis* included the palm of a child signifying 'stop' as a form of resistance, and each child wrote down the name of a martyred child. They used ribbons to put up *takhtis* along the barbed wire surrounding the Punjab Assembly signifying both a message against terrorists as well as highlighting the barbed wire 'which had come to define public space in these times.' The AAC went on to create a number of other temporary installations, some with the cooperation of the local city government, and expanded the idea within Lahore that public art had an important role to play in standing up to extremism. In one of them, in an effort to portray political and ideological violence over a thirty-year period, they made public installations in the public garden, Bagh-e-Jinnah, in front of the Punjab Assembly building, about 127 cases of violence. The 360-foot long walk highlighted the event of each individual's attack and was up for three weeks. The artists wanted to make it clear that violence precipitated the events of 9/11, and that the roots are much deeper.

They have prioritized art installations that can gain a great deal of public attention instead of the wall stencils we have seen gaining traction in Karachi. One popular stencil that they created was of another kind—this was for one of their own, Raza Khan, an AAC member who was abducted on 3 December 2017 from his home in Lahore. In addition to being one of the non-artist members of the AAC, Raza Khan was the convener of 'Aghaaz-e-Dosti' (discussed further in Chapter 7). When he was disappeared, the AAC developed a dramatic stencil that seemed to appear everywhere on social media and in physical locales to raise awareness of Raza Khan's abduction, as seen in Figure 4.14. Of all their work, this seems to have had the most long-lasting impact as it effectively raised awareness through much of Pakistan's population that this was an abducted activist from Lahore during the seven months he was gone. In doing so, they brought greater attention to pleas for recovery of missing persons from Balochistan and Khyber Pakhtunkhwa as well. Indeed, this captures AAC's key goal of 'art as activism.'

Another significant effort in Lahore to use art to reclaim identity and meaning can be seen in the various activities of the Lahore Biennale. In the tradition of public art exhibitions elsewhere in the world, such as the Venice Biennale, it was envisioned to include both international and domestic art. Somehow, however, in the process of planning for the Lahore Biennale, given the enthusiasm of different groups to participate, art work by local people became more dominant and indeed more meaningful than even imagined possible by the organizers. Qudsia Raheem, the driving force behind it, is the Director of the Lahore Biennale Foundation (LBF). She always envisaged the LBF to be in partnership with other people and groups, that they would not be undertaking activities on their own. She was drawn to organizing a community art celebration because she sees a massive problem in the fact that people have become disconnected from their history. She believes that the younger generation has a very different perspective of society, which is why we are seeing a disconnect, and the insecurity is very severe. She was trying to think of a way of bringing people together to redress this disconnect and nurture hope. From this line of thinking, she developed the idea that the LBF would put on the Lahore Biennale to enable people to recognize the similarities and differences in each other and to celebrate them. She told me, 'THIS is what this Biennale is all about.'[16]

A big thrust of the LBF to nurture diverse voices has been through reaching out to creative people and organizations by 'open calls' for ideas, and then the LBF can provide mentorship and guidance to provide opportunities to its partners 'through a horizontal framework where many of these strands can exist' to help them carry out the idea. She was trying to find out how to do public art; the idea was to empower, not be powerful. The goal was to be a facilitator, to create a movement where other creative individuals, collectives, and foundations can become alive.

She realized that she needed to identify who the major stakeholders are to support these efforts and had to become a fundraiser, raising support either from cultural centres (e.g., the German Goethe Institute, the British Council), businesses (e.g., Habib Bank, Ferozsons Pharmaceuticals), universities (e.g., National College of Arts, Kinnaird College, LUMS), and from private creative sources. She also wanted to find ways to work with the government and have them take ownership of the Lahore Biennale activities and was able to receive support from the Lahore Parks and Horticulture Department, the Lahore Transport Authority, the Walled City Trust, the Commissioner of Lahore, and from the former Chief Minister, Shahbaz Sharif, directly. She is delighted when she sees the list of partners at the bottom of the LBF's website; she sees strength in it. The LBF doesn't own anything, they don't put a sticker anywhere.

The LBF had been engaged in a number of activities all leading up to the March 2018 Biennale events. The first open call for public art that LBF sponsored was 'City within a City' in November 2015, the initial attempt in its 'Art in Public Spaces' project. The goal was to identify a space where people come together without any regard to class, gender, or ethnicity, but they're using the same space. Istanbul Chowk on Mall Road was selected 'for its ever-evolving historical significance, and its centrality between the old and new Lahore.' Developed by Atif Khan, a teacher at the National College of Arts (NCA) located centrally on Mall Road, the site served as home to many pigeons, but also where people throw grains to the pigeons, where they look at and sit upon Kim's Gun (from Kipling's stories), and a Mughal statue appears to be shooting at the birds. The artist symbolically brings them together in the resultant project, 'Intersections',

Fig. 4.2: Early stencils used to cover hate language, painted late at night on the walls of Karachi, Rang dey Karachi, courtesy Munawar Ali Syed.

Fig. 4.3: Stencil of Abdul Sattar Edhi, Rang dey Karachi.

Fig. 4.4: Seeking to de-weaponize Karachi, Purskoon Karachi.

Fig. 4.5: Sample of stencils between Liaquatabad and
Nazimabad, Reimagining the Walls of Karachi.

Fig. 4.6: Stenciling at night, Reimagining the Walls of
Karachi.

Fig. 4.7: Reimagining the Walls of Karachi.

Fig. 4.8: Walls of Karachi 'Joyous Melodies' by Madiha Sarwar.

Fig. 4.9: 'Sowing Seeds of Peace' Walls of Karachi.

Fig. 4.10: Drawings of Peace on the Walls of Bahawalpur.

Fig. 4.11: Panaflex of Khwaja Farid's poetry in
Bahawalpur.

Fig. 4.12: Sculpture celebrating Reading and Writing in
front of Islamia College, Bahawalpur.

Fig. 4.13: Pearls of Peace mural at MUET festival, Jamshoro, Sindh.

Fig. 4.14: AAC's appeal to raise awareness about
Raza Khan's disappearance.

Fig. 4.15: Intersections, at Istanbul Chowk, Lahore.

Fig. 4.16: A bus stop on Canal Bank Road, Lahore, from the LBF's Intersections project.

Fig. 4.17: Marble compass at Lawrence Gardens, at the centre of 'Rooted'.

which envisions a dialogue between the government, art, and the public; the aim is to recognize art as a powerful and positive tool in shaping the everyday experiences of the city, bridging gaps, alleviating the public and initiating meaningful dialogue... 'Art in Public Spaces' is the beginning of yet another revival for the city's culture and arts, an investment in the artist community and an indicator of a firm belief in the arts as a fundamental right of the people.[17]

Atif Khan proposed a monumental, abstract birdhouse, which 'is in itself symbolic of the human desire for shelter and safety.' He sees that the presence of birds and nature, in a chaotic city, acts as a symbol of peace and serenity, as we can see in the two photographs in Figure 4.15. His artwork explores this idea and further contemplates upon Lahoris' identity as humans in a cityscape.[18]

A second public art project in 'Intersections' in the 'Art in Public Spaces' series—quite explicitly focused on the themes of this book—is 'Where the Bus Stops.'[19] In response to an open call for proposals in January 2016, six artists were selected to erect bus stops along Lahore's central routes so the project would be 'instrumental in creating infrastructural support that is mindful of the interests of all of its stakeholders, especially those of its end users.' In other words, comfortable, airy, appealing bus stops, designed by artists, were placed in Lahore's busiest areas on Jail Road, M.M. Alam Road, Gulberg, Dharampura, the Canal Bank Road, and by Punjab University, providing shelter from the rain in winter and from the glaring sun in summer. When I viewed these bus stops, shown in the two photographs in Figure 4.16, I could imagine a worker commuting in the morning, noticing how pleasant the bus stop is and thinking 'someone cares about me, who built this.'

This was Qudsia Raheem's aspiration in getting behind the 'Where the Bus Stops' project. She said 'it gives people the sense that they're a part of the community, they matter, and someone purposely built it for them, using artistic insight. The power of art seeps into you and you don't even know it. When you have hope, it's changing your perspective.'

A total of forty bus stops were built on the Canal Bank Road (13), Main Boulevard in Gulberg (5), Jail Road (12), and Mall Road (10).[20] Each bus stop has two sections, so it could be gender-segregated if users prefer, or families could occupy the separate sections. Each of the artists had their designs vetted through the Social Design workshop at LUMS.

In another LBF effort, 'The Stories We Tell,' also part of 'Art in Public Spaces', the theme was to embolden an intercultural dialogue and encourage Lahoris to both reflect upon and share their personal experiences and expand public discourse.[21] While much of the project focused on the oral component of storytelling, there was an important art dimension to it as well. Twelve decorated rickshaws were placed in different parts of Lahore, mostly near the Walled City, over six months in 2017, provoking curiosity and drawing attention to the project. The organizers describe the goals thus,

> The art of conversation and storytelling has played an important role in suturing together the cultural fabric of South Asia. This was how, for the longest time, histories were transferred between generations; survival narratives were created, exchanged, and relayed; and instructional anecdotes to sustain everyday life were passed on. The act of listening and hearing created collective wisdom and a sense of commonality across social divides, thereby sustaining intercultural and interclass dialogue.
>
> With public spaces becoming more and more stratified and co-opted by specific classes, the interaction between classes has become minimal, most of it happening in a space where the power and class dynamics dictate how stories will be shared, as well as who will tell and who will listen to them. [This] aims to bring conversational storytelling and sharing back to public spaces in the hopes of making the act of storytelling and experience-sharing a democratic one.

The rickshaws proved to be an ideal venue for what the organizers had hoped to accomplish as they drew upon the sentiment of tradition with which everyone could identify.

A final 'Art in Public Spaces' undertaking was 'Rooted,' eight permanent art installations in various parts of Bagh-e-Jinnah (Lawrence Gardens). It draws on Lahore's cultural ethos as a city of gardens as it 'aims to draw on local heritage by employing an approach that engages the surrounding community.' South of the Quaid-i-Azam Library, located within the garden, an Islamic star inlaid into the ground acts as a marble compass, as shown in the two photographs in Figure 4.17, pointing to seven meticulously chosen sites each marked by a marble seat sited to inspire introspection and solitude. The project encourages the viewer to explore and personalize undiscovered spaces in the park dotted with rare and historic flora.

All of these various activities led up to the culminating event, the Lahore Biennale itself, held 18–31 March 2018. Events were held at three main locations in the city: near the Lahore Fort within the Walled City, including the Shahi Hammam and Masjid Wazir Khan by Delhi Gate and the Faqir Khana Museum inside Bhatti Gate; Mall Road from the National College of Arts and the historic Tollinton Market and nearby Lahore Museum down to Lawrence Gardens and the Alhamra Art Centre; and Canal Bank Road from Dharampura to the Punjab University New Campus, including a light show held at the Canal Bank. For the LBF participants, this was the culmination of all of their activities, coming together. Every artist in the city of Lahore opened their studios to the public for the entire time so people could do 'studio hops.' The Lahore Biennale included over seventy-five distinct artists; the list is extensive with artists displaying their craft throughout the city:

1. **Lahore Fort:** Amar Kanwar, Asad Raza, Faiza Butt, Fazal Rizvi, Firoz Mahmud, Hamra Abbas, Huma Mulji, Iftikhar Dadi and Elizabeth Dadi, Imran Qureshi, Nadia Kaabi-Linke, Naiza Khan, Sadia Salim, Shahpour Pouyan, Shahzia Sikander, Shirin Neshat, and Rehana Mangi.

2. **Mubarak Haveli:** Aisha Khalid, Alia Syed, Asvajit Boyle, Ayesha Sultana, Ayesha Jatoi, Lala Rukh, Mahbub Shah, Minam Apang, Muhanned Cader, Rasel Chowdhury, T. Shanaathanan, and Zahoor ul Akhlaq

3. **Shahi Hammam:** Aisha Khalid, Imran Qureshi, and Manisha Gera Baswani

4. **Lahore Museum:** Ayesha Jatoi, Bani Abidi, Masooma Syed, and Waqas Khan

5. **Alhamra Art Centre:** Atif Khan, CAMP, Halil Altindere, Hira Nabi, Kay Walkowiak, Komail Aijazuddin, Naeem Mohaiemen, Naila Mahmood, Naima Dadabhoy, Naiza Khan, Salima Hashmi, Seema Nusrat, Shezad Dawood, and Shahzia Sikander

6. **Bagh-e-Jinnah** (Lawrence Gardens): Ali Kazim, Mehreen Murtaza, David Alesworth, Noor Ali Chagani, and Wardha Shabbir
7. **Canal Bank Road:** Awami Art Collective

Community groups, schools, local art collectives, and others all joined in together over two weeks to show off artistic displays they had created to symbolize and celebrate the city of Lahore and its inhabitants. Thousands of people participated with the result being, as Qudsia Raheem asserted, 'each student creating artwork becomes an artist.'[22] A second Lahore Biennale was held 26 January–29 February 2020 entitled 'Between the Sun and the Moon' and included new projects, workshops and a great deal of public outreach.

A local journalist, Asif Akhtar, had commented that 'locating the public in a city like Lahore can be a challenge for there is not one but many publics. Asking the question 'which public gets to converse with which art intervention?' is equally complicated.'[23] But what is not complicated is that each person participating reinforced their connection, their history, with the city of Lahore and felt part of a community of 11 million people. No untoward events occurred at either Biennale, nor terrorist acts or even rowdy or disruptive behaviour, just a community celebrating itself through art.

Notes

1. Adnan Adil, 'Pakistan's Urban Capital,' *The News on Sunday*, 28 August 2011, p. 29.
2. Based on data as of August 2016 in the World Population Review, accessible at: http://worldpopulationreview.com/world-cities/karachi-population.
3. Arif Hassan, 'Karachi Violence,' *The News on Sunday*, 4 September 2011, Policy section, p. iii.
4. This section is based on various meetings with Munawar Ali Syed in Karachi in February 2017 and 2019.
5. 'One wall at a time,' *Dawn*, 23 May 2017, accessible at: https://www.dawn.com/news/1183365.
6. Momina Khan and Hussain Ali, 'In Karachi: When hate on the wall disappears,' *Dawn*, 25 May 2015, accessible at: http://www.dawn.com/news/1184142.
7. This is based on meetings with Noor Jehan Bilgrami, who teaches at the Indus Valley School of Art, at her Koel gallery in Karachi in March 2017 and February 2019.
8. She conveyed all of this in an interview with me in February 2017.
9. More of the paintings of the 'Walls of Peace' project can be found on the website at: http://iamkarachi.org/what-we-do-2/what-we-do/wall-of-peace/about-iak-walls/.

10. Based on an interview with Jamil Yusuf in Karachi on 16 February 2017.

11. Based on an interview with Amin Hashwani in Karachi on 21 February 2017.

12. This section is based on interviews with Dr Nasrullah Khan Nasser in Bahawalpur on 19 November 2017.

13. This was written about in 'Jamshoro makes history with 22-feet watercolour mural,' *Dawn*, 17 February 2018, accessible at: https://images.dawn.com/news/1179484/jamshoro-makes-history-w.

14. Unpublished draft of Raheem ul Haque, 'Activism as Spectacle and Engagement,' p. 5.

15. Ibid., p. 6.

16. References to conversations with Qudsia Raheem are based on interviews conducted with her in Lahore during October 2017 and January 2018.

17. *See* https://www.lahorebiennale.org/projects/intersections.

18. Ibid.

19. This is based on discussions with Qudsia Raheem and the LBF website, accessible at: https://www.lahorebiennale.org/projects/intersections-where-the-bus-stops.

20. Ibid.

21. *See* http://www.lahorebiennale.org/projects/storieswetell.

22. Interview conducted with Qudsia Raheem in Lahore on 29 January 2018.

23. Asif Akhtar, 'The Lahore Biennale: Painting the City Red', *The Herald*, 18 April 2018, accessible at: https://herald.dawn.com/news/print/1398516.

5 | Religion Itself Counters Extremism

It is a powerful thing when communities come together and say *'Bas!'*—
'Enough!'—'Stop, in the name of religion!' It is in taking these steps that
the promise of real change appears on the horizon, enticing people who
have long felt victimized by violence to envision that their religion has
been misinterpreted to condone violence, or through their actions the
violence will finally cease. In Pakistan today, there are direct attempts by
groups to mobilize and consciously and deliberatively do something about
a prevailing situation using religion as their focal point of organizing.

This chapter is concerned with how religious leaders and faith-based
groups are mobilizing to counter violent extremism and religiously-
motivated violence in Pakistan. This includes efforts to promote interfaith
harmony and pluralism as well as efforts by religious minorities to mobilize
and stand up to extremism and injustice (e.g., the Christian Studies Centre
and other Christian activists, REAT, Pahel) in the wake of violence.

Before we can turn to religious leaders and others coming together to
promote interfaith harmony and pluralism and efforts to mobilize and
empower religious minorities, we must first look at how violent extremism
has focused, in part, on religious belief and especially that of minorities
in Pakistan.

BACKDROP ON WHY VIOLENT EXTREMISM OFTEN FOCUSES ON RELIGIOUS DIFFERENCES

The question of religiously-motivated violence and how to maintain
harmony between religious groups goes back to the colonial era. Offences
relating to religion, making it a crime to deface or destroy places of
worship in British India, were first codified by the British in 1860. They
were subsequently modified in 1927 following religious riots to ward off
'deliberate and malicious acts intended to outrage religious feelings of any
class by insulting its religious belief.'[1] The law emphasized that there would

be no discrimination against any religion, and it would be applicable to all. Pakistan incorporated the existing penal code, including these laws, when it became an independent state after Partition in 1947.

Heightened intolerance by a relatively small segment of Pakistanis against religious minorities—but increasingly, not just minorities but even for non-Salafi Sunni Muslims—is due to a variety of factors. There was a noticeable tilt towards Saudi Arabia after Zia ul Haq's February 1979 promulgation of his Islamization programme which encouraged more Wahhabi and Salafi interpretations of Islam.[2] There was now state-sanctioned emphasis on orthodox Sunni Islam in Pakistan which further aggravated historic ruptures between Sunnis with Shias, Christians and Hindus. Laws were changed, textbooks and syllabi were altered, all to feed into the new ideology of the state under Zia ul Haq. A Pakistani writer, Hassan Jafar Zaidi,[3] argues that this was a form of 'religious narcissism' on the part of the state, 'culminating into its logical end: religious extremism, violence and terrorism.' Simultaneously, this was also fuelled by the marked growth of *madrassas* (religious schools), presumably from funds originating in Arabia and the Gulf. It is estimated that over 3.5 million students are being taught in over 35,000 madrassas today belonging to the Deobandi, Barelvi, Ahl-e-Hadith (Salafi), and Shia sects, and the Jamaat-e-Islami also has its own madrassas.[4] While refutation (*radd*) of other sects has always been part of some madrassa education, A.H. Nayyar, a scholar of education in Pakistan, blames it for the unprecedented increase in sectarian violence and that 'madrassas have, not surprisingly, become a source of hate-filled propaganda against other sects and the sectarian divide has become sharper and more violent.'[5] Some madrassa students and faculty actively supported the Afghan Taliban and al-Qaeda, especially after the 9/11 terrorist attacks,[6] and were prominent founding members of the Tehrik-e-Taliban Pakistan (TTP), known for intolerance.

Another factor contributing to heightened intolerance towards other religious groups, documented by former CII Chairperson and world-renowned scholar of Islam, Muhammad Khalid Masood, are the religious narratives that have been generated by extremist sectarian, political groups.[7] Tracing the history of how nearly all sects and religious parties in Pakistan established student and militant wings since the 1950s, and how some of them have become violent since the 1960s, he argues that the student wing of Jamaat-e-Islami (Islami Jam'iyyat al-Talaba) was the first 'to use religious narrative "forbidding evil" and jihad to justify violence against what they considered un-Islamic acts and practices'.[8] This opened the floodgates for many other religious groups and political parties; by the 1970s, sectarian groups also began forming militant wings. The most notable examples he offers are Ahl-e-Hadith's Lashkar-e-Tayyiba and Ahl-e-Hadith Force, the Deobandis' Jaish-e-Muhammad, Sipah-e-Sahaba and Lashkar-e-Jhangvi, the Barelvis' Sunni Tahrik, and the Shia Sipah-e-Muhammad. Importantly, these groups have been able to make outrageous claims saying their positions are based on *fatwas,* unconstrained by any sort of moral or political control, such as when Lashkar-e-Jhangvi's Balochistan-unit declared that all Shias are *kafir* (non-believers in Islam) in 2012 and resolved that 'Every Shia must be killed and Pakistan should be purified from their "filthy" existence'.[9] While reviewing specific catechist texts and *fatwas* that have contributed to Taliban, Daesh, and other extremist religious narratives and the ways in which they have been applied by extremist groups today to foment hatred, discrimination, and anti-state tenets, he also finds profound holes in the doctrinal explanations and justifications for violence. For example, Masood contends that,

> A major argument in the terrorist narrative is the claim that the governance structure of Pakistan does not conform to Islamic laws. This claim does not match with the facts. The Objectives Resolution and the successive constitutions clearly recognized Islamic injunctions as the basis for law and governance in Pakistan, and even helped solve the apparent conflict between democracy and these points. The 1962 Constitution established the Council of Islamic Ideology for the Islamization of laws. The Council was assigned the job of reviewing the existing laws in Pakistan. Its final report submitted in 1997 suggested that almost 95% of existing laws were not repugnant to Islam, and proposed annulment and revisions for the rest of the laws.[10]

He shows how extremists speak about 'justice, shariah, and *khilafa* (caliphate) only to gain public sympathy and support' which can best be negated through adopting good governance practices by the state promoting justice, and not falling for the bait to respond with religious arguments but rather showing how the extremists' goals are political, not religious.[11]

A final factor contributing to heightened intolerance was the victory of the Islamist coalition, the Muttahida Majlis-e-Amal (MMA),[12] in the provincial Khyber Pakhtunkhwa election in 2003 (the first time in Pakistan's fifty-five-year history that an Islamist political party had success at the ballot box) and its sharing of power in neighbouring Balochistan. This political act opened an unfettered space for religious extremism in western Pakistan.[13] The MMA enabled violent, militant groups euphemistically known as 'the Pakistan Taliban'—including the Tehreek-e-Nafaz-e-Shariat-e-Mohammadi (TNSM) and later the Tehrik-e-Taliban Pakistan (TTP)—to gain footholds. It was during this period, on 14 December 2007 in Quetta, that the TTP came into existence. The effect was of great social cost to Pakistan, especially to interfaith harmony efforts.[14] This dynamic was further aggravated after Nawaz Sharif became Prime Minister in 2013 and the subsequent donation of $1.5 billion from Saudi Arabia to Pakistan 'to bolster the country's falling foreign currency reserves and help cement security ties between the two countries.'[15] Indeed, the unrelenting influence of religion on political activities precludes many political parties or politicians from speaking out against acts of intolerance. Some critics contend that the political government didn't respond to acts against religious intolerance so as to appease high officials within the Kingdom of Saudi Arabia, which may explain why only the military acted against violent extremists and rarely the police.

We have seen religious intolerance increase in many parts of Pakistan. Some people attribute this to two significant state actions in the past: the passage of the Objectives Resolution on 12 March 1949 and incorporation of the Second Amendment to the 1973 Constitution of Pakistan.

On 11 August 1947, Quaid-i-Azam Mohammad Ali Jinnah, in his famous Presidential Address to the Constituent Assembly of Pakistan three days before the country came into being, stated that his vision for Pakistan was that religion would not be a concern of the state and that no sectarian group would be dominant over any other,

> You are free; you are free to go to your temples, you are free to go to your mosques or to any other place of worship in this State of Pakistan. You may belong to any religion or caste or creed that has nothing to do with the business of the State.[16]

The Objectives Resolution, however, suggests a remarkably different stance on the role of Islam in Pakistan. A *Dawn* editorial captures its impact well,

> The opening sentence of the Resolution confirms the limits for the state as prescribed by God who has sovereignty over the entire universe. It declares that by His authority delegated to the State of Pakistan through its people, Muslims shall be enabled to order their lives in accordance with Islam...[17]

With this, Jinnah's view that religion was of no concern for the state was transformed into Pakistan becoming first a homeland for Muslims, and then finally, with the passage of the third Constitution in 1973, an Islamic Republic. However, it was a year later that the new Constitution had a notable impact on interfaith harmony with the passage of the Second Amendment on 7 September 1974 which declared Ahmadis were non-Muslims. Since then, Ahmadis have often been spurned and excluded from full participation in Pakistani society. Most recently, this dynamic manifested in September 2018 when Imran Khan appointed Princeton-based economist Atif Mian to the Economic Advisory Council. This was seen by many as a bold effort by the new government to appoint a highly qualified Ahmadi economist, but the government quickly rescinded that decision due to threats of countrywide protests by Islamist groups.[18]

A third state action that ultimately contributed to extremism and intolerance in Pakistan can be seen in the state actors' responses to the Soviet invasion of Afghanistan on 24 December 1979. This was a seemingly political act: the Soviet Union, which had longstanding ties with Afghanistan going back to the 1920s, was seeking to cement its control after a series of political assassinations had introduced a great deal of instability there. With some roughly 30,000 troops sent to invade Afghanistan, Soviet troops killed President Hafizullah Amin and installed Babrak Karmal in his place. But it was the United States' reaction to the event that infused religion into the scenario by deeming the Afghan opposition to be *mujahideen*, fighters waging a *jihad* (struggle, battle) which is a religious act. The US put out a clarion call to Muslims worldwide to fight against the Soviet Union in Afghanistan.[19] In this endeavour, a group called 'the Base' was formed in Peshawar, to outfit the new recruits in this so-called jihad and provide them with food, housing, weapons, and instructions. In Arabic, 'the Base' translates as al-Qaeda. Framing the Afghan insurgency into a religious act fed into already-burgeoning Salafi sentiments in Pakistan nurtured by the Zia ul Haq government after it declared its Islamization programme earlier that year, on 2 February. The Pakistan government's focus had now shifted to Islamizing laws and policies internally while supporting the *mujahideen* in what had now come to be termed a religious struggle in Afghanistan.

The watershed period when violent extremism began to manifest on a near-daily basis—and attacks against religious minorities heightened— was when the Government of Pakistan joined the US 'War on Terror' campaign following the attacks on the US on 11 September 2001. The following month, on 7 October 2001, the US attacked Afghanistan with the undeniable support of the Government of Pakistan. While there were explicit political and ethnic objections to the Government of Pakistan's actions, it seems that occurrences of violence based on religious difference also escalated within Pakistan. Christians, in particular, seem to have borne the brunt of this violence, although periodically Shias and non-Salafi Sunnis have as well.[20]

The first infamous attack on Christians in this new era of divisiveness was on 9 August 2002, which targeted a church within the grounds of the Taxila Christian Hospital, slightly northwest of Pakistan's capital Islamabad, in which four people died and twenty-five men and women were wounded. Just over a month later, on 25 September 2002, gunmen shot and killed seven Christians at the Institute for Peace and Justice, an NGO in Karachi.[21] Exactly two months later, on Christmas, two *burqa*-clad gunmen threw grenades into a Presbyterian church in Chianwala, northwest of Lahore, killing three young girls and wounding fourteen others who were attending the service. The following day, more grenades were found outside of the St. Thomas Protestant church in Islamabad.

Attacks against Christians continued in many parts of Pakistan; some observers think Christians were targeted as symbolic representatives of the west. Attacks were also increasingly provoked by charges of blasphemy. For example, over 3,000 people in November 2005 attacked Roman Catholic, Salvation Army and United Presbyterian churches in Sangla Hill, near Faisalabad, over an allegation of blasphemy by Yousaf Masih, a local Christian. Three months later, provoked by publication in Denmark of objectionable cartoons depicting the Prophet, protesters targeted churches and Christian schools throughout Pakistan. Other significant attacks against Christians occurred when a mob stormed a Protestant church in July 2008 just outside of Karachi, denouncing Christians as *kafirs* (infidels). The following year, Christians were unprecedentedly targeted including the looting and destruction of a few dozen Christian homes in Kasur, Punjab, soon followed by attacks on over a hundred Christian homes in Gojra, Punjab, in July. Both attacks were provoked by charges of blasphemy— desecration of the Quran—that have never been upheld. Punjab Governor Salman Taseer, a vocal supporter of reforming Pakistan's blasphemy laws, was assassinated by Mumtaz Qadri masquerading as one of his security guards on 4 January 2011. This act has had important implications for violent extremism in Pakistan, prompting marked divisions between those who mourned the murder of a courageous politician while others hailed his killer as a hero. Even though Qadri was convicted of murder and executed (on 29 February 2016), his death has galvanized extremists, especially within Barelvi circles. Riots soon broke out throughout the country— even the Islamabad Bar Association went on strike protesting Qadri's execution—given the view held by some people that Qadri was a hero of Islam who killed a blasphemer (Salman Taseer) who had showed support for a blasphemer (Christian, Aasia Bibi) and just his raising the issue of reforming the blasphemy laws was blasphemy itself.

Michael Kugelman, a South Asia analyst at the Wilson Center in the US, assesses the significance of Taseer's assassination and Qadri's execution for violent extremism in Pakistan,

> After the assassination, Qadri was seemingly lionized as much as Taseer was mourned. He was infamously garlanded and showered with rose petals during his initial court appearance… Qadri continued to enjoy the support of numerous religious conservatives as well as lawyers to the day he died. After word of his fate became known, spontaneous protests sprung up around Pakistan to condemn his execution…In effect, the Pakistani state hanged a man who was revered by the radicalized elements of society. This is no small matter, by any measure.[22]

Merely two months following Salman Taseer's killing, on 2 March 2011, Shahbaz Bhatti, the Christian Minister of Minorities Affairs, was assassinated, allegedly due to his efforts to reform the blasphemy laws. He was well known for his dedication to promote communal harmony and was reportedly despondent with how he saw that harmony unravelling in Pakistan. It unravelled further the next month, in April 2011, when 500 demonstrators attacked the Christian community in Gujranwala.

There are many other violent incidents which can be recalled, but a provocative one had an impact on the first group to be addressed in this chapter, the Interfaith Council for Peace and Harmony. In March 2013, the Christian Joseph Colony in Lahore was brutally attacked and over a hundred homes were burned allegedly because a local Christian man was said to have made some blasphemous remarks. Six months later, a suicide attack at the All Saints Church in the old quarter of Peshawar, the provincial capital of Khyber Pakhtunkhwa, killed seventy-five Christians. On Sunday, 15 March 2015, two Taliban suicide bombers attacked two churches—a Catholic and a Protestant—in Youhanabad, Lahore, home to more than 100,000 Christians, killing at least twenty-one people and injuring more than seventy. The year 2016 was a particularly violent one for the Pakistani Ahmadi community, consistent with much of the violence they had faced previously and since: these included a number of unprovoked deaths throughout the country just because the men were Ahmadis, threats in many areas, the emergence of hateful anti-Ahmadi banners at Lahore's Hafeez Centre (which the Punjab government eventually ordered to be removed), and on 1 March 2016, when the Punjab Housing and Town Planning Agency in Chiniot began an auction of residential and commercial plots, they explicitly excluded Ahmadis and their non-Ahmadi relatives from bidding in the auction.[23] Then there was the attack in Sindh's Ghotki district near Sukkur in July 2016, when two Hindu men were shot at a tea stall during a mob attack following the arrest of a Hindu man the previous day for desecrating a Quran.[24] Local observers contended that the suspect was a drug addict with mental issues who had converted to Islam a few months earlier and began living in a mosque. Tensions ran high as over 150 people were arrested on rioting charges, and the local Hindu community began to feel targeted.

These events underscore the general belief among some in Pakistan that violence in the name of religion against people with other religious beliefs is acceptable. But this appears to manifest as violence more when mobs are provoked by leaders using hate rhetoric.

What is often overlooked are instances when tolerance has occurred. For example, madrassas have been growing in number in Sindh, prompting many political analysts—especially those based elsewhere, outside of the interior of Sindh—to comment that we will be seeing more sectarian violence in Sindh as a result of this. However, numerous Sindhis commented to me that 'madrassas will not change the character of Sindh, but rather Sindh will change the character of madrassas.' Admittedly doubtful, I thought I would challenge that observation when I visited a Hindu temple in Halani, Ranipur district, in upper Sindh.[25] The temple has long shared a wall with the neighbouring mosque, which was recently replaced with a Deobandi madrassa. Thinking this would disprove the indigenous Sindhis' observations, I queried the *pandit* (Hindu priest) at the temple about any increased acts of animosity towards the temple as well as the Hindu devotees who were attending it since the madrassa has been operational. He was quick to point out that relations with them have been extraordinarily good, that the madrassa students celebrate Holi[26] with them, and invite them to *iftar* meals during Ramadan. In effect, madrassa education does not necessarily lead to intolerance as there are other factors that may contribute to that intolerance as well as factors that may counter it.

The state, too, has made an effort to promote interfaith harmony by instituting a name change in the accountable ministry. The Ministry of Religious Affairs had long existed in tandem with the Ministry of Minorities Affairs, which had briefly been renamed the Ministry for Interfaith Harmony. Soon after the 2013 election, the PML-N government merged the two ministries to create a Ministry for Religion and Interfaith Harmony. Various leaders and activists celebrated this event, that the state was finally acting on promoting harmony and empowering religious minorities. However, a glance at the Ministry's website[27] shows that this is a change in name only, that the Ministry is mostly focused on Pakistan's Muslim population. Even the homepage of its website proclaims its mandate as such,

> The Ministry of Religious Affairs is responsible for the pilgrimage beyond Pakistan, Muslim pilgrims' visits to Iran for *ziarat* and

Saudi Arabia for Umra and Hajj. It is also responsible for the welfare and safety of pilgrims and *zaireen*. The main activities also include research based Islamic Studies, holding of conferences, seminars, training education of ulemas and *khateebs*, exchange of visits of scholars of Islamic learning with the liaison amongst foreign and international institutions.

There is no mention here—or anywhere else on the website—of the Ministry's efforts to ensure or promote interfaith harmony or of any involvement it has with non-Muslim concerns. It is today engaged with creating an official National Commission on Interfaith Harmony (discussed later in this chapter) but has not yet completed doing so. Indeed, in late September 2018, former senator Farhatullah Babar said that 'despite constitutional guarantees, religious injunctions and international covenants signed by Pakistan, the rights of minorities have been shrinking, and intolerance toward them by the state and society is increasing.'[28]

RELIGIOUS LEADERS' EFFORTS TO PROMOTE INTERFAITH HARMONY AND PLURALISM

Religious leaders throughout Pakistan have vowed for roughly a decade to do something about the violence occurring between communities and have been mobilizing other religious leaders to take action. In particular, Muslim 'ulema have begun organizing themselves into groups with the hope that they and their constituencies can prevent occurrences of violent extremism in the name of religion in the future. An important priority for many has been syllabus reform in madrassas to ensure that genuine interpretations of the religion are being taught rather than extremist ones with little bearing on what they perceive the religion actually espouses.[29] These faith-based networks have then reached out to include other religious leaders as well in their groups. Christian leaders have also played important roles in promoting interfaith harmony, especially in urban centres in Pakistan.

This is exemplified in the make-up and activities of the Lahore-based Interfaith Council for Peace and Harmony (ICPH). The religious leader of the Badshahi mosque, Imam Abdul Khabir Azad, has been organizing other religious leaders to have open communication with each other to promote interfaith harmony. His father, Maulana Syed Mohammad

Abdul Khadr Azad, who had been Imam of the Badshahi mosque for thirty years, was a founder of interfaith harmony in Pakistan, traveling all over Pakistan promoting that message; Imam Abdul Khabir Azad has dedicated himself to 'follow in his footsteps.'[30] He has organized other Muslim as well as Christian religious leaders in Lahore to meet periodically, discuss challenges to communal harmony, and overall mobilize their congregations into accepting people of faiths other than their own. As chairperson of the ICPH, he has been especially effective in mobilizing other religious leaders to come together in response to crises, first through their annual conferences and now, in the past decade, in response to crises and other events as they occur. He says, 'Today, the world has turned into a global village and we should embrace each other for global peace and interfaith harmony.' What animates him to do this is his understanding of Islam,

> The Quran says that we should respect each other. Our Prophet says that for you to be great people, be peaceful. People of the Book[31]—Muslims should get along with them.

He and the other religious leaders in his group became a symbol of interfaith harmony following the violence that occurred at a Christian-majority neighbourhood in Badami Bagh, Lahore, the Joseph Colony, on 9 March 2013. A Christian man, who it later turned out was falsely accused of blasphemy, was taken into custody at a police station on the blasphemy charge so as to placate a mob after the allegations of blasphemy spread throughout the neighbourhood. The mob, consisting of over 7,000 people, returned the next day and ransacked Christian homes, setting about 125 homes on fire (some colony residents claim the number to be higher, at 165).[32] It was finally at the intervention of Imam Abdul Khabir Azad and his group of other religious leaders who had rushed over to Badami Bagh that finally persuaded the mob to disperse and leave. He recounts what occurred,

> I went there with my team of all sects: Shia, Barelvi, Deobandi, and Ahl-e-Hadith. I went there and said to the people—there were thousands of people who were very angry, and they wanted to do more destruction—I went there and told them 'Like you are going, Islam does not give you permission. I am the Imam of Lahore and

I have come with love, but you must put the *tashuddud* [violence] aside. We want that you have to put this aside—Muslims need to meet with Christians peacefully...' I told them if someone did something wrong, then it's the work of the police and the laws to punish them. It's not their work to do this and bring this violence throughout Pakistan. Now—there were thousands of people who had sticks and other weapons in their hands—I got them to calm down.

From then on, the group of interfaith leaders began to meet even more regularly, attending each other's religious and family celebrations. The following year, in November 2014, there was an attack on a Christian man and his pregnant wife in Kot Radha Kishan, a town southwest of Lahore. They had allegedly desecrated a copy of the Quran and a mob of 4,000 people threw their bodies into a brick kiln where they burned to death. Imam Azad led a delegation of the Interfaith Council for Peace and Harmony to visit the house of the victims on the Friday following the incident to condole their family and declared that the act was against the teachings of Islam. Bringing together leaders of all faiths, he said that Islam doesn't allow people to take law into their own hands when a judicial system exists in a country, and people should rely on it. He appealed to the masses in general, and religious leaders in particular, to report problems to law-enforcers instead of inciting religious emotions.[33]

An active member of the ICPH, Maulana Zubair Ahmad Zaheer is the *Naib Ameer* (head imam) of the prominent Markazi Jamiat Ahl-e-Hadith Pakistan and director of the Jamia Umer bin Abdul Aziz mosque at Firdous Market in Lahore. He considers that he and other 'ulema have been struggling towards interfaith harmony and peace for the past 45 years.[34] He has spent quite a bit of time in jail after speaking out for Christians' rights, first during the Zulfiqar Ali Bhutto's government in the early 1970s, and then later when Zia ul Haq had decreed separate elections for Christians. Imam Zaheer had strongly condemned this decree for which he was sent to the Kot Lakhpat jail for a month and was later sent to the Gujranwala jail for twenty days for speaking in favour of the Christian community in Hafizabad. Firdous Market houses about 150 Christian families, and he opens the mosque for them to use when they have a funeral or any other function where they need space. He has also hosted the Catholic leader of Lahore, Bishop Shaw, at his mosque. On Eid, his mosque gives local Christian children money, cakes, and sweets; on Christmas, the local Christian leaders give treats to the Muslim children in the neighbourhood. He feels these are small ways to encourage interfaith harmony, and the children grow up with positive feelings about other religions.

He was a part of the delegation that rushed over to the Joseph Colony at the time of the attack in 2013, 'to try to cool down the angry people.' They also went to churches and met with Christian religious leaders and, he says, 'gave them a message of peace and love.' He sees that the group has been playing a very important role in countering extremism, resulting in a markedly improved situation between religious groups,

> We have brought together good-thinking 'ulema—Deobandi, Barelvi, Shia, and Catholic Archbishop Sebastian Shaw, Church of Pakistan Bishop Alexander John Malik Shah and now Bishop Irfan Jamil—they're all coming and going, appearing on television, saying we must end the hatred. It's starting to work…For interfaith harmony, you have to try hard. If you don't want to live like you're in a jungle, you have to have dialogue. Dialogue with justice. Everything will be better.

Imam Hafiz Syed Qasim Raza Naqvi, a Shia leader in Lahore, has run his madrassa, the Jamiat'ul-Muntazar, for the past twenty-three years.[35] He has been actively involved with the Interfaith Council for Peace and Harmony for the past eleven years. He was with the group when it went immediately to the Joseph Colony and returned a few more times with books and other things for the children there. He went to assist Christian communities at various other times when they needed help as well. When interfaith conflict is at its height, he sees Shias as having suffered as much as Christians, but it also hurts the entire society,

> Any time any group is harmed, it is a harm for Pakistan. It's a harm for us…No 'alim should have any fatwa against other Muslims. Sunnis and Shias: no one ever thought they would fight against each other. We (members of the Interfaith Council for Peace and Harmony) are now trying to explain to each other that God's command is that, if you kill someone, it's like you're killing a whole community. We are saying to our congregations, 'You have your

religion, we have our path, and there's no justification for killing each other.'

He considers that the Prophet gave a command that 'you do my work, but don't force others' and that true followers of all religions should do just that. He recalls visits to his madrassa from the late Barelvi leader, Sarfaraz Naeemi Shaheed (father of current Jamia Naeemi madrassa head, Dr Raghib Naeemi) and that Imam Azad's father, Abdur Rehman Azad, went with him to Iran for *ziarat*, a pilgrimage to sites associated with the Prophet and his family members. He and Ahl-e-Hadith leaders, like Maulana Zubair Ahmad Zaheer, frequently attend each other's programmes, and a local Christian leader, Alexander John Malik, used to come to his madrassa on Shia religious events. We therefore see that many leaders of different religious communities in Lahore have sought to cooperate with each other and promote interfaith harmony for a very long time. While interfaith relations in the country have deteriorated in the past two decades, these leaders and their sons have taken up the mantle and are stepping up their efforts.

Each of the religious leaders I spoke with in the ICPH think that interfaith conflict escalated during Zia ul Haq's government, as people were encouraged to build large mosques—setting themselves up as competitors—and the government allowed conflicts to simmer, such as the Shia-Sunni conflict in Jhang. But the promotion of understanding and accord between religious leaders is having a big impact, at least in Lahore. Imam Naqvi says,

> The bad work exists, but we're trying to get past it. There is an *ayat* (verse) in the Quran that we have to promote peace. The *silsila* (chain of continuity) that is progressing will continue. The 'ulema are working for this. The best work is that everyone should attend each other's programmes, in happiness or sadness, marriages and deaths, and religious functions. In this, it will give a sense of being together. Peace will grow from this. While the *awam* (the masses) don't attend each other's functions, they see their leaders doing so and it makes a big difference in their minds. It makes a big difference in their actions. Their hearts will change with time.

His words reverberate with those of Deobandi leader, Imam Azad of the Badshahi Mosque, who thinks that the religious leaders who have come together in the Interfaith Council for Peace and Harmony are doing something important, exciting, and innovative,

> We people—you know, we are ambassadors of our Prophet— we tell people not to fight with each other. At this time, we are talking about interfaith harmony. At one time, 30–40 years ago, there was no interfaith harmony. We didn't go to each other's churches, and we didn't get together. So for the future, we hope to further cultivate this. There is not just one platform for interfaith harmony, there are thousands. We now have a mission and thousands of people are with us.

Maulana Zubair Ahmad Zaheer, the Ahl-e-Hadith imam, wants to see religious leaders come together and develop a section about *all* religions in the education syllabus. He and many others participating in the ICPH assert that an introduction to the basics of all religions is important to foster interfaith harmony in Pakistan. Maulana Zaheer contends,

> Everyone should know, and then they won't think wrong about other religions. We need to identify what are the good things in each religion and write this book to be used in schools. We must show that the goal of all religions is the same.

In 2013, a branch of the Lahore Grammar School had introduced a course on Comparative Religion which was met with demonstrations and riots.[36] He considers that had the school brought the 'ulema together as they were developing the course, they would not have had a problem introducing it. They're the authorities on religion, and their voices would be more respected than those of the politicians who had supported it. The ultimate goal of such education is to foster peace,

> Peace and a calm environment will be achieved when all religions come together and don't fight. Research is necessary to find commonalities, to understand correctly. That's Islam. People's senses and hearts shouldn't try to force change. To stop others from worshipping is wrong.

Another prominent member of the group is Dr Raghib Naeemi, Principal of the Jamia Naeemi Hanifi Barelvi madrassa in Garhi Shahu, a working-class area of Lahore.[37] It is the largest institution of the Barelvi movement in Pakistan and was founded by his grandfather in 1953. Promoting interfaith harmony is truly at his essence: his grandfather was friends with Imam Abdul Khabir Azad's father and they worked together—two Deobandi and Barelvi leaders—to transmit the message of harmony. His father, Mufti Sarfraz Ahmed Naeemi, then Principal of the Jamia Naeemi madrassa, had been an outspoken critic of the TTP for over a decade. He had been speaking out against religious leaders advocating violent extremism since October 1998 when he issued his first *fatwa* against them from the Jamia Naeemia. He had brought together a large number of 'ulema at the Jamia Naeemia, including then head of the Jamaat-e-Islami, Qazi Hussain Ahmad, and gathered them together in support of the *fatwa*. He had continued to oppose the extremists and in May 2009, he participated in a conference of Islamic scholars convened by the Pakistani government that criticized suicide attacks and the beheading of innocent Muslims as unIslamic. Following the military attack on the Swat Taliban in May 2009, he declared that it was incumbent on the Pakistan military to eradicate the Taliban or else, he feared, they would 'capture the entire country, which would be a big catastrophe.' He was also a strong advocate of female education and using computers in schools, which also differed markedly from the Taliban's rigid interpretation of Islam.

Sarfraz Naeemi became a victim of extremist violence when a Taliban suicide bomber entered the Jamia Naeemi madrassa and detonated his explosives in the vestibule leading to his office on 12 June 2009, just after he had given the sermon at the Friday prayers.[38] Two days earlier, on 10 June 2009, he had brought more than 1,500 'ulema, *pirs,* and other religious leaders together at the nearby Aiwan-e-Iqbal Hall in Lahore where they spoke out against the Taliban. Students and faculty were still at the Jamia Naeemi madrassa and witnessed the explosion; the mark of where the explosion blew up a part of the floor remains as a poignant reminder of the violent assassination. Baitullah Mehsud, TTP head at that time, later confessed that the TTP had recruited the young man to be a suicide bomber.

Raghib Naeemi recalls that his father used to say he was dedicating his life to the Pakistani nation, the police, the army, and the Prophet. In light of his father's reputation as a dedicated, pious religious leader, Raghib Naeemia considers that his father's assassination was a wake-up call for Pakistan,

> Everyone in the army and police opened their eyes and said, what happened? OK, this is against the society and the people.[39]

As a teacher, his favourite class to teach is 'methods', because students can then do actual, viable research. He has sent Jamia Naeemia students to various parts of Lahore to conduct interviews with imams at mosques to find out whether the imam is a graduate or a *hafiz qari* (someone who has memorized the Quran and knows the actual pronunciation). Of the imams who were interviewed, his students found that 95 per cent of them were simple undergraduate degree-holders working in mosques as *imam khatibs* (the person who leads the Friday prayers and gives the sermon); only 5 per cent of the imams are graduates either from Islamic studies or from madrassas. To him, this means,

> They have no capability or capacity to give the *juma* [Friday] sermon, they don't know the meaning of the Quran, and they don't know with an inner sense the meaning of Islam. They are not giving the true message of Islam at the *juma* sermons. They are just giving a general message, not the entire message of Islam. And they may certainly be distorting it; they don't know the depth of any matter, and they don't know how to draw on Islam to help resolve daily matters. The situation is worse in far-flung areas, where there are no big cities. This is happening everywhere in Pakistan, this is why we don't have peace and harmony.

He is also a member of the Ittehad Bain ul Muslimeen (IBM) committee, established by the Punjab's provincial government to 'maintain religious harmony, brotherhood, and tolerance.' They meet twice or thrice a year, brainstorming on ways to promote interfaith harmony. During Muharram, IBM members 'go to far-flung areas to promote Shia-Sunni co-existence, especially at that time.' The IBM issued a Code of Conduct to maintain interfaith harmony, including such items as: no person belonging to any sect will be declared *kafir* (infidel) or *wajibul qatal* (worthy of death) and no speech will be made against any sect creating hatred; public meetings will be arranged jointly and addressed by 'ulema of all schools of thought to support national unity and religious harmony; 'ulema of all sects will be given due respect and protection of places of worship of all schools of thought will be ensured; slogans hurting people's feelings, creating hatred and provocation will be avoided completely; and the government will ensure, according to shariah, to protect life, property, and places of worship for non-Muslims. Strict legal action would be taken against those desecrating the life and property and places of worship of non-Muslims and there will be a complete ban on hate material.[40] Reflecting on the importance and utility of this Code of Conduct in preventing violence amongst adherents of different religious groups, an editorial in the *Daily Times* espoused,

> This is a country where, as far back as 1954, the Munir Report described how not one religious leader of the different sects could agree with the other on the definition of a Muslim. And that was a relatively manageable situation. However, now, we have an overload of hate-based material, intentions and elements that wish to cause strife, making Pakistan a living hell for all its minorities, including those within the state-sanctioned fold of Islam. This newly proposed code is a step in the right direction but it needs to be respected, adhered to and implemented for it to have any effect.[41]

Raghib Naeemi acknowledges that there is a lot of work to be done in Pakistan to promote interfaith harmony, even within his own Barelvi movement. It was a Barelvi, Khadim Hussain Rizvi, who essentially shut down the national capital Islamabad in November 2017 over the controversial issue of the need for government servants to believe in 'Khatam-e-Nabuwwat', the finality of the Prophet. He told me that Khadim Hussain Rizvi often shouts and uses abusive language and is against educating women. He said that 'these groups are emerging in our sect now (the Barelvis), and they are extremists.'

However, he considers that it is difficult for them to raise their voices against Khadim Hussain Rizvi because there is so much social media support behind him and his group, which is influencing a lot of young men. He acknowledges that not only interfaith harmony is important but inter-sect harmony as well. His hope for harmony in the future lies in his students,

> But we can prepare our students, and I think these students will bring harmony in the society, even if they are less in numbers. We need to educate people in both Islamic education and modern education—we are lacking in both. 'Ulema really need to use a better approach in educating society about Islam; it is a matter of society, not about the students.

A number of Christian leaders are also active members of the Interfaith Council for Peace and Harmony. Archbishop Joseph Coutts has been an outspoken leader for many years whose advocacy for interfaith harmony is praised by many other ICPH members. He is quoted as seeing himself as a conductor—not of musicians but of religious leaders from various faiths, 'We all are musical notes; each note has a specific identity but when played together, spread peace.'[42] He has made inter-religious dialogue a priority ever since he came to head the Archdiocese of Karachi in 2012. He regularly attends programmes, seminars, and conferences promoting interfaith harmony. Reflecting on the work of the Karachi diocese for the past sixty years, mostly in the arenas of education, healthcare, and reaching out to the greater community at times of natural disaster, he says that it's now time for a major shift to promote a culture of harmony. In December 2017, at a rally to celebrate the Prophet's birthday organized by ICPH, he said,

> It's time to promote harmony. That is our new motto. We have to learn it and teach it. Now we are tasked with restoring harmony to this seaport city by welcoming people from different customs and traditions.[43]

He entered the College of Cardinals in Vatican City on 29 June 2018, though he remains the Archbishop of Karachi as well.

Another key Christian figure promoting interfaith harmony, peace, and cooperation is Father James Channan (Figure 5.1), Director of the Lahore

Peace Centre.[44] He considers that Zia ul Haq played an unfortunate role by pitting religious communities against each other in Pakistan,

> If I look at Pakistan before 1979 and afterwards, there is a huge gulf in tolerance, acceptance, religious freedom, and openness of the country. Although Pakistan was made an Islamic state in the Constitution of 1973, but Zia is really the person who damaged peaceful relations amongst communities in Pakistan. The strict kind of Islamic shariah that he promoted—he was so narrow-minded. He did not believe in democracy, in political parties, or in minorities—who had an equal role in the Pakistan movement—he put that aside. He created gulfs between different Muslim groups, especially Shias and Sunnis. He came down hard on women, that they should cover their heads with the chador. He also nurtured those groups that were extremist in nature.

He considers that Christians in Pakistan today 'live in a state of fear and uncertainty, and we don't know what will happen, when or where. These extremists are everywhere.' But on the positive side, he looks to the 'ulema who are members of the Interfaith Council for Peace and Harmony, notably Imam Azad of the Badshahi mosque, Maulana Zubair Ahmed Zaheer and others who are taking stands to promote interfaith harmony. He has the Lahore Peace Centre participate in their activities as well as organize some of their own, to bring harmony between people, especially Muslims and Christians. Together they celebrate international days of peace including International Women's Day every 8th of March, the Symphony of Peace Prayers in mid-May, and the biggest celebration, the International Day of Peace on 21 September. Other activities include breaking the fast—*iftar*—with Muslims during Ramadan, celebrating Diwali and Holi with Hindus, and inviting different groups to their Interfaith Christian programmes. Their magazine *UMANG* (*Wishful Thinking*), published every three months, provides coverage to a wide range of national and international programmes on interfaith harmony.

He considers it a very positive development for interfaith harmony that federal and provincial governments organize Christmas day with various public events and give prominent coverage to Christmas programmes. During the Christmas period in 2016, a Christmas Peace Train ran from

Islamabad to Karachi and stopped at all the major cities on its route. There were no passengers on the train, a recognition that it would have been too risky in these times of violence. The train was brightly decorated with paintings and photos on each of the eight bogies, including pictures of Christian leaders who had worked with Jinnah, Christian army leaders, and others. There was also a large photograph of Father Channan's Peace Centre on the train, depicting him and others praying for the victims of the Gulshan Iqbal attack that had occurred on the other major Christian holiday, Easter Sunday. In every city where it stopped, the train was welcomed by local religious leaders. He, Imam Azad, and other ICPH leaders as well as the head of the provincial assembly and the Railways Minister inaugurated its arrival in Lahore on Christmas Eve, 24 December 2016. Twenty television channels covered its journey and arrival.

Father Channan credits the advocacy of religious leaders who support interfaith harmony throughout the country with the Government of Pakistan's decision to merge the Ministry of Religious Affairs and the Ministry of Minority Affairs in 2013 to become the Ministry of Religious Affairs and Interfaith Harmony. In 2017, the federal government drafted a bill to create an Interfaith Harmony Commission. Father Channan organized a meeting of fifteen religious scholars and human rights activists after receiving the draft of the bill and hopes that the comments they submitted will be incorporated into it.

The plan now is that the Interfaith Harmony Commission will be comprised of eighteen members: seven official members will be from the ministries of Human Rights, Foreign Affairs, Capital Administration, Interior, Law, the Council of Islamic Ideology, and the Ministry of Religious Affairs and Interfaith Harmony. The eleven non-official members will include four from the Muslim community (one each from Deobandi, Barelvi, Ahl-e-Hadith, and Shia sects), two from the Christian community (one Catholic, one Protestant) and two Hindus, one Sikh, one Zoroastrian, and one Baha'i. Father Channan credits the various religious leaders who have provided input into the formation of the Interfaith Harmony Commission with suggesting such a balanced representation of religious groups on it. He keeps at it, trying,

We keep on playing our positive role, to contact political and religious leaders, to create a sense of interfaith harmony and peace in Pakistan. Some steps must be taken to overcome this terrorism—the government should develop a syllabus to promote interfaith harmony in the schools. They should not allow hate speeches to take place; they must take action against them.

He echoes Maulana Zubair Ahmed Zaheer who also wants government schools to teach about all religions. In schools, all Muslim students are required to take Islamiat courses on their religion but that leaves them ignorant about other religions. Promoting understanding will go far towards lessening violence against those of other religions. He persists in his work, convinced that,

> There is hope, there is a chance. The most important thing is that 'instead of cursing the darkness, we must light the candle of hope.' That is what keeps me working, advocating for peace. While there are many thorns in the way, there are many roses that come up. In Pakistan, there are hundreds of peace and harmony groups that have come up, working all over the country. There is no survival of Pakistan without dialogue.

He considers that there are a number of other steps the government should also take to counter violence that is committed in the name of religion. He contends that it is vital that schools improve, and all materials that foment hate are removed from all syllabi. In its efforts to educate every Pakistani, the state must minimize the gulf between regular schools and madrassas. In addition, the electronic and print media should play a more positive role in building bridges between different religious communities and breaking the walls of non-acceptance and violence. He also observes that parents have a very important role to play because starting from home, children should be encouraged to grow up to be non-violent. He advocates banning Kalashnikov toys and pistols for children 'and they should have footballs in their hands' keeping them active and healthy.

He laments that many of the extremist religious groups, such as Jaish-e-Mohammad and Sipah-e-Sahaba, that were banned under Pervez Musharraf's government have returned with new names. He is dismayed that as the government is frightened of them, it has also given them so much room. Instead, at the grassroots level, religious leaders should be encouraged to promote peaceful coexistence and interfaith harmony. He also suggests that the Friday sermons be prepared centrally and delivered throughout the country, like they do in Turkey, a sentiment I heard repeatedly from different religious leaders, including Muslim leaders. Even more than these deliberate efforts, Father Channan thinks that people throughout the country must begin to envision a peaceful society,

> There is a need to promote interfaith harmony at every level of our lives. We need to promote this not only at the level of religious experience, but we must respect our neighbours, no matter what their religions. All of us must become bridge-builders and break all links with terrorism. We should reach out to others, and find ways to build trust between us.

He observes that since many 'ulema in Pakistan are saying the same thing, this is a sign of hope. The 'ulema, too, are fed up with what is happening—the violence—in the name of Islam.

Peter Jacob[45] of the Centre for Social Justice in Lahore is also an active participant in Interfaith Council for Peace and Harmony activities. He earlier worked for twenty-six years with the National Commission for Justice and Peace, reaching out to marginalized groups, not just Christians, to achieve their rights in a variety of arenas: work, housing, legal assistance, etc. But they constantly lived in fear of non-state actors and when his health began to deteriorate due to stress, he left. He started the Centre for Social Justice in October 2014 by conducting assessments of peace-building efforts in Punjab by churches, NGOs, and others, resulting in a 2015 publication, 'Building Peace from the Bottom,' and has since commissioned other reports assessing minorities' treatment. He seeks to build a rights-based approach to peace-building while asking for three pragmatic actions from the state:

1. Curriculum and textbooks, nationally, must be changed to remove hate speech.
2. Blasphemy laws should be substantially changed as these have disproportionately targeted the Christian minority.

3. Finally, establishment of a National Commission for Minorities which has been promised for many years but does not exist to date.

He and others at the Center for Social Justice have been working to curb violence on a number of fronts because,

> Since this challenge is multi-faceted and has a variety of responses, all approaches are important. The most important are those which help us form an alternative narrative, alternative views. This is the biggest tool that forces on the other side have used—a narrative that is supposedly enforced by everyone, including the state...Anything that builds hope is important. But the counter narrative—for instance, after the APS attack—was powerful. We were singing songs, 'we have to teach the enemies' children.'

Bishop Irfan Jamil,[46] the Protestant Bishop of Lahore representing the Church of Pakistan, has also developed close ties with the 'ulema involved in the Interfaith Council for Peace and Harmony. His is one of the eight dioceses within the Church of Pakistan, and his diocese's arc is from Sahiwal in southern Punjab to Lahore. Each of the eight dioceses has their own bishop, and each bishop is deeply involved in interfaith harmony. He advocates conflict prevention and building bridges between people in groups at the grassroots level. He sees that there has to be a transformation in thinking and only the two most influential social institutions can change this: one's family and the schools. How someone is taught to behave within a family is very consequential, as many people are socialized to believe that if you have an enemy, they are your enemy your whole life and nothing can change that. Schools are where the mind develops. He says,

> We have to change the thinking, change the mindset, so things can move. We can do this. People come here to pray on Sundays, or to mosques on Fridays: they come for peace. So, we try to do things within the faith.

By religion having become politicized, he sees a greater separation at his school between Christian and Muslim students today than has existed in the past. He finds this disheartening and has instituted programmes at his school to bring students from different religious communities together in discussions. He sees efforts to promote interfaith harmony working at their best at a time of crisis, with people coming together offering both physical and emotional help. 'We're trying to show people that they are walking together on the road, and this is making a difference.' During the Joseph Colony and Gulshan Ravi violent events, he joined other Christian leaders and key 'ulema and travelled to those places, urging people to promote harmony despite what occurred as it is the only way to move forward. Whenever Imam Azad invites him to participate in events, or he invites Imam Azad and other 'ulema, these efforts bring them closer. They all went together to Kot Radha Kishan in November 2014 to condole the family of the Christian couple who were incinerated there.

But he sees his struggle with the grassroots, his own congregation, and other religious leaders' congregations. He feels that there should be more places and areas where Christians and Muslims can be seen together, not just at disasters. Then they can share the true spirit of being human and promote understanding of each other: how they live, how they die, and people come to understand and finally care about each other.

When asked about what he saw as prospects for peace between communities and eliminating violence in the future, his response is that it is 'a continuous struggle' that they need to remain vigilant about. Whether conditions will improve or not is very unpredictable since they vary as the political situation changes. He hopes that whoever enters the field of doing religious work will be an educated individual who understands what interfaith harmony is and has internally pledged to focus on promoting religious harmony and understanding between groups. More than tolerance, the need of the day is to promote acceptance of other faiths. He considers that if people in Pakistan can learn to live in harmony and work collectively, the country will develop. 'People don't want to 'hear' what religion is, but rather they want to 'see' what it is. We should be practicing it, not just talking.'

We have seen in Lahore where sudden, explosive violent acts have occurred, clergy have been taking action, going to the sites of violence and through their actions, have tried to communicate what it is that Bishop Jamil is saying: they have been practicing faith as a means to counter violence and extremism. The network of religious leaders under the umbrella of the ICPH in Lahore continues to be strengthened due to both proactively building a sense of community between religious groups by sharing festive occasions as well as rushing to sites of violence and publicly offering assistance. We should not lose sight of how courageous these actions are because those untouched by the sentiments they espouse could quickly turn against them as well.

The Lahore Interfaith Council for Peace and Harmony is in no way the only organization of its kind but is rather merely the one being highlighted here, given its impact in much of Punjab, the most populous province of Pakistan. There is the Pakistan Council of World Religions, otherwise known as 'Faith Friends' in Peshawar, the Peace Education and Development Foundation (PEAD) in Swat, Peshawar, and FATA, the Interfaith Harmony group within the Islamic Research Centre at Bahauddin Zakariya University (BZU) in Multan, and 'ulema nearly everywhere are speaking to their congregations about the traditions of the Prophet in interacting with and promoting peace with people of other groups.

What stands out about 'Faith Friends' is that it was initiated by the Diocese of Peshawar whose then bishop visited a few Muslim leaders and scholars in 2004 with the dire plea to work together and build interfaith relationships during that period of heightened intolerance. The outcome was the Pakistan Council of World Religions which reached out the following year to include Hindu and Sikh members as well. Headed in Peshawar since 2005 by Qari Ruhullah Madani,[47] he credits the strength of the Pakistan Council of World Religions—the 'Faith Friends'—as being comprised of religious leaders from many religions, sects, and constituencies. It has since spread out to other areas of Pakistan. He recalls that when it was started, the situation in Peshawar was very bad,

> It was very hard to talk about interfaith harmony and peace at that time. We had internal problems then too: everyone would say if you were talking about interfaith harmony, you were some sort of agent. They said this about their own people too. In this area, the agencies' role was very big—and it still is. It was very difficult… But I see the base of intolerance's roots is religious people. I wanted to help fix this wrong thought.

He was trying to include the top level of religious leadership in Khyber Pakhtunkhwa in the Council as 'they know their religion, and people would listen to them.' They held special programmes for university and madrassa students, lawyers, and media workers. It was difficult to do so at the outset as most people had no concept of what they were endeavouring to do. He emphatically noted that they had to keep asserting they were not starting a new religion but that their goal was to promote peaceful coexistence among the followers of various religions. He noted it was especially tough at the outset,

> People would meet each other but would never shake hands. There was a kind of social gap among them. They would eat together but sit separately. In Peshawar, Muslims don't go to any church; Christians don't go to any mosques. This was very difficult work.

'Faith Friends' members remain quite active. Recently, in November 2017, they organized a meeting attended by Muslim, Sikh, Christian, and Hindu leaders in a madrassa in Khwazakhela, Swat, to promote interaction amongst all religious groups, at a religious level. He felt that while it is easy to hold an interfaith activity in a hotel or an open area, it's very hard to hold such an activity in a madrassa. He had to tell the 'ulema who were attending that they should understand that meeting with other religious leaders, 'is not something un-Islamic…We are following our own Prophet by doing this. So, after saying that, there was no resistance.' He attributes the importance of what they were trying to accomplish to challenges from the past as well as recent conflicts,

> When you are trying to make some change at the social level, that is one thing; but to change mindsets at the religious level, this is the hardest thing, not only in Pakistan but in the entire world…In our society, in the subcontinent, there is no single religion. Every religion is here. People would live with each other in the past. They did business with each other—but religiously, there was no contact, even in the old days. They were not enemies, but they had no contact at the level of religion.

These days, he contends, war is not only fought on the battleground but is fought to win the hearts and minds of people. Attacks on churches and mosques in this area had never happened before the US attack on Afghanistan in October 2001 and the Government of Pakistan's subsequent

Fig. 5.1: Father James Channan.

Fig. 5.2: Samples of PEAD students' calligraphy.

Fig. 5.3: Unprecedented Christmas Cake cutting, 22 December 2018 at the Council of Islamic Ideology headquarters in Islamabad.

رواداری تحریک کے چیئرمین سیمسن سلامت کی قیادت میں
امن کاروان کی لاہور ریلوے سٹیشن سے کراچی روانگی

Fig. 5.4: Rwadari Tehreek members seeing off the Peace Train in Lahore as it departs for Karachi.

Fig. 5.5: A one-off effort, symbolically portraying that water faucets are for everyone to use, regardless of religion.

support for that attack. But he considers that Pakistan is now on the right path to peace. A strong majority of Pakistanis know that other religions should not be openly criticized and if we do criticize other religions or their beliefs, then we'll go ten years backward. People's sensitivities will escalate. In addition, now when some people advocate disharmony and don't talk about peace, the media usually criticizes them.

Another concern he had, that exists not only in Peshawar but in many parts of Pakistan, is the big problem of lack of exposure to other ideas and of what is happening elsewhere in the world. Outsiders no longer come to the area for tourism or to travel around the country. While local people could learn much from other people's experiences, there is far less presence of outsiders here.

Madani's apprehensions are echoed by PEAD leaders who engaged in conflict analysis to promote social cohesion in Khyber Pakhtunkhwa. PEAD's origins were not faith-based. Begun in 2002 in the wake of the 11 September 2001 attacks, PEAD's founders had the specific goal of making a social contribution and changing people's perceptions. One of PEAD's founders, Sameena Imtiaz, said they wanted to develop a programme to teach people to deal peacefully with day-to-day conflicts, to accept the differences they confront, and share other conflict resolution skills.[48] The Friedrich Naumann Stiftung Foundation provided funding the first year to support PEAD's training efforts which they used to develop a training manual, *The First Step toward Peace*, which focused on teachers to help students become aware of others in the world. PEAD gradually became involved with interfaith harmony efforts through reviewing curriculum for the Khyber Pakhtunkhwa government in 2010. Sameena Imtiaz was one of the founding members of REAT (discussed below) in 2014, enabling PEAD to extend its outreach on a national level. PEAD helped REAT develop a national media training campaign on how to report on minorities.

Tariq Hayat, who had been involved in other peace-building activities with PEAD since 2011, began to work in 2013 on UNICEF's initiative, 'Strengthening Social Cohesion and Resilience' in war-torn, terrorism-affected areas of Khyber Pakhtunkhwa and FATA.[49] The goal was to identify how various kinds of people understood what ties were binding the society together and what was contributing to ripping it apart. When asked these two questions—what are the connectors within the society and what are the dividers?—he found that some people considered religious leaders as the connecting threads of the society, although others felt that it was religious leaders who were dividing them. So collectively, they realized these religious leaders could play a dual role: with the right learning opportunities, enabling environment, and encouragement they could get past the trust deficit and bring people together to promote true social cohesion. In Swat, they met with local religious leaders and others to identify how 'ulema could be included in their efforts to encourage social unity and a sense of belonging among different groups within the area. Tariq Hayat built on the discussions he had with 'ulema in the Swat chapter of the Wafaq-ul-Madaris to launch a pilot calligraphy project, 'Calligraphy for Peace', between November 2013 and March 2014 that included students from six madrassas. They were looking to see how such activities could strengthen connections between people, enhancing tolerance and respect. They taught children studying in madrassas how to do calligraphy using selected verses from the Quran along with peace motifs. Glancing over the calligraphy is a moving and humbling experience, as seen in the three drawings in Figure 5.2.

He has been working closely with madrassas for some time, but in 2014 ventured into a new phase to work with regular schools and madrassas together, including female madrassas, in Swat, Peshawar, and Kohat. They linked every madrassa with a nearby government school and brought the children together to talk. Both sets of students realized that they had the same desires and needs, but the madrassa students were largely cut off from any government support for other activities. Tariq Hayat felt that engaging with each other would go far in promoting understanding in the long-run, and diminish the lure of extremism and violence. He has been encouraged by various religious leaders to think differently about harmony. He has sought to involve madrassa students in temporal activities, bringing them into 'the outside world.' For example, he organized mega sports events for them in 2015, 2016, and 2017 and, most recently, in late August 2018. He organized a mega cricket tournament for madrassa students in Peshawar, the Zalmi Madrasa League, at Arbab Niaz Stadium, which included students from twelve madrassas representing different Muslim sects. Even the Haqqani madrassa from Akora Khattak—said to have taught many Taliban—fielded a team in the tournament. For the final match,

Dr Qibla Ayaz, Chairperson of the Council of Islamic Ideology, along with Christian, Sikh, and Hindu leaders, were the guests of honour.

He believes that these efforts indirectly counter extremism by sensitizing future prayer leaders, which can make a huge difference. There is usually no interaction between madrassa children and other school children— they were always 'the other.' His efforts, therefore, are about decreasing misperceptions. He says,

> If there's a process of breaking down isolation and negative perceptions, then peace can become a possibility. If we can enable teachers, the undeclared leaders of their communities, to do this then support and sensitization must also be provided. We must adopt this collaborative approach. We have tried to avoid any kind of ambiguity, and transparency has been there in everything we have done. Now local teachers have created conflict resolution committees and they are visibly contributing to bringing people together in whatever activities they engage in.

Another way of going about availing religion itself to counter extremism can be seen in the activities of the Interfaith Harmony group in Multan, founded in 2010 within the Islamic Research Centre at Bahauddin Zakariya University (BZU). It is comprised of local religious scholars concerned with research, interfaith harmony, and dialogue and includes Christians, Hindus, Sikhs, and most Muslim sects (Deobandi, Ahl-e-Hadith, Barelvi, and Shias). Dr Abdul Khadoos,[50] then director of the Islamic Research Centre, said he deliberately started the Interfaith Harmony group at a university because 'If you sit in a mosque, you can't reach these objectives— so we brought them to the neutral university.' The various religious scholars deliberately sit together twice a year, sometimes for a conference and sometimes just to talk about current issues and communicate. They have finally announced that 'we are one nation in Pakistan, and Pakistan is a country for peace and harmony.' Representatives from the group have participated in conferences promoting interfaith harmony throughout the country, to be able to bring in the voice of Multan into the dialogue. They participated in a meeting of interfaith harmony groups from throughout Pakistan at the International Islamic University (IIU) in Islamabad in September 2017 when they helped draft a resolution concerning teaching about religion in Pakistan. Similar to what 'ulema in the Interfaith Council for Peace and Harmony in Lahore advocate, the resolution advocated that the subject of Comparative Religion should be changed to be *the study* of all religions, not of comparing them. This change has now been implemented in universities in Pakistan, although lower-level schools are more reluctant to do so given the bureaucratic hassle of changing any course syllabus.

He credits another effect the Interfaith Harmony group has had is that of making students at both the university and at madrassas aware of the nature of the other group,

> It comes to their minds that we can all sit together and meet. In the beginning, our students were very close-minded and conservative, especially about Christianity. So we had them meet and talk twice a year. Last year (2016), for the first time in the history of the department, I took twenty-five students plus two teachers to a church. At the church, we cut the Christmas cake with the Father. First we had the meeting, then they said 'you should eat.' A few of our more conservative students, showing their naiveté and lack of exposure, asked me if the food was halal!

> Our group now goes to churches periodically. For the past two years, we have all gone to celebrate Christmas at the Pastoral Institute of Christianity (Protestant Church of Pakistan) and at a Catholic Church. When the time came, I told my students that it was time to pray. The students went to the washroom to do *wazu* [ritualistic cleansing prior to a Muslim prayer] and the Christians there enthusiastically welcomed it.

The Centre is also actively engaged in establishing a new syllabus to create a counter narrative to terrorism and extremism that will have an impact throughout the university. In early 2018, faculty started to develop a series of new courses along these lines to create a counter narrative. Then BZU Vice Chancellor, the late Dr Tahir Amin, chaired the provincial board that met regarding this syllabus. In late November 2018, the idea for creating this syllabus for a counter narrative against extremism was discussed at a meeting of eighty vice chancellors of Pakistan's public sector universities. Non-state actors have already taken the initiative to propose the syllabus, and for it to be fully implemented will require continuing dedication of teachers tasked with the syllabus.

Dr Khadoos envisions that achieving interfaith harmony 'is a long journey, a marathon race' that will only see results from the various efforts they are making now in a generation or two. But at least they're having a start in Multan.

At the International Islamic University (IIU) in Islamabad, Dr Muhammad Zia ul Haq is a Professor of Shariah and Islamic Law and heads the Islamic Research Institute (IRI).[51] He sees the IRI as having a very important task: the reconstruction of contemporary Islamic society in Pakistan. He has been a strong advocate of social justice courses and programmes and considers that the authentic message of Islam regarding dialogue, peace, and social harmony amongst people of all religions has been lost. He has developed various projects at IIU to promote greater understanding about what Islam actually says about social harmony, society, and peace. For example, he received a thematic grant project in 2017 from the Higher Education Commission (HEC) to develop an action plan to bring in universities in advancing a national counter narrative to violence, extremism, and terrorism as part of the reconstruction of Pakistani society, transforming the perception of social differences while encouraging awareness of Islam's history of jurisprudential traditions.[52] Additional goals for the project to counter violent extremism are:

1. To demonstrate mainstream Islamic teachings against the violent tendencies of its militant adherents.
2. To prepare Muslim scholars, particularly in Pakistan, to strive to resuscitate a non-violent and enlightened Muslim culture that is receptive to new ideas and cognizant of Islam's principled but adaptive history.
3. To contribute to presenting the Islamic worldview as a moderate way of life, a rival to the volcanic voices of radical adherents.
4. To disputing the morally bankrupt ideologies of the extremists and militants.

To achieve these ends, he has initiated various research programmes at the IIU through the IRI, many under the moniker Paigham-e-Pakistan, the message of Pakistan to counter extremism. For example, he convened a national seminar 'Reconstruction of Pakistani Society in the light of Mithaq-e-Madinah' (the Charter of Madinah) on 26 May 2017 which brought together 'ulema representing all Muslim schools of thought in the country. He was able to get the group to support a *fatwa* unanimously—the first time this kind of *fatwa* has been issued on this subject in Pakistan—that refutes terrorism and extremism. As of February 2019, more than 6,000 'ulema had ratified the *fatwa*, including the Imam-e-Kaaba (in Makkah, Saudi Arabia), the Sheikh-ul-Azhar (Ahmed el-Tayeb, Imam of the Al-Azhar University in Cairo), and the grand muftis of Russia, Kazakhstan, Thailand, and Croatia, among others.[53] In another project, they have provided two-day training sessions on the importance of the peace narrative, inclusiveness, and on understanding the challenges confronting Pakistani society to 800 faculty members including scholars, religious leaders (imams and 'ulema) and faculty members who already teach at universities and are members of civil society. This is part of the IIU's priorities to change curricula and education policy along with policies of other important institutions so as to inculcate peace in Pakistani society. The IRI organized a two-day national conference at the University of Gujrat on 13–14 March 2019, entitled 'Challenges to Inter-faith Harmony in Pakistan: Strategies and Solutions.' This is an example of how Dr Zia ul Haq is using the central position of the IIU on Islamic discourse in Pakistan to identify substantive ways to implement tolerance, peace, patience, and interfaith harmony, and not merely say this is something that should be done in an ideal world. Pakistan's very future is at stake here, as he says,

> It is tremendously essential to emphasize on the significance of Interfaith Harmony through educational seminars, universities, media, workshops, and public meetings in Pakistan. The lack of collective common sense, religious misconceptions, unfair and unjust election procedures for minorities, misinterpretation of jihad, the partial and prejudiced religious discourse, the migrations of the non-Muslims from Pakistan especially Hindus, insecurity of the holy sites of minorities, unjust distribution of socio-economic resources, the absence of non-Muslim literature in the national educational curriculum, and misuse of blasphemy laws are some remarkable challenges to Interfaith Harmony in Pakistan.[54]

Another outcome is the establishment of the Paigham-e-Pakistan Centre for Peace, Reconciliation and Reconstruction Studies at IRI. Dr Zia ul Haq said that the Centre organizes conferences and other activities,

> to promote peaceful coexistence and interfaith harmony in an Islamic perspective. It will advance the Islamic tradition of peace and peaceful coexistence rooted in the Quran and Sunnah.[55]

It has begun offering a six-month undergraduate diploma programme in Peace and Conflict Studies as well as a postgraduate diploma at the MA level.

They also agreed upon a strong national declaration, the resultant Policy Declaration for the Promotion of Interfaith Harmony and Coexistence, which takes a powerful stand such as we can see in the following selected (ten of twenty-one) clauses:

1. All citizens of Pakistan, irrespective of their faith, shall have the protection of law and rights such as right to life with dignity, right to property, right to education, protection of family and faith, right to profess and practice their religion, right to employment without discrimination, and the right to not be discriminated in curriculum.

2. The religious sentiments of all communities are very important and reciprocal for each other. Such social and religious reciprocity requires mutual respect and tolerance in the subjectivity of faith.

3. According to clause 16 of Mithaq-e-Madinah (the Charter of Madinah), all Muslim and non-Muslim citizens of Pakistan shall be treated with absolute equality.

4. Places of worship, religious leaders, and religious sentiments of all religions be respected.

5. Interfaith religious and theological differences may not be debated without strictly following the ethics of disagreement.

6. Interfaith dialogue is a legitimate tool for advancing harmony and coexistence. It should be promoted as a policy for maintaining peace, harmony, and coexistence in society.

7. Religion-based hate speech must be discouraged and shall be penalized under the Anti-terrorism Act 1997 by considering them crimes against the state.

8. The word 'minority' should be replaced with 'non-Muslim citizens of Pakistan' in all official documents including enacted laws and the Constitution of Pakistan.

9. A subject of interfaith harmony, tolerance, and peaceful coexistence should be introduced as a compulsory subject in all primary and higher secondary schools of Pakistan.

10. The system of education should be improved in a way where interfaith harmony and peaceful coexistence is promoted.

It is important to realize what is behind the Paigham-e-Pakistan and other programmes being initiated by the IRI: the IIU, which has been stereotypically perceived as the bastion of conservative Muslim values now comprises scholars who are taking a stand and saying 'enough' to 'the volcanic voices of radical adherents' and are striving to recapture what they perceive as authentic Islam. They are also engaged in substantive curriculum revisions, again to get authentic Islam back in the classrooms and thwart the misrepresentation of the religion as they perceive has been done by 'the morally bankrupt ideologies of the extremists and militants.'

A key figure today in Pakistan who is striving to achieve interfaith harmony and bring groups together in this undertaking is Dr Qibla Ayaz,[56] former Dean of the Faculty of Islamic and Oriental Studies of the University of Peshawar and, since early November 2017, Chairperson of the Council of Islamic Ideology (CII). The Council's mandate, stated in the 1973 Constitution, is to ensure that no laws are in conflict with those of Islam. Dr Ayaz notes that all religions promote peace, and especially Islam, whose name itself means peace,

> What the meaning of the word is, should be seen in the reality. Islam came in an environment of violence, and then ended the violence and the area became peaceful. So the origin of Islam is to end communal wars and bring harmony to society.

> The Treaty of Medina was one of the first things the Prophet did. In it, Jews and the Prophet agreed on certain clauses guaranteeing freedom of religion. And of course, living together peacefully, acting upon their own customs.

He is proud of the litany of 'ulema who have spoken out against extremism in Pakistan and even against the hateful rhetoric espoused by the Taliban and other extremist groups. Some, such as the Barelvi leader Sarfraz Naeemi in Lahore and Maulana Hassan Jan in Peshawar, were killed for speaking up against the Taliban. He thinks that few others take such stands now which he attributes to fear as being 'the major reason why no one is speaking out and disputing their interpretation of religion.'

He plays a prominent role in the nationwide discussion of syllabus reform in the teaching of religion. He thinks that the current terminology being used in Urdu to denote 'interfaith harmony'—*bain-ul-mazhahib*—is confusing because some people think it is developing some sort of mixture of religions as they don't know the history behind the concept. He wants to introduce other titles for courses that are more direct, such as 'How non-Muslims should be treated in a Muslim-majority area,' 'How Muslims should behave toward non-Muslims,' and 'How should Muslims behave in a non-Muslim majority area?' He considers that these sorts of themes will promote better interfaith relationships without annoying anyone while giving students confidence they're being educated on important issues.

Since being appointed Chairperson of the CII, Qibla Ayaz has been focused on the state's policy for interfaith relations in Pakistan. The Ministry of Religious Affairs and Interfaith Harmony first developed a draft, and since December 2017 the CII is working on it. This is an important part of the role he sees himself playing as the CII's Chairperson. As it is a constitutional body with an official recognition, he now has the opportunity to go to universities and other gatherings as an official representative. For example, in December 2017, he addressed a gathering of 10,000 people in Bannu, Khyber Pakhtunkhwa, pronouncing that 'If you want to make Pakistan a strong country, you cannot kill your fellow man…if you hope CPEC will change the economic and political scenario, you have to change how you think and promote harmony.' He is now able to use this official platform to convey the message that he has promoted throughout his professional career teaching Islamic Studies at the University of Peshawar: that the path to a prosperous and peaceful Pakistan is to promote interfaith understanding and trust.

Pakistan has a bulging youth population and a larger concentration of the youth are in universities, especially with the BSc degree programme. He sees important opportunities in addressing them, engaging them in dialogue and seminars like he did in Bannu. He also wants to make senior faculty members 'change agents' and engage with NGOs to persuade the state—the ministries of Interior, Education, Religious Affairs, and the HEC—to communicate the message of interfaith harmony in their spheres of influence. He is convinced that this is a requirement for achieving a prosperous Pakistan. He is also working with an *alim* who enjoys a good rapport with the ISI (Inter-Services Intelligence, the Pakistani equivalent of the FBI). He is encouraging him to reach out to the army and ISI to explain why a peaceful Pakistan is important. He is optimistic that there is a change occurring in ISI's optic as, for the first time, the army chief is on record saying that the Good Taliban/Bad Taliban duality doesn't exist whatsoever.

Throughout Pakistan, cutting the Christmas cake together has become an annual ritual in interfaith harmony circles, as we already heard from people in Lahore, Peshawar, and Multan. The CII has held seminars on interfaith harmony and participated in Christmas events elsewhere as they have occurred. However, for the first time in its history, the CII organized a Christmas cake-cutting forum and ceremony within its headquarters on 22 December 2017 (as shown in Figure 5.3). It included representative religious leaders from most Muslim sects as well as Catholic, Protestant, Hindu, and Sikh communities, Qibla Ayaz, and this author. The symbolism of the moment was not lost on the audience as each speaker commended the CII for its openness and spoke of what they are doing with their own community to promote interfaith harmony, awareness, and peace.

It is in part due to the charisma and stature in their communities that the religious leaders discussed herein have rarely encountered any protest to their efforts to promote harmony. It is also the carefulness with which they engage with communities and act deliberatively in their communications. Perhaps, too, they are espousing a message to promote peace and harmony between communities that the vast majority of Pakistanis truly want to hear.

EFFORTS BY NON-MUSLIM RELIGIOUS GROUPS TO MOBILIZE AND FOSTER EMPOWERMENT

Members of non-Muslim religious minorities have been mobilizing not only to ensure their rights and safety but also to expand the counter narrative that they are not the enemy in Pakistan. We see this notably among Christian leaders throughout Pakistan because Christians have borne the brunt of sectarian violence against non-Muslims in the country. As in the Joseph Colony and Kot Radha Kishan attacks, charges of blasphemy often precede the violence. Hindu leaders are also galvanizing their communities to ensure their safety and claim their rights.

Father James Channan of the Peace Centre, Peter Jacob of the Centre for Social Justice and Bishop Irfan Jamil in Lahore, each discussed earlier in this chapter, have been playing active roles in groups promoting interfaith harmony while also trying to expand the counter narrative regarding Christians. In Rawalpindi, Jennifer Jag Jivan, Director of the Christian Studies Centre (CSC), has been working tirelessly to promote understanding about Christianity and Christians in Pakistan for many years, as has Samson Salamat of the Centre for Human Rights Education in Lahore. Their style of operation is quite different from those religious leaders discussed earlier in this chapter as their focus is explicitly on educating their own constituencies and others about their religion, leading to greater confidence and feelings of empowerment within the community. Yet each in their own unique way is also contributing to interfaith harmony.

Jennifer Jag Jivan is the Director of the Christian Studies Centre (CSC) in the Rawalpindi Cantonment.[57] The National Council of Churches, overseeing Protestant churches in Pakistan, founded the CSC in 1967 with the goal to improve Christian-Muslim relations and to assist churches in understanding Islam. The CSC has only two projects specifically for Christians; the rest of its activities are focused on interfaith harmony.

A very popular programme the CSC has been running for the past thirty years is a three-year course, mostly for Christians, to enable them to understand their Christian faith in relation to other groups. Participants receive a diploma in Basic Theology and Christian Formation at the end. It was launched during the height of Zia ul Haq's Islamization programme when Christians were concerned about their safety and security given the new Hudood laws and the introduction of separate electorates.

The second programme for Christians was started by Charles Amjad Ali and the Presentation Sisters in September 1988, namely the Institute of Theology and Christian Formation. Classes on Christian theology are held every Wednesday. In addition, however, they also give participants time to explore their own prejudices. She sees that after taking these classes—even while taking the classes—the Christian participants become,

> More confident in their faith, interacting with others, and understand that we're all part of the human family. We also explore how Christians can play a more vibrant role as citizens of the country. How do we engage ourselves in economics, social justice issues, and theological debates—focus on reflecting on the inner faith and what it says to them in relation to what is happening around them.

Jennifer Jag Jivan considers that the Christian community has responsibilities at the local, national, and global levels, and they learn about these responsibilities in the class over a course of three years, every Wednesday. But in addition to what is taught in these two classes, offered only to Christians, the CSC strives to bring people together throughout the country to share cultural perspectives based on the concept of 'composite heritage.' At these forums, people generally don't talk about religion but rather discuss cultural issues that they have in common such as that they,

> come from the same land, wear the same clothes, eat the same food…we look at commonalities in Pakistan, such as cultural actions regarding women including dowry, *karo kari*, and forced marriages. We also discuss things like forced conversions and emotional blackmailing.

The CSC has now trained hundreds of individuals and has worked with a wide range of organizations from throughout the country since 1998. Peter Jacob (of the Centre for Social Justice in Lahore) has been closely associated with the CSC and Samson Salamat (of the Centre for Human Rights Education in Lahore) was trained by the CSC. The staff of CSC have become resource-persons for other organizations to work with various kinds of groups focused on peace and social harmony. For example, they have run these trainings with groups of women lawyers; women lawyers practicing in the Lahore High Court held a cultural event in 2017 which will now take place annually. They are also working with the NGO Salifi, in Khyber Pakhtunkhwa, which is working for interfaith peace, and with women's groups in Balochistan that put on interfaith festivals there. The CSC is 'reclaiming cultural spaces that have been lost' as they make a conscious effort for smaller organizations to have direct outreach bringing people together, finding commonalities, while also critiquing the culture and exploring how they can interact and relate with each other, not only about cultural activities. Jennifer poignantly notes,

> Until it doesn't rest in the minds and hearts of the common people,
> it can only be at a surface level or the government level where these
> things take place, and not permeate to the grassroots.

Importantly, the CSC runs peace projects related to interfaith harmony and human rights involving writers, poets, lawyers, teachers, parliamentarians, journalists, media workers, grassroots activists, and religious scholars. In Faisalabad, for example, they have been bringing people together in forums—for lawyers, teachers, and journalists—and formulating peace committees. They often invite officials in the local government to join them too. CSC staff continue to serve as watchdogs when any problems break out, such as those surrounding sensitive issues like blasphemy. They have a successful track record of good cases, positive stories—when blasphemy charges could have been lodged and riots could have happened—but instead, people in the peace committees came together and actually diffused the situation.

When queried if Jennifer thinks the CSC's efforts are making a difference, she says she sees hope. Thirty years ago, there were hardly any interfaith efforts but now she contends that there are hundreds of organizations working on it. She claims that,

> There are pockets of hope, people are aspiring, now you see people
> like the 'ulema in Lahore—this is significant because it contributes
> to the larger picture of peace-building. All people look at peace-
> building differently, but as long as there are symbolic aspects

playing a role in peace-building, this is promising. It is for civil society, writers, and activists to take this deeper. The narrative at the government level, while still cosmetic and hasn't sunken in, has started to be vocalized. We all have to play our bit, to do whatever we can do. It's not easy, in terms of challenges of security and finances and the way you are looked at, but then you do find individuals, organizations, and people where there is growth. You have to create spaces...sometimes civil society has not been in such a great space, and the space for them is shrinking. But imagine if these places didn't exist...

Samson Salamat works with the Centre for Human Rights Education in Lahore.[58] He had previously worked for the National Commission for Justice and Peace on human rights education with a focus on religious freedom and also counselled victims of blasphemy allegations. His desire to create the Centre came from his conviction of the importance to create a cadre with a focus on human rights education. He proceeded to introduce a three-week participatory course on Democracy and Human Rights in 2010 and later developed a second course on Peace and Tolerance that revolves around the concept of non-violence. In these courses, he and his team have trained hundreds of human rights defenders. But when the attack on the Army Public School occurred in December 2014, they realized they had to start a movement to counter violent extremism. So in 2015, after the National Action Plan was developed by the Government of Pakistan, they founded Rawadari Tehreek, a Movement for Pluralism. Their objectives in founding the movement were to go directly to the people and launch an awareness campaign on the importance of religious diversity and pluralism; to act as a pressure group, putting pressure on the government, the military, and other stakeholders to implement the National Action Plan; and to bridge the gap between different religious communities. Samson Salamat became the National Chairman of Rawadari Tehreek and Deedar Ahmed Mirani of Sukkur, a founder of Pahel, became the national vice chairman.

According to their official literature, Rawadari Tehreek,

aims to generate a debate on the importance of religious tolerance and respect of diversity in a multi-religious society and to remind the government, political forces, state's institutions, and other stakeholders their responsibilities to seriously address trends of hatred, violent extremism, and intolerance in the society which has created an atmosphere of fear among the citizens and have riddled the public life, particularly of those belonging to religious minorities.

Salamat claims that Rawadari is not an interfaith movement—he says that most interfaith movements are just activities on the surface—but is much more than that, with far deeper roots. He considers that interfaith activities are useless unless they are integrated into the grassroots communities where the problem exists. Salamat has brought together thousands of people from different walks of life and from different faiths to talk about issues facing local communities and how to act collectively to solve them. He contends,

> Interfaith has failed when you can't talk about the conflict zones. If you can't talk about the problems, how are you going to solve them? So we must talk about revising the syllabus, the hate speech coming from madrassas, etc.—that's the understanding of interfaith. It's more important for us to attract grassroots people, not the leaders. We don't want to play on religion as we are dedicated to religion being a personal matter.

Rawadari engages in both local and nationwide activities, and has leadership groups in each of the four provinces. They have organized groups—Rawadarians—in about fifty districts in Pakistan that hold internal elections. In their respective areas, each group holds seminars on the importance of religious diversity, anti-extremism, respect, and non-discrimination at schools and colleges. They have developed an Oath for Peace that they ask students and teachers to take at the end of the event. Rawadari members also frequently go on 'Goodwill Exchange Visits' to temples, shrines, churches, and other religious sites to do away with misperceptions of other religions and promote better relations, one-on-one, amongst adherents of different faiths. Under the banner of Rawadari Tehreek, the districts organize people to celebrate Holi, Diwali, Eid, and *iftar* parties.

Rawadari's best-known national event is the annual Rawadari Caravan which begins with a few hundred people in Lahore, sometimes proceeding by train, sometimes by road (as seen in Figure 5.4). Hundreds of people come to rally support wherever the caravan stops. For example, in April 2017, the caravan went by train from Lahore to Sukkur (in upper Sindh), then continued by road to the shrine of Sachal Sarmast in Khairpur, Lal Shahbaz Qalandar in Sehwan, Shah Abdul Latif Bhittai in Bhit Shah, and from there to Hyderabad and then Karachi. At the end of the Caravan, they celebrate the Rawadari Festival, an opportunity to express unity against hate speech, extremism, and terrorism. Another important national event occurs on 16 December to commemorate and memorialize the 2014 APS attack in Peshawar. Rawadari holds roughly fifty activities on that one day throughout the country, consisting of rallies, candle vigils, and conferences. They have proposed that the Government of Pakistan declare 16 December as the National Day to Counter Extremism, but the state has not yet responded.

Rawadari Tehreek engages in a number of one-off activities as well. For example, they organized a one-day hunger strike in twelve cities in February 2017 to protest violent extremism in the country and social awareness campaigns are seen in Figure 5.5. They mobilize small caravans to Sufi shrines from Lahore to Pakpattan, Lahore to Kasur, etc. as they are inspired by the peaceful message of Sufism. They send recommendations, frequently—at least every quarter—to the prime minister, chief ministers, and the heads of political parties with their message of peace and countering extremism. Only once, they received an acknowledgement from the head of Pakistan Awami Tehreek, Tahir-ul-Qadri's party, otherwise nothing else. They claim all of these various activities are necessary as the 'stakes in sanity' are higher than ever before, and they are doing whatever is necessary to achieve 'a saner and safer Pakistan.'

Rawadari receives funding from a variety of different kinds of groups, including the US-based National Endowment for Democracy (NED), the Taiwan Foundation for Democracy, Equitas, and Freedom House. They have never taken funds from a bilateral donor; Salamat thinks that would make them indebted to the donors, to some extent, saying, 'We want to be free in our work, because it's a movement.'

Salamat considers that their greatest achievement has been the ability to mobilize people and have them act and take a stand, especially when there is an emergency. In that event, he gives a call and their teams go into action wherever possible. He notes,

People are voluntarily working, and they are not asking about each other's religion. They are coexisting. When we started, there was an atmosphere of terror and dread. We have facilitated people coming out of that tension.

Rawadari has come to be identified by the orange scarf they give out at functions. When they began using it, the colour sparked some confusion as it was originally thought to be the colour of Hinduism. It took them about six months to convince people that it is a colour that has long been identified with Sufism, and is just a symbol of the group. But the orange scarf powerfully captures the spirit of the organization and what it aims to achieve when Rawadarians stand before crowds wearing it—their own religion incognito.

Pahel Pakistan shares Rawadari Tehreek's goals and has collaborated with it extensively.[59] Founded in 2009, Pahel—meaning protection and promotion of human rights and democracy—began to focus on extremism in Sindh in early 2014 following a series of attacks on religious shrines and religious leaders. The first two were in February 2013:

1. On 6 February 2013, a blast tore through Dargah Pir Hajan Shah Huzoori in Marri village near Shikarpur, killing four and injuring twelve others, including Syed Hajan Shah, the Gaddi Nasheen (a descendant of the saint and custodian of the shrine). Investigators believe the incident was suicidal and was the first suicidal attack in interior Sindh.

2. On 20 February 2013, a blast targeted a religious rally near Jacobabad that killed one person and injured twelve others. A remote-controlled bomb planted on the roadside was detonated when a vehicle carrying the *pir* of Qambar Sharif, Syed Hussain Shah, was passing by. In this attack, Syed Hussain Shah was seriously wounded besides twelve others, while his grandson, Shafiq Hussain Shah, died.

Deedar Ahmed Mirani, the director of Pahel in Sindh, remembers those attacks as direct assaults on Sindhi culture and, in Shikarpur, especially on Shias. The Shia community was specifically attacked by the Taliban which took responsibility for the attacks. He reflected that,

As Sindhis, we think of our culture as consisting of *ajrak* [traditional cloths], *kalaam* [lyrical poetry], folk songs, folk stories, etc. As a Sindhi, I am a custodian of a 5,000-year-old culture. Sindhi is a non-violent culture, friendly, full of hospitality. This was our culture, but it's no longer our culture today; that culture is dying. The extremism is killing our culture.

Before Partition, Hindus and Muslims lived together happily in Sindh. We would attend each other's weddings and funerals. We would celebrate religious festivals together: Holi, Eid, etc. We believed in diversity. Sindhis believe more in Shah Abdul Latif Bhittai than in formal practices of separate religions. It's for humanity; it's Sindhi. But now they've been making it 'more Muslim.' When I go to Shahbaz Qalandar (the shrine in Sehwan), it has become a Shia *dargah*. Now everyone identifies this as Sunni and that as Shia, but Sachal Sarmast and Shah Abdul Latif never identified as such. The worst damage is that Sindh's identity as a peaceful place is getting lost.[60]

Prior to 2014, Pahel's activities focused on involving youth in four districts (Shikarpur, Jacobabad, Larkana, and Kashmore) in their Human Rights Watch groups. After three days of training, they would return to their districts. Pahel began to team up with Rawadari Tehreek in 2014 and has since become active in all nine districts in upper Sindh. They have opened a platform for religious people to sit together and have a dialogue. But Mirani bemoans that while he and other participants would prefer to speak boldly and honestly, he feels they have been prevented from doing so as they have been threatened and abused by enemies of peace and harmony.

What makes Pahel a distinct faith-based organization is that they encourage pilgrimages to religious locations, and in particular to all kinds of religious places—Hindu *mandirs*, Shia *imam bargahs*, Christian churches, Sikh *gurdwaras*, and Muslim *masjids*—as a way to promote understanding and peace. The goal is not just to go see the site, but to meet with the religious leaders who can tell them what that religion says about peace. Along with this, they actively advocate participating in Sindh's various religious festivals that have historically been celebrated collectively. For example, on the Hindu festival of Holi, members go to temples and throw the *rangoli* colour. They also gather together to cut the Christmas cake as well as the Prophet's birthday cake. He says that for this type of activity at religious festivals, they promote an atmosphere of love and diversity.

When queried about his opinion as to what caused the change in culture of religious tolerance in Sindh, Mirani first pointed to what is and is not being taught in madrassas,

> First, the madrassas. They teach hate, and the children become like robots. They don't teach humanism, peace, etc. They barely teach the regular syllabus; they don't teach the other *fiqhs* [Islamic schools of law] but are putting a 'chip' into their mindsets about religion. A base of hatred is set from a very young class. They teach about Mohammad Bin Qasim bringing Islam here, and that Hindus are our enemies. Whatever you study—physics, biology, other sciences—they incorporate the study of Islam into it as well. People open schools, and they just become businesses. But the regular schools' syllabus has hatred in it too, in all of the syllabi, whether in Sindh, Punjab, or elsewhere. Finally, we have no regulatory authority that can control the mosques, and especially the Friday sermon.

The Pahel team decided there should be some 'ideological nourishment' so they published *The Pluralism Book*. It addresses intolerance and offers thought-provoking insights about peace. Thus far, it only exists in the national language, Urdu, though a Sindhi version is in production and they are hoping to translate it into other regional languages. They come out with a monthly newsletter with Rawadari Tehreek that addresses the principles of secularism, capitalism, and other ideologies, especially the peaceful dimensions of all religions.

A final organization that actively embraces the concept of this chapter, how religious leaders and groups themselves are countering extremism, is REAT.[61] The acronym comprising its name is Right of Expression, Assembly, Association and Thought. This is a network of twenty-five civil society organizations created in June 2013 that has been working on the issue of minority rights and advocates for equal citizenship for minorities in Pakistan and freedom of religion, using the slogan 'we may be different but we are all equal.' Its vision is 'a socio-politically and economically just and peaceful society in which religious minorities can access and exercise their right to life, liberty, and dignity with freedom.' Krishan Sharma, Chairman of the REAT Network, explains why he, a Hindu man, feels discriminated against in Pakistan, because 'the state considers Hindus as allies of India; Hindus have no voice.' REAT explains the necessity for the organization that,

> The space for human rights is shrinking in Pakistan. There is growing intolerance resulting in attacks on human rights of all citizens. However, the religious minorities are placed on a higher risk as there is associated legal and institutional discrimination against them…discrimination based on religion is also widespread in the society. Terrorism, institutional and legal discrimination, and societal stereotypes have increased the vulnerabilities of religious minorities manifold. Addressing the situation is a daunting task as it requires a series of efforts.[62]

With its main office in Islamabad, it is also active in Sindh (in Umerkot, Tharparkar, Mirpurkhas, Hyderabad, Larkana, and Jacobabad), Punjab (in Bahawalpur which houses many Christians and Hindus; Khanewal which includes Shantinager, the Christian minority town that was burned in 1997; Nankana Sahib, a site of pilgrimage for Sikhs; and Chiniot, which houses many Ahmadis), in Swat in Khyber Pakhtunkhwa, and in the provincial capital of Balochistan, Quetta. REAT provides 'a platform for religious minorities in Pakistan to share their grievances and challenges, while also serving as a forum to raise collective voices for their rights at the provincial level and in targeted districts where the rights of the religious minorities are most at risk.'[63]

Similar to Rawadari Tehreek, REAT has availed interfaith religious celebrations (e.g., Holi, Christmas) as a way to promote understanding between different communities. They are also utilizing Sufi shrines to promote brotherhood, coexistence, and tolerance, in the conviction that Sufi philosophy is a counter narrative to that of the Taliban.

REAT and its partners have reached out to the Pakistani state to secure their rights on the basis that the Constitution says that the state is bound to provide protection to its people, especially that of life and liberty. Towards this end, they have signed Memoranda of Understanding with the Federal Ministry of Human Rights, the Ministry of Interior and the Department of Minorities at the provincial level. REAT has drafted a number of bills including 'Hindu Marriages Registration,' stopping forced conversions, and stopping forced marriages of religious minorities to Muslims. In addition, in its efforts to protect religious minority communities and provide legal aid, REAT has established a helpline in each district where they operate, with a Universal Access Number (UAN) that anyone can call from anywhere. They have formed groups of human rights defenders comprised of local journalists, civil society activists, lawyers, political party workers, and local trade union leaders along with office bearers of the local Hindu and Christian populations. They have promoted local capacity-building by identifying fifty people in each district who can act quickly in the event of a violent outburst, who can analyse threats and spring into action promoting conflict resolution. Through this, they have diffused many cases of blasphemy charges. REAT has published six books on what political parties say about minorities to keep the public informed. In another book, *Ripple Effects*, they have recorded information on seventy cases that have been diffused with their 'early warning system.'

A REAT human rights defender, Jasbir Singh, took a stand against the Government of Balochistan to demand the protection of the Sikh *gurdwara* in Quetta. Prior to 1980, Sikhs had prayed at the *gurdwara* in Quetta, but the land belonging to it was taken over by the Education Department that established a school on it. The Sikh community was now deprived of their place of worship and their constitutional rights. After being ignored by provincial government officials who he had lobbied, Jasbir Singh sought out the support and expertise of the REAT network. REAT provided invaluable legal assistance in filing the case at the Quetta High Court. Of the experience, a writer in a REAT Network Newsletter contends,

> It is a small milestone in the empowerment of human rights defenders and minorities who are now beginning to utilize legal avenues to not only bring attention to their rights but importantly, to seek redressal. The forcibly taking over of a place of worship adversely impacted minority communities who already felt vulnerable and added to fears that their places of worship were not safe...fear was replaced with steps towards self-empowerment and as a result the Sikh community began to feel protected.

Another conflict that was resolved as a result of REAT's early warning committee's timely intervention between Muslims and Christians was in district Nankana Sahib in Punjab. After the Principal of a public school accused the Principal of a local Christian school of forcibly teaching the Bible to Muslim children at the school, others picked up the issue and began to provoke religious clashes. When the early warning committee spoke to the accuser, he denied the allegations. After investigating it further and bringing the case to the district police administration, they found that both parties of the conflict 'were involved in baseless accusations and speculations as a result of a business rivalry' and that personal and business issues 'were being molded to a religious clash.' A strong warning was issued to both parties with the threat that they could be faced with terrorism charges if the conflict didn't desist, which it did.[64]

In this chapter, we have seen how many people from throughout Pakistan are taking stands *in the name of religion* to stop extremists from using religion as a justification for violence. Coming from all religious backgrounds, they are meeting with members of other religious communities promoting understanding, interfaith harmony, and diffusing crises. A theme we have consistently seen is an effort to recapture indigenous cultural values and interfaith cooperation and to be mindful of what is being taught to children.

Notes

1. Government of Pakistan, *Pakistan Penal Code (Act XLV of 1860), October 6th, 1860 (with Amendments)*, 2012. Accessible at: http://www.pakistani.org/pakistan/legislation/1860/actXLVof1860.html.

2. There are numerous scholarly works on the impact of Zia's Islamization programme on Pakistani society. *See* for example Anita M. Weiss (ed.), *Islamic Reassertion in Pakistan: The Application of Islamic Laws in a Modern State*, Syracuse, Syracuse University Press, November 1986, Vanguard Press, 1987; Christophe Jaffrelot, *Pakistan: Nationalism without a Nation?*, London, Palgrave Macmillan, 2002; Husain Haqqani, *Pakistan: Between Mosque and Military*, Washington, DC, Carnegie Endowment for International Peace; Distributor, Brookings Institution Press, 2005; Farzana Shaikh, *Making Sense of Pakistan*, New York, Columbia University Press, 2009; Faisal Devji, *Muslim Zion: Pakistan as a Political Idea*, Cambridge, Massachusetts, Harvard University Press, 2013; and Farahnaz Ispahani, *Purifying the Land of the Pure: a History of Pakistan's Religious Minorities*, New York, Oxford University Press, 2017.

3. Hassan J. Zaidi, *State & Religion in the Perspective of Muslim History,* Lahore, Idara-e-Mutalaa-e-Tareekh, 2015, pp. 63–4.

4. Estimates vary widely on the number of madrassas in Pakistan and the number of students attending them. Umair Khalil in his study 'The Madrasa Conundrum: The state of religious education in Pakistan,' estimated this figure in 2015; it has likely grown since then. His study is reported in 'Report says over 35,000 madrassas operating in Pakistan', *Pakistan Today,* 31 July 2015, accessible at: https://www.pakistantoday.com.pk/2015/07/31/report-says-over-35000-madrassas-operating-in-pakistan/. An exceptionally useful, well-written account of madrassas is in Tariq Rahman, 'The Madrassa and the State of Pakistan' *Himal South Asian,* 13 September 2016, accessible at: http://himalmag.com/the-madrassa-and-the-state-of-pakistan-tariq-rahman/.

5. Quoted in Rahman, Ibid.

6. In particular Sufi Mohammad, founder of the TNSM in Dir, is said to have brought thousands of madrassa students to Afghanistan in October 2001 to support the Afghan Taliban.

7. Muhammad Khalid Masud, 'Analysis Paper: Religious counter-narratives against violent extremism,' for the Pakistan Peace Collective, Federal Ministry for Information, Broadcasting and National Heritage, Government of Pakistan, n.d., 34 pp.

8. Quoted in K. Muhammad Masud, 'Analysis Paper: Religious counter-narratives against violent extremism', Pakistan Peace Collective, Federal Ministry for Information, Broadcasting and National Heritage, Government of Pakistan, n.d, p. 4.

9. Ibid., p. 5.

10. Ibid., p. 26.

11. Ibid., pp. 20–30.

12. The 2003 MMA was a coalition of six Islamist parties: Jamaat-e-Islami, Jamiat Ulema-e-Islam (Fazlur Rehman group), Jamiat Ulema-e-Islam (Samiul Haq group), Jamiat Ulema-e-Pakistan, Markazi Jamiat Ahl-e-Hadith, and Tehrik Nifaz Fiqah Jaferiya (a Shia party). The political configuration did not change until after the February 2008 general elections.

13. A discussion of the socio-political impact of the MMA provincial government can be found in Anita M. Weiss 'A Provincial Islamist Victory in NWFP, Pakistan: The Social Reform Agenda of the Muttahida Majlis-i-Amal' in John L. Esposito and John Voll (eds.), *Asian Islam in the 21st Century,* New York, Oxford University Press, 2008, pp. 145–73.

14. The TNSM was founded in Malakand in 1989, though its influence exploded during the MMA government. A discussion of the social costs of militarism on interfaith harmony in Pakistan can be found in Anita M. Weiss's chapter 'Pakistan' in Arjun Guneratne and Anita M. Weiss (eds.) *Pathways to Power: the Domestic Politics of South Asia,* Rowman & Littlefield, 2014, South Asia edition published by Orient BlackSwan, India, 2015, pp. 216–21. *See* also Khadim Hussain, 2013.

15. F. Bokhari, 'Saudi Arabia gives financial aid to Pakistan', *Financial Times,* 14 March 2014, accessible at: https://www.ft.com/content/d40980de-aa88-11e3-9fd6-00144feab7de#axzz3sFxTtR1S.

16. The entire 11 August 1947 Presidential Address to the Constituent Assembly of Pakistan is accessible at: http://www.pakistani.org/pakistan/legislation/constituent_address_11aug1947.html.

17. 'Objectives Resolution: the root of religious orthodoxy', *Dawn*, 20 June 2010, accessible at: https://www.dawn.com/news/881205.

18. Ahmadis are followers of Mirza Ghulam Ahmad, who lived in northern India in the late 1800s and purported that he was a prophet of Islam. Islamist opposition to Ahmadis is based on the concept of *Khatam-e-Nabuwat*, the Finality of the Prophethood, that there are no prophets after Prophet Muhammad (PBUH). The issue of Atif Mian's appointment and the quick rescission is covered very well in Amir Wasim 'Analysis: What drove PTI govt to reverse Atif Mian's nomination', *Dawn*, 10 September 2018, accessible at: https://www.dawn.com/news/1432021/analysis-what-drove-pti-govt-to-reverse-atif-mians-nomination.

19. For more about the US involvement in and support of the Afghan insurgency, *see* Ahmed Rashid, *Descent into Chaos: The U.S. and the Disaster in Pakistan, Afghanistan, and Central Asia*, Penguin, 2008, Steve Coll, *Ghost Wars: The Secret History of the CIA, Afghanistan, and bin Laden, from the Soviet Invasion to September 10, 2001*, Penguin, 2004, Mary Ann Weaver, *Pakistan: In the Shadow of Jihad and Afghanistan*, Farrar, Straus and Giroux, 2002, and Mubarak Ali *Pakistan in Search of Identity*, Aakar Books, 2011.

20. An outstanding discussion of the foundations of religious militancy in Pakistan and its influences elsewhere in the world can be found in Syed et. al., 2016.

21. A heartfelt account of the victims of this attack is provided in Nafisa Hoodbhoy, Aboard the Democracy Train: A Journey through Pakistan's Last Decade of Democracy, Anthem Press, 2011, pp. 159–60.

22. Michael Kugelman, 'What Does the Execution of Mumtaz Qadri Mean for Pakistan?' *The Diplomat*, 1 March 2016, accessible at: https://thediplomat.com/2016/03/what-does-the-execution-of-mumtaz-qadri-mean-for-pakistan/.

23. Kunwar Khuldune Shahid, 'Nightmare without End: Will minorities continue to be persecuted and murdered in the name of religion?' *Newsline*, 17 February 2017, pp. 66–8.

24. A good account of what apparently transpired is found in Hanif Samoon 'Hindu youth killed as communal tensions rock Ghotki after 'sacrilege' incident', *Dawn*, 27 July 2016, accessible at: https://www.dawn.com/news/1273509.

25. This incident occurred on 10 January 2018. I appreciate that Dr Altaf Aseem, retired professor from Shah Abdul Latif University in Khairpur and inaugural-holder of the Sachal Chair, accompanied me to the mosque and temple.

26. Holi is a colourful Hindu spring festival.

27. *See* http://www.mora.gov.pk

28. This was reported in 'Intolerance towards religious minorities in Pakistan increasing: report', *Pakistan Today*, 26 September 2018, accessible at: https://www.pakistantoday.com.pk/2018/09/26/intolerance-towards-religious-minorities-in-pakistan-increasing-report/.

29. The Pakistan-based NGO, PILDAT, has documented the challenges of madrassa syllabus reform, from the perspective of youth in Pakistan, in 'Madrasa Education 2014: Challenges, Reforms and Possibilities', March 2015, accessible at: https://www.google.com/url?sa=t&rct=j&q=&esrc=s&source=web&cd=1& ved=2ahUKEwjR8_v41vLdAhUKFnwKHciiDHgQFjAAegQICRAC&url= http%3A%2F%2Fyp2014.youthparliament.pk%2Fdownloads%2FCR%2 Feducationandyouthaffairsstandingcommitteereport pdf&usg=AOvVaw2s2xp QARDyiCJ-L7DOQ8v4.

30. This section is based on interviews held with Imam Abdul Khabir Azad at the Badshahi mosque in October 2017.

31. The expression 'People of the Book' includes followers of the three books Muslims consider to be revealed by God: the Old Testament, the New Testament, and the Quran, which comprise Jews, Christians, and Muslims.

32. *See*, for example, the *Dawn* news reports on the incident, 'Dozens of houses torched as mob attacks Lahore Christian locality' at: https://www.dawn.com/news/791408 and '125 Christian houses burnt over blasphemy' at: https://www.dawn.com/news/791491.

33. For a report of the incident and what Imam Azad did and said about it *see* 'Religious scholars demand justice for murdered Christian couple', *Dawn*, 8 November 2014, accessible at: https://www.dawn.com/news/1143038.

34. This section is based on interviews held with Imam Zubair Ahmad Zaheer in Lahore in October 2017.

35. This section is based on interviews held with Imam Hafiz Syed Qasim Raza Naqvi at his madrassa in Model Town, Lahore, in November 2017.

36. A good recount of what transpired at LGS is found in Ameer Gilani 'Teaching Comparative Religion: Lahore Grammar School did the right thing', *The Express Tribune Blogs,* 19 September 2013, accessible at: https://blogs.tribune.com.pk/ story/18908/teaching-comparative-religion-lahore-grammar-school-did-the-right-thing/

37. This section is based on interviews held with Dr Raghib Naeemi at the Jamia Naeemia madrassa in Garhi Shahu, Lahore, in November 2017.

38. BBC News, 'Bomb kills senior Pakistan cleric,' 12 June 2009, accessible at: http:// news.bbc.co.uk/2/hi/south_asia/8096776.stm

39. Dr Raghib Naeemi told me this at the Jamia Naeemia madrassa in Garhi Shahu, Lahore, in November 2017.

40. The IBM's complete Code of Conduct is accessible at: http://lahoreworld. com/2013/12/02/ittehad-bain-ul-muslimeen-committee-issues-code-conduct/.

41. 'A bid to end sectarian strife', *The Daily Times*, 3 December 2013, accessible at: https:// dailytimes.com.pk/106698/a-bid-to-end-sectarian-strife.

42. Ayyaz Gulzar, 'Archbishop leads "symphony" of religions in Karachi,' *La Croix International*, 3 May 2018, accessible at: https://international.la-croix.com/news/ archbishop-leads-symphony-of-religions-in-karachi/7502#

43. Ibid.

44. This section is based on interviews held with Father James Channan at his office at the Peace Centre in Lahore in November 2017.

45. This section is based on interviews held with Peter Jacob at the Center for Social Justice in Lahore in November 2017.
46. This section is based on interviews held with Bishop Jamil at the Cathedral School on Mall Road, Lahore in November 2017.
47. This section is based on interviews held with Qari Ruhullah Madani in Peshawar in February 2018, and with Dr Qibla Ayaz at the University of Peshawar in 2017 and subsequently after his appointment to head the Council of Islamic Ideology at its headquarters in Islamabad at various times in fall 2017 and winter 2018.
48. This section on PEAD's founding and its early focus is based on interviews held with Sameena Imtiaz in December 2017.
49. This section is based on interviews held with Tariq Hayat at his office in Peshawar in February 2018 and in Islamabad in January 2019.
50. This section is based on interviews held with Dr Abdul Khadoos and others at BZU in Multan in November 2017.
51. This section is based on interviews held with Dr Muhammad Zia ul Haq and others at the IRI in Islamabad in December 2017 and February 2019.
52. These and other details of the proposal are included in the IRI application to the HEC for the project 'Reconstruction of Pakistani Society in the light of Sirah of the Prophet Muhammad (Peace be on Him),' to span 1 May 2017 to 31 May 2018.
53. Told to me by Dr Muhammad Zia ul Haq at the IRI office in IIU in Islamabad in February 2019.
54. Background on two-day national conference at University of Gujrat on interfaith harmony, 13–14 March 2019.
55. Dr Muhammad Zia ul Haq in Islamabad in February 2019.
56. As noted earlier in this chapter, the recounting of Dr Ayaz's views is based on a number of discussions with him in Peshawar and Islamabad in 2017 and 2018.
57. This section is based on interviews held with Jennifer Jag Jivan at the CSC in Rawalpindi in February 2018.
58. This section is based on interviews held with Samson Salamat in Lahore in January 2018, and various Rawadari Tehreek publications.
59. This section is based on interviews held with Deedar Ahmed Mirani in Sukkur, upper Sindh, in January 2018 and on various Pahel documents.
60. *See* Chapter 2 for a discussion of how the poetry of Sachal Sarmast and Shah Abdul Latif Bhittai is a foundation of resistance poetry in contemporary Sindh.
61. This section is based on interviews held with Krishan Sharma in Karachi in February 2017 and on various REAT documents.
62. REAT Network, *REAT Network Progress Report 2013-15*, REAT Network, Islamabad, n.d., p. 1.
63. Ibid., p. 2.
64. Both of these events are written about in the *REAT Network Newsletter,* vol. 2, issue 2, 2016, p. 7.

6 | Innovative Educational Efforts

Pakistan is proud of her youth, particularly the students, who are the nation builders of tomorrow. They must fully equip themselves by discipline, education, and training for the arduous task lying ahead of them.

Quaid-i-Azam Mohammad Ali Jinnah
Lahore, 31 October 1947

The plea of the founder of Pakistan, Mohammad Ali Jinnah, for the country to facilitate educating all of its children in preparation for 'the arduous task lying ahead of them' is one which remains unrealized. But the dearth of schools adequately preparing students in Pakistan for the myriad roles they can play in the country's future economically and politically pales in importance to the reality they could play as social unifiers, inculcating values of acceptance of diversity, negotiation when disputes arise, community responsibility (more than just to one's own family), and personal responsibility to the surrounding environment. This could go far in countering violence and extremism as students would then grow up to shun participating in violence as an option as they grow older. However, there is a need to have constructive systems in place before education can perform this role.

Indeed, one of the most important institutions that affects individuals' values and priorities are schools, as that is where much socialization occurs in the contemporary world. While in the pre-industrial past, the process of socialization was largely accomplished by families and religious institutions, in most parts of the world this process has largely been taken over by schools. As they prepare students for professions, they also prepare them for participation in the society at large. Pakistan's schools, however, have not prioritized this kind of preparation, as A.H. Nayyar and Ahmed Salim argue,

Governments everywhere use education to further the process of nation-building. Through the teachings of history, language, and social sciences, children are given what the state believes should be part of their shared identity and perspective for understanding the world. However, from the very beginning, the educational system in Pakistan has been aimed at reinforcing one particular view of Pakistani nationalism and identity, namely that Pakistan is an Islamic state rather than a country with a majority Muslim population.[1]

Pakistan's schools, falling short of providing a sound and constructive education, result in many social dislocations including, for some, seeing extremism as a viable option for achieving goals. Hence there is a sense of urgency among many people and groups in Pakistan to envision schools that will not only provide a solid education but also inculcate a passion for living in a peaceful, flourishing community. With this in mind, following an overview of the history and extant tripartite system of education that now exists in Pakistan, this chapter focuses on something exciting and innovative that is occurring in two private, not-for-profit education systems that are located in areas that have experienced the greatest violence from extremism. Both the Bacha Khan Trust Educational Foundation in Khyber Pakhtunkhwa and the Zoya Science Schools in southern Punjab are seeking to provide an outstanding educational foundation for their students while also inculcating a sense of social responsibility and, in the words of Muslim sociologist Ibn Khaldun, 'asabiyyah'—group feeling, social solidarity, and a sense of shared purpose. What they have been able to achieve is quite remarkable, not only in providing good quality education but also in going very far in countering violent extremism.

EDUCATIONAL LEGACIES AND CURRENT CHALLENGES IN PAKISTAN

Educational institutions have an extensive legacy in Muslim communities worldwide and were historically closely tied to religious education. In South Asia, the two best known Sunni schools were the Darul Uloom Deoband (established in Uttar Pradesh in 1866) and the Darul Uloom Nadwatul Ulama (established in Kanpur in 1894), each dedicated to a revitalization of Islam through providing religious education. As with madrassas of the past, their focus was on imbuing students with knowledge of religious history, law, practices, and rituals. These contrasted greatly with the educational institutions the British Raj was establishing in British India, especially after they banned Arabic, Persian, and religious education in such schools after 1835. This action complemented English becoming the official language of the Raj and the medium of instruction in British schools.

Sir Sayyid Ahmed Khan is said to have looked at the declining state of Muslim communities in British India and considered that they were causing their own erosion by not incorporating the knowledge and science of the West into what was being taught in their schools. It was as if Muslims were completely disconnected from the new society that the Raj was constructing in British India, either due to political loss (the Mughal defeat to the British in 1857) or their refusal to attend British schools. In response, he created the Mohammadan Anglo-Oriental (M.A.O.) College at Aligarh in 1875 which brought together young men from prominent Muslim families throughout British India, and later established the Muhammadan Educational Conference in 1886.[2] M.A.O. College actively incorporated teaching science, philosophy, English, and other subjects more commonly associated with the West alongside providing religious education. Importantly, what came to be known as the Aligarh movement played a seminal role in developing a cadre of young Muslim men dedicated to greater political autonomy and later independence from Britain, and who formed the All-India Muslim League in 1906. They also, in desiring wives who could be their companions, were at the forefront of supporting female education, easing some of the extreme restrictions on Muslim women's activities associated with purdah, advocating restrictions on polygamy, ensuring women's legal rights under Islamic law, and overall raising women's status, mobility, and opportunities in the wider society.

A few elite schools for boys were created by the British—either by members of the Raj itself or by Christian missionaries—in the area that today comprises Pakistan. In Lahore, the British opened the Punjab Chiefs' College in early 1886, which was renamed Aitchison College in November of that year. Other prominent early schools include Sadiq Public School in Bahawalpur, Army Burnhall College in Abbottabad, Lawrence College in Murree, Islamia College in Peshawar, and the Presentation Convent

Schools in various parts of the country. There were a few similar-level schools established for girls in various parts of the country as well.

We can see that there were indeed a number of excellent schools in Pakistan at the time of independence in 1947. But what is also important to note is that the colonial legacy of education left a situation where these schools were attended by elites who were socialized into seeing themselves as the country's leaders and part of a unified class through the usage of English; educational opportunities for the rest of the population were largely ignored. There were merely 8,413 primary schools in the whole of Pakistan at independence and 2,598 secondary schools;[3] today, there are 164,630 primary schools and a total of 78,002 middle and secondary schools.[4] But what can we understand about the *quality* of instruction in these schools, especially those dedicated to serving the majority of children in Pakistan and especially their efforts in inculcating a sense of civic obligation and Ibn Khaldun's *asabiyyah*?

This question has fuelled a great deal of research, debates, and development assistance engagement in Pakistan for a long time given the recognition of the failure of government schools to provide viable education which has unduly harmed that very group—children of the poor—which it claims to be dedicated to serving. General Zia ul Haq, to serve his politico-ideological agenda, mandated a change in the medium of instruction in public schools in the early 1980s to Urdu, further truncating the line between quality in private and public education. New private English medium school systems (e.g., Beaconhouse, Grammar, City School, Roots, among others) were developed for upper-middle and elite children while the English proficiency of the mass of the population declined, essentially limiting their knowledge of and engagement with the rest of the world.

When educational expenditures make up less than 3 per cent of the country's national budget, what can we expect will be the final outcome for government schools?[5] The various Five-Year Plans[6] and the newfound attention on reaching some of the Sustainable Development Goals (SDGs)[7] have all had the objective of achieving universal primary education and roughly 75 per cent enrolment in secondary education. But the overall development budget is once again facing marked cuts, making it clear that this cannot be achieved, albeit Pakistan's future will continue to be precarious if it is not. In addition, investment in education and creation of good schools has been a victim of political pandering and imbroglios in Pakistan: it's one of those situations where everyone talks about the existence of massive problems and yet often fall short on offering solutions, underscoring the lack of prioritizing truly fixing the problems. As there is still no national consensus on such things as how to share water, the rights women inherently have and, for our concerns here, what comprises a 'good education' aside from having 'served time' as a student, how best to respond to these challenges?

On the part of the state, the federal government had declared that education would be compulsory but this has often been overlooked. How can we understand that the Government of Pakistan had approached this with sincerity when Nasim Ahmad Aheer of Jauharabad served as Minister of Education in 1986–7 despite having only a 5th-grade education? How can someone who has never prioritized education for himself be at the helm of a national education system and understand what is to be done? In 2010, the state finally put some weight behind this wish when it mandated that free education will be provided throughout the country and attendance will be compulsory, making education a fundamental right for every child in Pakistan when it incorporated Article 25-A, into the country's Constitution,

> Article 25-A. The state shall provide free and compulsory education to all children of the age of five to sixteen years in such manner as may be determined by law.[8]

But that same year, following the enactment of the Eighteenth Amendment to the Constitution, many legislative and executive powers were devolved to the provinces, including primary and secondary education. So now the responsibility to provide 'free and compulsory education' is in the hands of each province, including syllabus creation, funding, oversight, etc. Importantly, there is no federal mandate included on what must be taught, especially the inclusion of any kind of civics education that could imbue students with a sense of responsibility to the larger society.

Indeed, instead of teaching social responsibility, a study done by the Sustainable Development Policy Institute (SDPI) found that curricula and textbooks in most government schools are largely insensitive to religious diversity within the country, fuelling discrimination and bias. It argues that curricula and textbooks are,

> heavily laden with religious teachings, reflecting a very narrow view held by a minority among Muslims that all the education should be essentially that of Islamiyat...Pakistani nationalism is repeatedly defined in a manner that excludes non-Muslim Pakistanis from either being Pakistani nationals or from even being good human beings. Much of this material runs counter to any efforts at national integration.[9]

A separate study commissioned by the US Commission on International Religious Freedom (USCIRF) found similar problems with what is being taught in government-funded schools in Pakistan. The Pakistani authors argue that public schools have long been part of the problem in provoking disdain, misunderstanding, and animosity towards religious minorities in Pakistan. They found that primary and secondary school textbooks often 'foster prejudice and intolerance of religious minorities, especially Hindus and Christians. Such intolerant references are not restricted to Islamic Studies textbooks: they are found in both early elementary and more advanced Social Studies texts used by all public school students, including non-Muslims.' These results are eye opening about what is often taught in government schools,

> Public school textbooks used by all children often were found to have a strong Islamic orientation, while Pakistan's religious minorities were either referenced derogatorily or omitted all together. Hindus, one of Pakistan's religious minorities, were described in especially negative terms, and references to Christians were often inaccurate and offensive. Madrassa textbooks generally portrayed non-Muslims in one of three ways: 1. kafirs (infidels) or *mushrakeen* (pagans) 2. *dhimmis* (non-Muslims living under Islamic rule), or 3. *murtids* (apostates, i.e. people who have turned away from Islam). Non-Muslims were never described as citizens with the constitutionally-protected rights which accompany citizenship.[10]

The report also describes that interviews with public school and madrassa teachers demonstrated that they 'had limited awareness or understanding of religious minorities and their beliefs and were divided on whether a religious minority was a citizen. Views expressed by teachers about Ahmadis, Christians, and Jews often were very negative. Interviews showed that these biased sentiments were transmitted and held by the students.'[11] As a result of the study, USCIRF recommended that the US government urge the Government of Pakistan and appropriate provincial authorities to set national textbook and curricula standards that actively promote tolerance towards all persons, move quickly to implement improved guidelines for textbooks used in public schools, replace current public school textbooks with ones that exclude messages of intolerance, hatred, or violence against any group based on any differences, and ensure that a madrassa oversight board is empowered to develop, implement, and train teachers in human rights standards.[12]

In another section of *The Subtle Subversion*, the SDPI researchers identified detailed materials being used in public education curriculum that are 'insensitive'—at the least—to religious diversity and understanding. For example, the researchers found that the Urdu curriculum (first and second language) for classes VI–VIII created by the National Curriculum Committee for the National Bureau of Curriculum and Textbooks states that the objectives of teaching the Urdu language is 'to create love for religion and respect for personalities' and therefore students must have,

1. Belief in the Unity of God, and know that Allah is the creator of the universe;
2. Must regard Islamic ways as the best of all…(and)
3. Must be aware of the blessings of jihad, and must create a yearning for jihad in his heart.[13]

Another author in the study questions the appropriateness of 'a distinct overloading of religious contents' in the Urdu curriculum.[14] A second example he offers is from the Pakistan Studies Curriculum for Classes XI–XII, again created by the National Bureau of Curriculum and Textbooks, that includes the statement that 'the Islamization of all institutions of Society is a means towards achieving the goal of an Islamic Society as embodied in the Objectives Resolution.'[15] This is patently untrue as there is nothing mentioned in this regard in the Objectives Resolution nor among curricula goals either nationally or provincially.

Public school textbooks are not considered extreme when compared with Muslim religious schools, *madrassas*, which offer a 'third estate' of educational opportunities in Pakistan. As mentioned earlier, they have long existed to provide religious education to Muslims in South Asia, but Zia ul Haq encouraged their unprecedented expansion in the early 1980s in his quest to bring Pakistan closer into Saudi Arabia's orbit; his government even went so far as to consider a madrassa degree as the equivalent of other educational degrees. Madrassa students could receive an education without the burden of their families' having to pay school fees or for school uniforms. In many instances, religious schools would offer a student's family essential grains (rice, wheat, etc.), cooking oil, or even money to help towards a sister's marriage. Families considered that at the least, their son would learn to read the Quran and lead prayers, which has a moral benefit. They also surmised, and appropriately so, that their son could earn a living later on by teaching children the Quran and their prayers, as many families have a *maulvi sahib* (religious tutor) visit their house daily to do so.

One of the largest and most controversial of these madrassas is located on the Grand Trunk (GT) Road, a half hour's drive east of Peshawar at Akora Khattak in Khyber Pakhtunkhwa. It was run by Maulana Sami ul Haq until his murder in November 2018. Many people say that the madrassa at Akora Khattak's most famous alumnus is Mullah Omar, the late leader of the fallen Taliban in Afghanistan, although when I visited this decidedly male enclave I was told that they only gave him an honorary diploma. I saw roomfuls of boys moving back and forth in place reciting the Quran or prescribed prayers. I saw no evidence of any other kind of education being provided.

Every Muslim sect runs madrassas in Pakistan, and most of them comply with Government of Pakistan's requirements to register with the authorities and teach math and science courses, in addition to religion. The curriculum of those madrassas that are registered are not significantly different from those in schools run by the government. Both kinds elevate Muslims over others, but do not support or promote violence. It is only a small percentage of madrassas that essentially compel students to engage in rote memorization and constant repetition, often advocating violence as a means to recapturing an authentic Islam but also not preparing students to be functional adults later. Back in 1997, long before the 9/11 attack and the subsequent US attack on Afghanistan which directly brought Pakistan into the imbroglio, Pakistani journalist Muhammad Ali Anwar observed that different sects often hate each other and wrote that,

> Holy war against non-believers is one of the important teachings of the *madaris*, and this has indirectly led to the creation of sectarian hatred because each sect believes the other to be heretical. While it may be said that religious schools are meeting a need for education among lower-income families, that too is because the state has abdicated its role to educate the people. In the process, a lot of intolerance is being spread.[16]

A.H. Nayyar's more recent study found that a significant minority of madrassas in Pakistan continue to provide ideological training and motivation 'in those who take part in religiously-inspired violence in Pakistan and abroad.'[17] A former Chairperson of the PMEB (Pakistan Madrasah Education Board) told me that in his official position, he had the opportunity to review the syllabi of many different sects' *madaris* in Pakistan and found no tolerance in any of them.[18] He found this to be true especially in the private *madaris* he encountered which resisted the mandatory registration. They didn't want to be affiliated with the government as they were afraid they would have to be accountable, and that the government would see their funds and where they came from.

Few madrassas are teaching about peace or taking stands to counter violence and extremism.[19] Indeed, the actors behind reforming madrassa curriculum and syllabi are not the teachers and students of the madrassas themselves, but instead are outside interests comprising the Government of Pakistan, external donors, and educational practitioners from within Pakistan. While some activists consider that some madrassas are distorting and misrepresenting the message of Islam, they are playing only a small role behind madrassa syllabus reform. The big impetus is the pressure being placed on the Government of Pakistan by many different countries to curtail extremism in the country, and a glance at what is being taught in some madrassas reveals that students are rarely taught about acceptance of diversity.[20]

A Memorandum of Understanding, signed in October 2010 between the Pakistan Ministry of Interior, which oversees the madrassa system, and the five main madrassa boards in the country was an attempt to better regulate their curriculum and financing, and required registration but without any penalty for those that demurred.[21] The Wafaq-ul-Madaris (Federation of Madaris) is a self-regulatory entity, rather different from the 'madrassa oversight board' the USCIRF had recommended in 2011 be created and empowered to develop, implement, and train madrassa teachers in human rights standards and to provide oversight of madrassa curricula and teaching standards (as cited earlier in this chapter).[22] In September 2015, the National Counter Terrorism Authority (NACTA) agreed that indeed some of the *madaris* in the country were inciting conflict and violence,

> During the War on Terror and consequent terrorism in Pakistan, it was found that some of the terrorists were informally schooled in some of the *madaris*. Although the suspect *madaris* were placed under intense scrutiny, a need was felt to bring all the *madaris* under a registration framework, reforming of their education system and curricula and their mainstreaming into the formal education framework.[23]

In response, NACTA finally developed a registration mechanism for madrassas and announced that it would allow only registered madrassas to operate, and there would be the penalty of closure for those that did not (but of course, first, they would have to find them). In addition, it established two committees—one for secondary education and the second for higher education—comprised of both madrassa and government officials for reviewing curricula and determining degree equivalents.

However, after speaking extensively with 'ulema throughout Pakistan between 2017and 2019, I have found that the only viable, functional monitoring is internal, conducted by the 'ulema and their madrassa boards, and which exists solely within those madrassas that have registered with the state. When I queried the head of one of the five major boards about what his madrassa's syllabus is including to promote peace, I found little understanding even of my questioning. For example, when I asked if they teach anything about the sectarian strife happening around them, he responded, 'No—we just teach.' I asked if they teach about social problems, and his response was 'No, the syllabus is about the Quran and the hadith; they talk about social issues.' Finally, I questioned that aside from the existing syllabus, do they teach anything else to promote inter-faith harmony? And he said, they do not, except for encouraging 'people to speak truth with all.'[24] From such examples, how can we understand the utility of monitoring madrassa curriculum so as to stand against violence and extremism when an important, registered madrassa board offers no pathway for doing so themselves?

What we do know is that as of this writing today, in 2020, only 56 per cent of Pakistan's population is literate; the sheer magnitude of what that number means is sobering when we realize that roughly 97,192,630 Pakistanis are illiterate. There remain an inordinate number of out-of-school children (OOSC); the NGO Alif Ailaan estimates that 25.02 million Pakistani children between the ages of 5 and 16 will soon join the ranks of Pakistan's illiterates. Among children of primary school-going age, roughly 20 per cent are not in school and more than half of those children are girls. The proportions increase at higher levels of education.

We can understand the importance of school systems like the Bacha Khan and Zoya Science Schools when we see the challenges of educating poor, rural children in Pakistan as cited in the Alif Ailaan report, especially as the researchers found 'vast' regional and economic disparities, with the greatest gaps in Khyber Pakhtunkhwa,

> For both girls and boys, access to schooling is more difficult in rural areas and the gap widens at higher levels of education. Similarly, children from the poorest families are more likely to be out of school compared to their counterparts belonging to richer families.[25]

Two small, privately-funded school systems are contributing models of how to inculcate communal respect, welcoming diversity, and environmental responsibility while delivering an outstanding free education to poor girls and boys in areas that have been wracked by violent extremism, something the public education system still finds elusive seventy-three years after independence.

BACHA KHAN EDUCATIONAL FOUNDATION SCHOOLS IN KHYBER PAKHTUNKHWA

The Bacha Khan Trust, a legacy of the work of Khan Abdul Ghaffar Khan (1890–1988), popularly known as Bacha Khan, as well as that of the Khudai Khidmatgar movement, formed an auxiliary institution, the Bacha Khan Trust Educational Foundation (BKTEF), in line with its priorities to promote social reform in March 2007. Its mandate was to work towards the 'promotion and development of peace, human rights, interfaith harmony, and socio-economic uplift of the society through an extended educational programme in the north-western parts of Pakistan: Khyber Pakhtunkhwa and FATA.'[26] It was inspired by Bacha Khan's earlier Azad School initiative that aimed to offer modern technical and vocational education to bring about social change and a society based on social justice, non-violence, gender equality, and pluralism. Initiated in 1921, it opened fifty-seven schools between 1921 and 1923; at its peak, it included 134 schools throughout the northwest. The schools, which incorporated Pashto as the medium of instruction as an ethnic identity marker, were to be an important vehicle for Bacha Khan to bring about a society free of biases and social injustices.

A related inspiration for the Bacha Khan schools was the Khudai Khidmatgar (Servants of God) movement that Bacha Khan had founded in 1929 as a call for socio-cultural reforms. Being under heavy pressure from the British who had forced him in and out of jail in the 1920s, he made the appeal that Pakhtuns had to get past their endless fighting with each other if they could ever defeat the British. Scott Baldauf argues that Bacha Khan called for a reform of Pakhtun culture itself with the adoption of a disciplined moral cause,

> While others called for jihad, or holy war against the British infidels, Badshah (Bacha) Khan called for a reform of Pashtun culture itself. It was not Britain's superior numbers, weapons, or even culture that kept Pashtuns subjected. Instead, it was the Pashtuns themselves, through endless land feuds and tribal bickering. Badshah Khan knew that Pashtuns could never defeat the British through violence that required money, arms, and complete secrecy, three things that were in short supply on the

impoverished frontier. A disciplined moral cause, on the other hand, was cheap, and required only thousands of Pashtuns with attitude.[27]

Bacha Khan was highly cognizant of the challenges facing Pakhtuns under British rule, but advocated that changes had to be achieved internally. He said,

> The history of my people is full of victories and tales of heroism, but there are drawbacks too. Internal feuds and personal jealousies have always snatched away the gains achieved through vast sacrifices. They were dispossessed only because of their own inherent defects, never by any outside power for who could oppose them on the battlefield.[28]

Members took an oath in joining the movement with each stating,

> Since God needs no service…I promise to serve humanity in the name of God. I promise to refrain from violence and from taking revenge. I promise to forgive those who oppress me or treat me with cruelty. I promise to devote at least two hours a day to social work.[29]

The last point is very telling: service to one's community was the hallmark of the Khudai Khidmatgar movement and remains the central philosophy behind the Bacha Khan schools. Managing Director Dr Khadim Hussain told me that the Bacha Khan Education Foundation's alternative education model promotes critical thinking, the development of multiple skills, the development of civic and aesthetic senses, and environmental consciousness. For the latter, students are tasked with the responsibility of keeping their classrooms and their schools clean. Where possible, many schools have students tend the community gardens within the schools' premises.[30] The goals of the Bacha Khan schools, therefore, are not simply education—which they deliver very well—but inner transformation of each student to see themselves as a social actor and reclaim indigenous identify. Khadim Hussain is working to establish 'a critical educational network in all the nooks and corners of Pakhtunkhwa on the vision of the national legend, Bacha Khan' which, at its core, emphasizes critical thinking, creative faculty, modern skills, and building on local, indigenous knowledge. The Foundation is providing high quality education free of cost to children without any discrimination regarding language or religion. A principal at a Bacha Khan School said that the schools aspire to develop in students values of democracy, tolerance and interfaith harmony, and that 'our focus is to make our children confident, self-reliant, and productive citizens realized through imparting hard and soft key skills.'

The Bacha Khan School System began with the BKTEF opening two co-educational primary schools in Peshawar and Charsadda in September 2007. With the assistance of local communities throughout Khyber Pakhtunkhwa and FATA, it opened an additional ten schools the following year, spanning the area from upper Dir in the north to Hangu district in the south. Three more Bacha Khan schools were added in 2015, making the total today fifteen schools. All schools serve children from nursery to Class 6 and, depending on space available, may go up to Class 10, as shown in Table 6.1.

Table 6.1: Bacha Khan schools by location and grades taught		
Name	Location	Grades
BKS Pabini	Village Pabini, District Swabi	Nursery to 7th
*BKS Shahbaz Garhi	Village Shahbaz Garhi, District Mardan	Nursery to 8th
*BKS Dargai	Village Sidrajowar, Dargai, District Malakand	Nursery to 8th
BKS Totakan	Village Totakan, District Malakand	Nursery to 9th
BKS Gandigar	Village Gandigar, District Upper Dir	Nursery to 10th
BKS Landi Kotal	Landi Kotal, Khyber Agency, FATA	Nursery to 7th
BKS Karak	Karak, District Karak	Nursery to 8th
*BKS Takht-e-Nasrati	Village Chata Banda, Takht e Nasrati, District Karak	Nursery to 8th
BKS Thall	Thal, District Hangu	Nursery to 6th
*BKS Nauthia	Old Darul Kafala, Nauthia, Peshawar	Nursery to 10th
BKS Shoghore	Shoghore Valley, Chitral	Nursery to 9th
BKS Kohat	Kohat	Nursery to 8th
*BKS Mathra	Kandi Payan, Mathra, Peshawar	Nursery to 9th
*BKS Swat	Mingora, District Swat	Nursery to 8th
*BKS Charsadda	Wazir Bagh Korona, District Charsadda	Nursery to 10th
*Personally visited by the author. Source: BKTEF website[31]		

The BKTEF offers a training academy for teachers in its Peshawar headquarters. Its unique style of teaching, as explained by Khadim Hussain, is based on interactive teaching-learning methodologies that encourage independent, critical thinking. Students are urged to question things and move away from the self-imposed discipline that is socially mandated for students at most other schools. In addition, the academic environment nurtures cooperation and collegiality; violence of any type is absolutely forbidden. It also incorporates a cultural education component which includes visual arts, performing arts, crafts, and folklore in all classes. These connect students with indigenous values as well as with modern technology. The trainings are offered quarterly and consist of three types: 5-day basic teacher training; five-day science and social science teacher training; and language training in English, Urdu, and Pashto, in recognition that there is a big problem in teaching in other languages in the area. The BKTEF has developed tools for activity-based learning using the three languages. A usual training consists of 25–30 teachers who stay in the BKTEF guesthouse. Khadim Hussain estimates that they must have trained more than 3,000 teachers in the last ten years.

More than 5,000 students are said to be enrolled in the Bacha Khan schools today, with a 60:40 gender ratio of boys and girls in the co-educational schools. Between 2016 and 2019, I spoke with a few hundred students from seven of the fifteen Bacha Khan schools in different areas of Khyber Pakhtunkhwa.[32] Almost universally, boys and girls alike said they enjoyed having classes together and that essentially it was 'no big deal,' a marked difference from the vast majority of government and private schools in Pakistan that are single gender. For example, during a Class 3 mixed sex knitting activity, where the boys appeared as eager as the girls to learn how to knit, a student told me,

> Boys and girls should not only be entitled to uniform education but should also go to co-educational schools and interact with each other. We can only deliver Bacha Khan's message if we work together.

Students were consistently enthusiastic about their school. I have found this to be true in many parts of Pakistan, but with a significant difference: students in Bacha Khan schools could articulate *why* they liked their school, using specifics, even from an early age. When I spoke with a student in a Nursery class, in response to my question about the school, the student responded 'We love our teacher. We don't fight with one another. We learn ABC, 123, Alif Bae Pae' (i.e., English, math, and Urdu). The zero-tolerance policy for fighting and violence, consistent with Bacha Khan's philosophy, is very popular at every school I visited; students offered that they were happy with what they were learning and also not being beaten in schools (somewhat common elsewhere, I believe),

- It is peaceful here. They teach us skilled work. They also teach us well and don't beat us. Additionally, they take us to the lab and let us play games. They talk to us in a polite manner. We have a class period where we learn about Bacha Khan and during other class periods, we learn different subjects. We also get to present in the assembly about Bacha Khan, in front of other people.
- They don't hit us at this school. They teach us a lot about Bacha Khan: who he was, where he was born, what he taught.
- They teach us good things and we learn about non-violence. It has a friendly environment. There is no violence and/or beating. We play games here and do other activities. In other schools, they do not teach us Pashto but over here I learned Pashto. In this school, people are kind and gentle.
- The messages of peace in the textbooks here are beautiful.
- I don't have to go for tuition anymore as my teachers are very good at explaining. I'm not burdened with homework.
- I'll never beat my children regardless of how much they frustrate me.

Another thing they liked about their schools is that they could learn about their own culture—through stories, art projects, and even learning about Bacha Khan and his philosophy,

- When we open Bacha Khan *Baba's* books, it has such nice teachings which teach us about helping others and to spread that message among them, which is why we like this school.

- They teach us about Bacha Khan and what he did for Pakhtuns; they teach us about our culture. They also encourage us to do the same for other Pakhtuns.
- Before getting admitted in this school, I wasn't politically aware. I didn't know anything about Bacha Khan. I've seen how much of a difference we as students can make to better the world.
- I learned from Bacha Khan that you should not do injustice and treat everyone with love and care.
- They teach us Pashto as a subject, they teach us theatre arts and we get to learn how to play music and sing *tapay* (plural for spoken word Pashto folk poetry).
- I won't hesitate to talk to madrassa students about what I've acquired from this school. If they can feel free to preach to us about their beliefs, then why shouldn't I?

A student recited in traditional Pashto style *tapa* (spoken word Pashto folk poetry), 'I turn and cross the hairpin bends of the Malakand pass, give my salutations to the Bacha Khan School!'

Bacha Khan's philosophy and legacy is shared with students in many ways, both as part of their course materials and in quotes within colourful posters on the school walls as shown in Figures 6.1 and 6.2. Students' decorative work is displayed frequently as seen in Figure 6.3.

In response, explicitly, to what they have learned from Bacha Khan, students said, 'He taught us to share.' 'He taught us to love one another and not fight.' 'Non-violence.' 'Khudai Khidmatgari.' Many BK students' parents and grandparents are Khudai Khidmatgari supporters. In a primary school class, students enthusiastically raised their hands when queried if they have family members in Khudai Khidmatgar as seen in Figure 6.4.

When responding to questions pertaining to what they want to do when they grow up, the students were intriguing in that while they stated similar professions I have heard children tell me throughout Pakistan—doctor, teacher, pilot, police, join the army, even fashion designer—these students usually offered social reasons behind their choices. Nearly universally, they aspire to do something positive for their communities and be of service to other Pakhtuns; many desire to become peacemakers like the young girl in Figure 6.5,

- I want to be a peacemaker. I will do Khudai Khidmat (help people, for the love of God). I will write for people, in case they're too sick to write on their own. I will also help the elderly and be kind to the younger ones and I will not hold grudges against my friends.
- I will become a peacemaker and spread the philosophy of peace. Instead of aiming a gun at wrongdoers, I'll gift them with grains of wheat.
- I will bring peace between people who are fighting. I will have people love each other and not fight.
- I want to be a teacher at a madrassa. I will teach the Quran and other teachings about patience and tolerance.
- Just like Bacha Khan, I will serve the Pakhtun people.
- I want to be a teacher and pass on what I have learned here to the people of Swat.
- I will join the army and protect my country.
- A doctor, because I want to help people and provide quality treatment to children and those in need.
- An army officer, so I can serve the country and its people.
- I want to become a doctor to help the people of this country.
- As a doctor, I can help my brothers (community) and my elders and provide treatment to them.
- I will become a pilot so that I can help my country succeed.
- I will become a Khudai Khidmatgar, like Bacha Khan. I will help people and will serve as a peacemaker to those who are fighting.
- I will help people and spread the philosophy of non-violence.
- I will become a soldier. I will get rid of terrorists and improve schools.

Students were convinced they will be able to contribute to Pakistan and make it a better, more meaningful, and equitable country. They were enthusiastic to talk about what they will do for the success of the country and how they will 'help fix' Pakistan,

- We will bring peace to our country and we will educate ourselves. Whoever fights, we will stop them from fighting.
- And those children who do not go to schools, we will make sure that they get educated.

- I want to do a lot for my country. If we learn to behave and teach that to others too, this way our country will become a better place, where there will be no more fights and we will be a peaceful and successful nation.
- We won't fight in our country; we will bring peace and those who fight, we will stop them from fighting.
- I won't be cruel to anyone and will work for the success of our country and its people.
- I will serve the country and help it succeed.
- I will treat Pakistan well.

I also asked students—only those in Class 7 and older—what they would say to their brother or cousin if he said he was fed up and was going off to join the Taliban. I have heard many responses to this question elsewhere in Pakistan, virtually all of which have been concerned about a boy's well-being and for him to keep contact with his family. But I found the responses from students at the Bacha Khan schools highly distinctive, again with an overriding concern for the well-being of society. They said they would tell him this is not something good to do for society, that they have to work together to build a better Pakistan, and that violence is never the answer to anything. The maturity they displayed was notable and impressive.

In addition to the primary schools, Khadim Hussain said that in an effort to help reclaim cultural space, the BKTEF has also been providing training workshops to graduates of provincial universities in critical thinking, pluralism, and good governance. A variety of programmes enable them to do this. For example, they have been providing training in scripting, directing, and acting to youth, and have now adopted interactive theatre and other kinds of theatre forums as part of their leadership training. He runs a monthly study circle which many teachers from nearby Bacha Khan schools also attend. It often delves into more dense, theoretical works such as discussing a framework for democratic struggle, and lighter works such as a Calandar Mohmand's 1960s short story in *Gajjre* (Flower Bracelet). Another frequent participant is Bilal Khan from Malakand district; a rabab player (like Gulab Khel Afridi, discussed in Chapter 3), he is seeking to create an alternative narrative through his rabab. Khadim Hussain, who runs the study circles and invited Bilal Khan to participate in them, said,

> Bilal Khan plays songs which depict the indigenous, folk narrative which is pluralist, secular, pro-women—he considers women as humans—and he plays folk songs. There is no place for extremist violence in this culture. It's a narrative for a song that has sprouted from the soil. The soil has a long history of accommodation, tolerance, races, and ethnicities. Music itself is antithetical to extremism.[33]

They have also established BKTEF community education committees consisting of representatives of parents of students, elders of the local community, elected members of local governments, educators, and the school principal. Committee members feel entrusted in the success of the school and participate in the admission process, look at absenteeism (of both students and teachers), the drop-out rate and meet with students and parents to find out why they drop out, and address security issues in consultation with local political and other local enforcement agencies.

In 2016, the Bacha Khan schools extended the course designed for cultural curriculum to include visual arts, performing arts, crafts, and folklore. They decided to extend the crafts part to the schools' local communities to provide those who want to learn them with marketable skills. This is now self-sustaining, an 'institution within the institutions,' thanks to an initial injection of support from the Malala Fund. Khadim Hussain considers this is a vital change as girls and women have unduly been victims of terrorism and extremism and have lost their source of income; any earnings they used to bring in have disappeared. Now the Bacha Khan schools are offering courses in stitching, tailoring, working with clay, and the like to the community surrounding each school. Women can come to the school to make their craft and the school connects them to the market, or they directly make plans with shopkeepers and showrooms to sell their products. The community curriculum also includes basic literacy and math. There are, on average, thirty women per school, for the duration of three months, and each school offers these classes for four quarters, resulting in each school teaching roughly 1,700 women per year.[34]

Funding for this private school system that provides free education to children of poor families is always a challenge. The Bacha Khan schools, according to Khadim Hussain, have finally been able to move towards implementing a community-based school funding model. Until 2016,

80 per cent of the funding was from external donors (the Bacha Khan Trust as well as from USAID, FOSIP, NED, among others, and joined by the Malala Fund in 2015) and 20 per cent was from local donations. Recognizing that many international NGOs have been closed or threatened with closure in Pakistan, they knew they had to figure out a new way of funding the schools and ensure their survival. They made a push to do away with external funding so the schools are nearly fully sustainable through local communities, the BKTEF, and by members of the BK Education Trust who donate Rs1,000 per month (about $6). The latter is comprised of roughly three hundred people, all of whom are Pakhtuns with most residing within Pakistan though some live abroad in the diaspora. Khadim Hussain claims they learned important lessons for doing this from the building of mosques in Pakistan; they equated building and running the schools to the communities with building and running a mosque. This enabled them to convince the communities to sustain the schools, teachers' salaries, buildings, etc.

The community-based funding model has had an unexpected benefit in that the BKTEF leadership were able to convince the local district school administrations and the police stations that they were safe places. Since 2014, they had been pressured 'to have schools like banks, with cameras and guards,' but given the Bacha Khan schools' zero-tolerance policy for violence, having guns and security screeners in the schools seemed incongruous. They refused to keep armed guards or have people on rooftops with guns given how the schools always seek to counter the narrative of violence with non-violence along with everything they teach. Bacha Khan has left a legacy of non-violence, and the Bacha Khan schools stand for human dignity and cooperation, for the rights of people to govern themselves, to own their own resources, to move according to their will and wishes, and resist those forces that hinder or impede the rights of people or perpetrate violence. The curriculum is imbued with the importance of non-violence and the empowerment of communities. So the BKTEF agreed to install cameras, but refused to do anything related to guns. They were able to provide written assurances that the schools were actually protected by the local communities, and they could finally get rid of the guns. In response to the government's Rules of Business for Security requests, Khadim Hussain must frequently respond in detail about what they are doing for security.

Some letters have gone on for five pages as he elaborates on what the schools are about, how the local communities support them, and where the responsibility lies—within communities and their leaders—for protecting the schools.

These Bacha Khan schools are indeed a breed apart from mainstream schools and madrassas in Pakistan.

ZOYA SCIENCE SCHOOLS IN SOUTHERN PUNJAB

There is another private, not-for-profit educational system far from Khyber Pakhtunkhwa but in an area that has also experienced a great deal of violence—southern Punjab. The Zoya Science Schools prioritize STEM—Science, Technology and Math—subjects, while also teaching peace. They encourage students to work to build a better future for Pakistan, and also a peaceful Pakistan. The Zoya Schools are co-educational, and built right next to poor *bastis* (slums) so their students as well as their teachers can walk to the school.

The Zoya Schools' curriculum was conceived to highlight the work especially of Muslim scientists such as Al-Biruni.[35] George Sarton's *History of Science*[36] is the organizing framework for what Sarmad Khwaja, the founder of the Zoya Science Schools, is seeking to accomplish with the schools—a blending of scientific understanding with humanistic priorities. They have developed the curriculum using mnemonics, to make difficult concepts easy to understand and remember by designing experiments that children themselves can do.

Sarmad Khwaja, the founder and greatest benefactor of the Zoya Science Schools, had spent his career as a leading economist with the International Monetary Fund (IMF).[37] He hadn't imagined that he would someday start a group of primary schools but everything changed for him with the death of his beloved daughter, Zoya. She had studied at Queens University in Canada, then at Georgetown, followed by working at the National Institute of Health in the US as part of a team doing genetics research before entering Yale to do a doctorate in epidemiology. She fell ill and within three months she was gone; it was brain cancer.

Recently retired from the IMF, he decided to dedicate himself to educating children from poor families in Zoya's name, as a memorial to

Fig. 6.1: The principal at BKS Swat, surrounded
by Bacha Khan quotes.

Fig. 6.2: Bacha Khan quotes at another BKS school.

Fig. 6.3: Student work about the environment on display at
the BKS in Dargai.

Fig. 6.4: Students at a BK school whose families support the Khudai Khidmatgar movement.

Fig. 6.5: A student at a BK school who aspires to be a peacemaker.

Fig. 6.6: Banner of the Zoya Science Schools.

Fig. 6.7: Students performing an original play at Nala Khudadad Zoya
Science School, Kot Addu, southern Punjab.

her and to her passion for science and the empowerment of girls. Zoya passed away in 2010, at a time when there were devastating floods in southern Punjab. Social activists had arranged a camp near the Press Club in Islamabad to raise awareness regarding the tragedy and raise emergency funds. He met with them and discussed his desire to build a school there, that he would provide the funds if someone from the area provided the land. Mazhar Iqbal Jagliani's family agreed to donate a *kanal* (about one-eighth of an acre) for a school in the Kot Addu region outside of Multan. Many other people in the local community also contributed. The Jaglianis, a political family, were able to mobilize a lot of people to help build the first Zoya School, which was completed in 2012. Other schools were built in that wider region and in nearby Muzaffargarh.

Sarmad Khwaja had studied, as a young man, in the former Soviet Union, and the progressive ideas he had heard there gave him a framework for his educational philosophy: the need for empirical rigor to justify beliefs and ideas, especially about development. He realized that economics without statistics and without mathematics doesn't get respect. He had also been strongly influenced by his parents: his father had been very active in the trade union movement and both of his parents were school principals. There was a very progressive atmosphere in his home, part of the motivation to go to Moscow to study, rather than to London or the US.

So when he had the means to do something, he thought this was the time to put his ideas into action. His motivation was partially political, to start schools in the poorest areas of southern Punjab and hit the *zamindars* who had neglected their constituencies. He thinks the Zoya Science Schools are having that effect, and they can build even more schools by spreading the word further. But the other part of his motivation was to do something that his daughter, Zoya, would have appreciated. When he started to build the schools, it became a source of happiness for him when he started seeing children singing and learning. He said to me, 'You've lost one child, but you've gained 2,000 other children.' As of 2018, he had spent about $1.5 million, and intended to spend a lot more.

He also understood that for such schools to be viable and sustainable, the community has to take ownership of them. The goal is to have a local community give them the land for the school, he will establish it, and then give it back to the community for them to run it. In conjunction with this, he began a microfinance programme: all participants received a loan and upon receipt, they had to make a donation to the local school. Khwaja claims this had been very successful because there is so much demand for microcredit. He would then get a return of about PKR 40,000 per month which, added to the negligible amounts they charge for school fees, was enough to finance a school.

However, the area where he has been building the Zoya Science Schools is very conservative, dominated by landed, feudal interests who have rarely done anything productive for the local residents such as establishing schools or hospitals. He suddenly found out that a whispering campaign had begun, claiming that the school's benefactors were engaging in usury (charging interest, which is prohibited in Islam), started by those who opposed the kind of education he was trying to provide to poor children. Soon afterwards, despite the propaganda, the Zoya Science Schools were registered as a Section 42 Company with the Securities and Exchange Commission in Pakistan and were compelled to stop providing the microfinance loans as it was a school, not a bank. Khwaja is again just privately giving money to the schools. He has already given five of the schools as a gift to their community. In locations where the transfer process has been computerized, it took him a half hour to complete the transfer, but where they have *patwaris* (human record-keepers) it is taking an inordinate amount of time.

The pedagogical goals of the Zoya Science Schools share some similarities with those of the Bacha Khan schools, but a key emphasis is math and science (and no mention of Bacha Khan in this Punjabi environment). These are articulately summed up thusly,

> Zoya schools address the wider condition and needs of society. We promote citizenship in classrooms with posters on children's rights, songs on oppression, liberation, tolerance. Our classroom seating—4 children to a table–encourages discussion, dialogue, and argument. Our teaching responds to local needs: our math/science curriculum uses observation, experimentation, measurement, and verification (essential features of science) in our exercise to measure the Earth's Circumference. We use the local language, i.e. the language in which the children think—their mother

tongue. Basic medicine is taught by informing about 5 diseases common in villages and their 5 cures. Children take part in health/ mal-nutrition surveys. Our chemistry curriculum will analyse soils/water/crops in villages. Our children read world literature (Hemingway, Prem Chand, Rumi, Tolstoy, Gogol, Chekov) and learn about world music (Beethoven, etc.) through our rock opera Nawan Sij, which brings together our poems on science/tolerance/ children's rights into a musical story of a girl who wishes to know how big is the earth and finds out in Zoya school. We are also preparing a brief people's history of Pakistan for children in Saraiki from the lives and poetry of Faiz Ahmed Faiz and Habib Jalib.[38]

There are currently seven Zoya Science Schools, with six in district Muzzafargah and one in district Dera Ghazi Khan, as shown in Table 6.2. Three of the schools have fairly balanced gender ratios while boys are a significant majority in the other four. The schools in Garibabad, Daruhal, Nala Khudadad, and Usmanabad have been picked up as partners with the Punjab Education Foundation (PEF), so therefore are no longer supported by the Zoya Science School Network. The land, building, and other properties have been given as a gift to their communities and the title deeds have been handed over to the school administrators so that they conform to the PEF requirements.

Table 6.2 Zoya Science Schools by enrolment and location

School Name	Enrolment	Girls	Boys	Level	Tehsil/ Town	District
*Zoya SS, Garibabad	403	202	201	Elementary	Kot Addu	Muzaffargah
Zoya SS, Daruhal (by Hina Rabbani Khar's house)	307	160	147	Primary	Kot Addu	Muzaffargah
*Zoya SS, Nala Khudadad	157	75	82	Secondary	Kot Addu	Muzaffargah
Zoya SS, Essenwala	326	135	191	Primary	Kot Addu	Muzaffargah
Zoya SS, Usmanabad (biggest & oldest)	468	175	293	Elementary	Muzaffargah	Muzaffargah
Zoya SS, Ramzanabad	172	7	95	Primary	Muzaffargah	Muzaffargah
Zoya SS, Cheenwala	319	120	199	Elementary	Kot Chuta	Dera Ghazi Khan

*Personally visited by the author.
Source: Zoya Science Schools Annual Report[39]

The medium of instruction for science is Saraiki, the local language, to enable better understanding. They use poems and songs in Saraiki to teach the fundamentals of math and science including songs 'on Pythagoras theorem and its proof, Galileo and Heliocentrism, how Al-Biruni, Eratosthenes, Aryabhata measured the earth's circumference, circles, triangles, etc.' This captures the essence of using mnemonics for learning.

The banner of the Zoya Science Schools, as seen in Figure 6.6, symbolically reflects this pedagogical vision. It depicts a strong girl, the kind they want to graduate from the Zoya Schools. Khwaja described that the background is the sun, the light. The idea for the banner is taken from Edvard Munch's painting in the Norwegian parliament; the girl is Lady Liberty from a Delacroix painting, but dressed in local clothes; the head is Cindy Crawford when she was young; and the hand is from a Soviet war poster (The Motherland Cries for You). The girl is emerging from this new sun that has been made possible by the Zoya Schools. The lower hand is a fist, just as Athena emerges from her father Zeus, the core name of Zoya. Zeus evolved in Arabic to have 'Zo' as the core word, and it became Zoya. The website continues the description,

> From this outburst of hope emerges, as Athena from the head of Zeus, the resolute (marked by her clenched left fist), noble, courageous, and advancing figure of the girl of Zoya Science School, breaking free of the tyranny of ages and custom, daring to be the first drop of hope in an oppressive land, and Lady Liberty-like beckoning to a bright future.[40]

The areas where Zoya Science Schools are built are severely impoverished. The schools conducted a nutrition survey of the children in three schools—800 children—and found that 90 per cent of the children were short and underweight, stunted. Most of the areas where the schools are built have no other school nearby. Since then, they have begun the Ghazai (Nutrition) programme to provide food (a glass of milk and banana, twice-weekly) to over 650 children at the Zoya Science Schools in Daruhal and Essenwala.

I visited two of the Kot Addu Zoya Science Schools and spoke with many teachers and students there. One of the schools, in Nala Khudadad, is attended mostly by Shias, a community that has endured a lot of violence in southern Punjab. When I talked with students about terrorism, their responses made it apparent that they had personal experiences with violence. When I asked female students about how to bring about peace and eliminate violence and extremism, I received the following responses,

- A female student spoke strongly with resolve, and said that as a nation, we have messed up and brought ourselves to this point. We (her generation) are the only ones who will be able to bring the country out of this.
- Another girl said that we should live in love and harmony as a nation, without letting our differences violently divide us.

I spoke with girls in the Nala Khudadad Zoya Science School who were in their first year of FSc (11th grade). Many of them had studied elsewhere, but enrolled in this school because they were able to continue with their science studies here. It was nearby to where they live, so convenient because they could just walk to the school. When I asked them about what they aspire to do when they grow up, their responses were quite similar—but not identical—to what I had heard at the Bacha Khan schools,

- I enjoy and love my studies, and want to become a doctor to serve my community and my country.
- I would like to serve my country, either as a doctor or else join the military and become a pilot.
- I want to serve my country and my nation as a doctor.
- Peace is necessary for every country, and we should spread the message to the people that we should work hard towards having a peaceful society. We have to educate people and teach them how important peace is and the only way we can teach them this is from a place of peace and compassion.
- We all should study and become doctors and engineers and set an example for other girls, as well as for boys, so they can see that these girls can study and make something out of their lives, so they will follow us. People in our country need greater awareness.
- We need to get rid of the terrorism we have been living with, so we can live in peace and harmony.

- Education is key to a peaceful society. There are some madrassas where people are misguided, and the only way we can achieve our goals to live in a peaceful society is to teach people.
- We need to get rid of sectarian conflict so we can all become one nation and one country, period.

This girl was implying that 'we Pakistanis' should stop fighting against each other because of different beliefs.

Boys at the Garibabad Zoya Science School with whom I spoke tended to have less passionate responses, but it also seemed that many of these boys were stunted. This is one of the poorest communities where Zoya Schools have been constructed, and the boys were clearly happy that they are able to attend such a good school and not have to pay any school fees. When asked what they like about the school, responses were,

- The teachers are good because they explain things very well. They teach us with love and their knowledge gets transferred to us.
- We will try everything possible that we can do to work for peace. I will do anything I can to bring peace to Pakistan, even if I have to lose my own life in trying.
- Wealthy people should treat poor people respectfully, but they often don't. Otherwise poor people will just turn into terrorists. So poor people should be treated well.
- Becoming united as a nation is the only way we can actually work together to spread peace.
- I want to be in the army and protect my country.
- I want to become a lawyer so I can seek justice for people.
- I want to be a doctor because I want to help people; I have great interest in serving other people.
- I want to join the army so I can eliminate terrorism.

I asked these boys questions similar to what I had asked the older students at Bacha Khan schools, namely what they would tell a brother, cousin, or friend who told them they were frustrated and were leaving to join the Taliban. Some responses were less focused on the consequences of what would happen to their relatives and more about the social implications of the act of moving away and joining a terrorist organization. They said,

- I will advise him to be patient, because sometimes people make a decision when they are emotional, and later on they realize that the step they took had grave consequences.
- I would try to stop him, but if I can't stop him, then he will face the consequences by losing his life doing that, being a terrorist.
- I will try to convince him that the fruit that comes from being patient is sweeter, and tell him that the reward that comes from being patient is great. But if he doesn't listen to me…
- We would try to convince him that he should stay and work here, where there are business opportunities. You're not going to have these opportunities over there, because a person going from here to there doesn't get any chances.

They put on a powerful play for me when I was there, as seen in Figure 6.7. At first it seemed like the kind of play organized at schools throughout the country: everyone was invited to have a role in it. It began with children playing, and then they started to organize to walk to school. One boy said he had to stay back that day, because his father needed his help in the shop. Then we heard a big explosion followed by wailing: the boy and his father had both been killed by an extremist suicide bomber. Each of the student actors talked about a similar loss they had endured and I realized that for them, this was no work of fiction. This was a catharsis, an opportunity to express something that every child in the area had experienced. They had all been victims of violence.

I also visited the Garibabad Zoya Science School in a different part of Kot Addu. Teachers and students had similar stories to share with me about the appreciation they had for their school. Nearly all of them walked to the school from the nearby neighbourhood, so parents were not afraid to send their children out of concern for their safety. The students here put on a different kind of play for me that was written by one of their teachers. A feudal landlord comes to the Zoya School and adds an extra '0' to how much people owe him, so they are now in greater debt. A student, however, catches the mistake, and they all grab the landlord and beat him.

The awareness of the fraud was only possible because the student could read. This satisfaction is also captured in the Zoya Schools' anthem which, in Saraiki (a variant of Punjabi), declares that 'now our children won't be grazing the animals of the landlord; they will be thinking the thoughts of the country.'

I asked many students about the kind of job they would want to do when they grow up. As common in mainstream schools throughout Pakistan, they said they want to become doctors, engineers, computer scientists, and a few said teachers. But unique to other responses I've heard in regular schools in Pakistan but similar to what I heard at the Bacha Khan schools, when I asked why they gave this response, they said it is to make their contribution for a better, peaceful Pakistan. Both kinds of curriculum, at the Bacha Khan schools and the Zoya Science Schools, are proving to be powerful ways to claim authentic identity, imbibe knowledge, and counter violence and extremism.

Notes

1. A.H. Nayyar and Ahmed Salim, 'Glorification of War and the Military,' in A.H. Nayyar and Ahmad Salim (eds.), 2005, *The Subtle Subversion: The State of Curricula and Textbooks in Pakistan (Urdu, English, Social Studies, and Civics)*, Islamabad: SDPI, p. 79. Accessible at: https://www.sdpi.org/publications/files/State%20of%20Curr&TextBooks.pdf.

2. There are a number of excellent works that have been written about Sir Sayyid Ahmed Khan, the Aligarh movement and its influence on Muslims in British India. *See* for example David Lelyveld, *Aligarh's First Generation: Muslim Solidarity in British India*, Princeton, N.J., Princeton University Press, 1978, Hafeez Malik, *Sir Sayyid Ahmad Khan and Muslim Modernization in India and Pakistan*, New York, Columbia University Press, 1980 and Shafey Kidwai, *Cementing Ethics with Modernism: An Appraisal of Sir Sayyed Ahmed Khan's Writings*, India, Gyan Publishing House, 2010. *See* also Syed Masroor Ali Akhtar Hashmi, *Muslim Response to Western Education: a Study of Four Pioneer Institutions*, New Delhi, India, Commonwealth Publishers, 1989 which analyzes the four major educational institutions established by Muslim leaders in the nineteenth century in British India (e.g., Darul 'Ulum Deoband; Mohammadan Anglo-Oriental College, Aligarh; Darul 'Ulum Nadwatul 'Ulama, Lucknow; and Jamia Millia Islamia, Delhi).

3. This figure is for both public and private schools and includes schools in areas that are today in Bangladesh. Pakistan Bureau of Statistics 'Education' n.d., p. 175, accessible at: http://www.pbs.gov.pk/sites/default/files/50_years_statistics/vol1/12.pdf.

4. Pakistan Bureau of Statistics 'Pakistan Statistical Yearbook, 2016,' Islamabad, 2016, p. 126, accessible at: http://www.pbs.gov.pk/sites/default/files//PAKISTAN%20 STATISTICAL%20YEAR%20BOOK %2C%202016.pdf.

5. Pakistan government expenditures on education as a percentage of GDP in 2018 were 2.8 per cent, according to the UNDP *Human Development Report*, accessible at: http:// hdr.undp.org/en/countries/profiles/PAK.

6. Pakistan introduced its first Five-Year Plan, the first of a series of nationwide economic plans, targets, and development priorities, in 1948, although it did not become a formal policy until 1955. Pakistan is currently trying to achieve the goals outlined in the eleventh Five-Year Plan.

7. The SDGs succeeded the Millennium Development Goals (2000–2015) which were eight priorities for combatting global poverty, inequality and achieve development globally. The seventeen SDGs prioritize achievable, sustainable development. Pakistan met none of its MDGs and the state—under pressure from global donors—hopes to achieve at least some of the SDGs.

8. 1973 Constitution of Pakistan, Part II Fundamental Rights and Principles of Policy, Chapter I, Fundamental Rights.

9. A.H. Nayyar, and Ahmad Salim (eds.), 2005, *The Subtle Subversion: The State of Curricula and Textbooks in Pakistan (Urdu, English, Social Studies, and Civics)*, Islamabad, SDPI, p. vi, accessible at: https://www.sdpi.org/publications/files/State%20 of%20Curr&TextBooks.pdf.

10. Azhar Hussain, Ahmad Salim, and Arif Naveed. 'Connecting the Dots: Education and Religious Discrimination in Pakistan: A Study of Public Schools and Madrassas', Washington, D.C., United States Commission on International Religious Freedom (USCIRF), November 2011, pp. 10–11.

11. Ibid., p. 11.

12. Ibid., p. 10.

13. A.H. Nayyar, 'Insensitivity to the Religious Diversity of the Nation,' in A.H. Nayyar and Ahmad Salim (eds.), *The Subtle Subversion: The State of Curricula and Textbooks in Pakistan (Urdu, English, Social Studies, and Civics,* Islamabad, SDPI, 2005, p. 30. There are many more examples like this one—many even more divisive—identified in this study, though as it is tangential to this chapter we won't explore them further here.

14. Mohammad Pervez, 'Primary Education: A Critique of the Curriculum' in A.H. Nayyar and Ahmad Salim (eds.), *The Subtle Subversion: The State of Curricula and Textbooks in Pakistan (Urdu, English, Social Studies, and Civics),* Islamabad, SDPI, 2005, p. 105.

15. A.H. Nayyar 'Insensitivity to the Religious Diversity of the Nation' in A.H. Nayyar and Ahmad Salim (eds.), *The Subtle Subversion: The State of Curricula and Textbooks in Pakistan (Urdu, English, Social Studies, and Civics)*, Islamabad, SDPI, 2005, p. 43.

16. Muhammad Ali Anwar, 'Mushroom growth of Deeni Madaris', *Dawn,* 24 May 1997 writes that four sects have been the most prominent in creating such schools: Deoband, Barelvi, Ahl-e-Hadith, and Ahl-e-Tashi.

17. A.H. Nayyar, 'Insensitivity to the Religious Diversity of the Nation' in A.H. Nayyar and Ahmad Salim (eds.), *The Subtle Subversion: The State of Curricula and Textbooks in Pakistan (Urdu, English, Social Studies, and Civics)*, Islamabad, SDPI, 2005, p. 43.

18. Confidential interview conducted in Islamabad, December 2017.

19. Zahid Shahab Ahmed argues that peace education programmes have reached a minor fraction of the country's 35,000 madrassas in 'Idealism versus Pragmatism in Teaching Peace in Pakistan', *Peace Review*, vol. 30, no. 3, 2018, p. 333.

20. Chapter 5 discusses some 'ulema who are taking activist stances to counter violence and extremism in the country and teaching tolerance and acceptance of diversity in their madrassas. These, however, appear to still comprise a minority.

21. Azhar Hussain, Ahmad Salim, and Arif Naveed, 'Connecting the Dots: Education and Religious Discrimination in Pakistan: A Study of Public Schools and Madrassas' Washington, D.C., United States Commission on International Religious Freedom (USCIRF), November 2011, p. 9. The five madrassa boards are: Wafaq ul-Madaris al-Arabia (Deobandi); Wafaq ul-Madaris al-Salifia (el-e-Hadith); Tanzim ul-Madaris (Barelvi); Rabta ul-Madaris (Jamaat-e-Islami); and Wafaq ul-Madaris (Shia).

22. Ibid., p. 10.

23. This is from NACTA's (National Counter Terrorism Authority) policy on Madaris reforms, accessible at: https://nacta.gov.pk/madaris-reforms/.

24. Confidential interview conducted in Multan, 16 November 2017.

25. Alif Ailaan, '25 Million Broken Promises: The Crisis of Pakistan's Out-of-School Children', Islamabad, Alif Ailaan, 2014, p. ix, accessible at: https://www.alifailaan. pk/25_million_broken_promises_gallery-pubs.

26. From the BKTEF website, accessible at: http://bkefoundation.org/index. php?option=com_content&view=article&id=63&Itemid=67.

27. Scott Baldauf, 'Pashtuns are not all warrior fire', *Christian Science Monitor*, 16 January 2003, accessible at: https://www.csmonitor.com/2003/0116/p12s01-lire.html.

28. This quote is on the BKTEF website, accessible at: http://bkefoundation.org/index. php?option=com_content&view=article&id=85&Itemid=103

29. D.G. Tendulkar, *Abdul Ghaffar Khan: Faith is a Battle*, New Delhi, Gandhi Peace Foundation, 1967, p. 59.

30. This section is based on various interviews held with Dr Khadim Hussain in Peshawar between 2017 and 2019.

31. *See* http://bkefoundation.org/index.php?option=com_content&view=article&id=69 &Itemid=97.

32. All of the quotes attributed to students at Bacha Khan schools that follow were gathered during this time period. For the purpose of confidentiality, I am neither identifying the name of the student nor the location of the school. Aneela Sulaiman provided invaluable help translating Pashto statements for me.

33. Conveyed in an interview at a study circle held at the BKTEF headquarters in Peshawar, January 2017.

34. Conveyed to me in an interview with Khadim Hussain in Peshawar, 30 January 2019.

35. Abū al-Rayḥān Muḥammad ibn Aḥmad al-Bīrūnī (973–1052) was an Iranian polymath who was an astronomer, mathematician, ethnographer, anthropologist, historian, and geographer; he published extensively on astronomy and mathematics.

36. George Sarton (1884–1956), a Belgian-born chemist and historian, is considered the founder of the discipline of the history of science and sought to make connections between the sciences and the humanities. He traveled throughout the Muslim world in his scientific pursuits.

37. All references to Sarmad Khwaja in this section are based on interviews with him in Islamabad and extensive email correspondence.

38. From a page on the Zoya Science School website, accessible at: https://zoyaschool.edu.pk/meeting-zoya-school-higher-education-commission-chairman.

39. 1 July 2018–30 June 2019, p. 6.

40. This is from the Zoya Science Schools website, accessible at: https://zoyaschool.edu.pk.

7 | Communal and Social Actions

Fig. 7.1: *Sheema Kirmani and Hyderabad WAF members dance defiantly at the tomb of Lal Shahbaz Qalandar in Sehwan following the terrorist bombing, February 2017.*

There are numerous arenas where communal social activism is occurring today in Pakistan, and countless examples can be presented of direct attempts by groups to mobilize and consciously and deliberatively do something against violent extremism. There are copious one-off events, such as when dancer Sheema Kirmani[1] and women from the Hyderabad Women's Action Forum (WAF) raced to the *dargah* of Lal Shahbaz Qalandar in Sehwan, Sindh, in February 2017, four days after violent extremists sought to destroy it and killed nearly eighty-five people in the attack.[2] In front of the shrine, as shown in Figure 7.1, they defiantly danced the ecstatic Sufi *dhamaal*[3] as an act to tell the terrorists that they cannot stop the celebration of the mystic. Notwithstanding the importance of such discrete acts, this chapter is instead concerned with actions that bring communities together and mobilize them to bring about long-term change. Of the many possibilities, the ones selected have the determination that they actually *are* having an impact and making a difference, and their inclusion provides insights into the wide spectrum of ongoing communal actions in Pakistan to counter violent extremism in myriad ways.

This chapter focuses largely on groups standing together to advocate for better lives and peaceful environments, as these kinds of activities have the most pervasive and long-lasting effect. It explores the Bhittai Social Watch Advocacy (BSWA) in Khairpur, Sindh and their priorities to facilitate communities' success in conflict resolution as a counter to extremism, the Pashtun Tahafuz Movement (PTM) that is struggling to get the injustices perpetrated against Pakhtuns acknowledged and stopped, Lok Sujag's efforts to deliver health information and local news in southern Punjab, the Orangi Pilot Project (OPP) that counters extremism through fighting poverty in Karachi, and Khwendo Kor's Viable Village project that seeks to reconstruct social relations from the ground up in villages in Khyber Pakhtunkhwa, the former FATA area and a few in Sindh.

The above, comprising the bulk of the chapter, is followed by an exploration of three small group initiatives as examples of communal social activism happening throughout the country but at a more individual level. These include critical thinking messages found in Creative Frontiers' *Paasbaan* comic books to promote youth to make choices in thinking about violent extremism, Aghaaz-e-Dosti's efforts to promote understanding between Pakistani and Indian children, and Taangh Wasaib's Peace Park in Sargodha, Punjab that enables the local community to gather together, resolve conflicts, and speak out for peace. Finally, this chapter concludes by looking at the modest activities of communal social activism underway in Pakistan to reclaim cultural space occurring in public venues including The Second Floor (T2F) in Karachi, Khanabadosh in Hyderabad, and Books n' Beans and the Last Word in Lahore.

GROUPS STANDING TOGETHER

There are a number of groups in Pakistan that exist with a key goal to promote conflict resolution within communities. One example is the Bhittai Social Watch Advocacy (BSWA), located in Khairpur, Sindh. BSWA is engaged in a variety of activities, all with the goal to bring communities closer together which, in turn, deliberatively repels the lure of extremism.

A group of social activists in village Sadarji Bhatyoon, district Khairpur, led by Khadim Hussain Mirani came together in 1995 over concern for the lack of basic educational facilities, health services, and annual flooding of the nearby Indus River which profoundly affected the lives of poor people in the area. They formed BSWA, initially called the Bhittai Social Welfare Association, under the Sindh Provincial Welfare Act (the Voluntary Social Welfare Agency [Registration and Control] Ordinance 1961).[4] 'Bhittai' was adopted from the name of the Sindhi poet, Shah Abdul Latif, who had taken the name 'Bhittai,' the place where he had settled and who, they felt, spoke to all Sindhis, regardless of class or religion. From the outset, BSWA's vision has been to build a peaceful and prosperous society,

> to empower the marginalized community through building their capacities and align them with state organs or nation building institutes. Hence they can enjoy their social, political, economic, and cultural rights in (an) eco-friendly environment.

As they transformed from a voluntary social welfare association to a mid-level development organization, they changed the name to Bhittai Social Watch & Advocacy (still BSWA).

BSWA's thematic areas are to promote peace and harmony, human rights, healthcare, education, sustainable livelihoods, disaster risk reduction, and climate change. These themes are captured in their eight objectives,[5]

1. To educate and capacitate the marginalized communities for their legal and basic human rights;
2. To develop support mechanisms with district and local governments for initiating and streamlining community development programmes;
3. To take efforts to harmonize public and private institutions to provide effective education at various levels;
4. To create awareness among people of Sindh regarding environment and climate change;

5. To ensure participation of women in all development activities and introduce tools and methods for the economic well-being of women;

6. To capacitate farmers to use sustainable agriculture techniques;

7. To sensitize communities on sustainable development and social, economic, ecological, and cultural effects of mega projects on human life and their livelihood;

8. To highlight indigenous culture through traditional celebrations and relevant cultural activities aiming to educate people for change.

Their activities have become deeply concerned with the social impact of tribal conflicts, why intolerance has been growing among groups and tribes, and how best to promote peace and harmony at the local level. They realized the need to address intolerance and tribal conflicts after the devastating 2010 flood, when BSWA engaged with various groups in twelve nearby flood-affected areas to teach people how to fend off the annual natural disaster of floods. The area was also becoming overwhelmed with local conflicts and terrorism. BSWA conducted a study in 2012, to understand both the historical prevalence of tribal conflicts in the interior of Sindh as well as how they have become more intense and widespread. They concluded that the cause behind this is political,

> Political factors have significantly enhanced the severity, complexity, and frequency of the conflicts. The dictatorial regime of General Zia ul Haq is believed to have manipulated social conditions in Sindh to escalate tribal conflicts. Zia gave unconditional powers to feudal lords/*waderas* in Sindh, and even police remained under their virtual control. The massive flow of weapons, particularly during the Afghan war period, has also contributed to escalation of conflicts. Moreover, unchecked supply of arms continues to prevail even today.[6]

Therefore, they set out to address conflict resolution between groups in the flood relief work they were doing as well as in their educational programmes. Khadim Mirani said that in the area where they were working, one of the groups was the Narejo tribe who were often viewed as criminal provocateurs, essentially 'the most wanted' at the local level. The few schools their children could attend only went up to Class 5. BSWA also set out to improve the schools and help children be successful in them. They taught students to care for the environment, 'to live beside nature' and not to cut the trees as this leads to disastrous flooding. They also worked with children on their mental attitudes too, 'if something bad happens, they shouldn't just fall apart.' They pointed out to students and to community members that there is a connection between the natural environment, people getting frustrated and fighting,

> We talk to people about protecting their environment. Like in the River Indus area, those areas where there are no trees, there is a huge problem for livestock. We want to give them a cultural environment where they can survive.

When they thought they were finished, the Narejo pleaded with them not to leave so that their children wouldn't grow up to be like them. BSWA continued working there and were able to get the Sindh Education Foundation (a partnership between the World Bank and the Sindh government) to support the schools they had helped develop.

Their work building schools and strengthening school management committees, based on community participation, is also at the heart of their efforts to promote conflict resolution given education's salience to counter extremism and promote communal harmony. They work with the local community and with the Sindh Education Foundation (an effort of the Government of Sindh) to build schools in remote areas and to oversee their functioning, particularly the enrolment of girls, recordkeeping, and other operations. At one of the schools I visited in the Narejo area, depicted in Figure 7.2, I saw three young girls sitting outside the school while it was in session. They were waiting for the cousin of one of the girls. They told me they would like to attend the school too, but their fathers forbid it. I realized then that it takes time for such new institutions to take hold in remote areas, despite the state's mandate that every child is entitled to receive education.

Another central priority for BSWA has been its Peace My Rights campaign, initiated in 2010 in response to the expanding tribal conflicts, the rise of extremism, growing violations of basic human rights, addressing the law and order situation as well as poor governance, and brainstorming on best practices possible for local actions and interventions.[7] They adapted the traditional village *katchahries*[8] into the Peace My Rights campaign. All community members were to be welcome, unlike in the traditional *jirgas* where elites have greater influence. Khadim Mirani considers that in a *katchahri*, 'they try to sort things out peacefully—but in the *jirga*, they will decide things for their own interests.' He sees the local *katcahri* as a positive institution where people sit together and resolve things. They identify someone who is neutral—not biased—sometimes even from a different area to help the process. As per the local cultural tradition, the arbiter is fed, though not given any payment (so being an arbiter doesn't become a commercial endeavour).

In Sajjan Mahesar in district Taluka Kingri, a village about an hour's drive from Khairpur, BSWA has engaged with residents since the onset of the Peace My Rights campaign. Before someone in the village came to Khadim Mirani and asked for BSWA to assist them, generations-long feuds had become the norm here. When villagers met with me in January 2018 as depicted in Figure 7.3, they retold stories of individuals from one tribe being shot by individuals from another, and a virtual revolving door of men being picked up by the police on charges laid out in FIRs.[9] The village had become dysfunctional, with crops not tended, communal and family relations suffered, and no advances were being made such as building a school for the village children. But today, nearly a decade later, following BSWA's consistent engagement with the villagers and working with them on conflict management techniques, the village has become a wholly other place. When a conflict erupts, the villagers gather at a *katchahri* and work it out amicably. The community has joined together and built a school and even developed a collective savings effort to purchase an ambulance for the village to help anyone get to Khairpur in an emergency.

BSWA has scaled up the Peace My Rights initiative with the Amun Dost (Peaceful Friends) Network. They created the network to bring together local peacemakers just as, with the Sindhi tradition, all villagers regardless of creed become involved whenever there is a religious celebration. For example, during the Shia rituals associated with Ashura,[10] local Sunnis help arrange for water and Hindus help carry the flags. When Sunnis celebrate something such as the Prophet's birthday, other communities become involved. So too with Christian holidays and Hindu festivals. In an effort to recreate the interfaith ties that had traditionally existed but which were being dissipated with the rise of violent extremism, BSWA set out at both the town (union council) and district levels to identify authority figures—religious leaders, teachers, singers, poets, and even traditional storytellers—who can intervene to help resolve conflicts. They have since scaled up that network and also brought in various local civil society organizations in thirteen districts to create the Sindh Amun Forum. It holds regular quarterly meetings and comes together quickly if there is a crisis. For example, in 2014, in Larkana, there was a blasphemy allegation that a Hindu had burnt some pages of a Quran which sparked a violent reaction and some Muslims set out to destroy a local Hindu temple. As soon as BSWA heard about what was happening, they activated their networks. They all went to Larkana, supported the Sindh Amun Forum network, and calmed the community.

Another incident occurred in the Khairpur area in 2012. A Shia-Sunni conflict erupted and the local police put the area under curfew for two days. Members of the network communicated with one another and they decided to write *Amun Mere Haq* (Peace is My Right) on a banner and organized an Amun rally; everyone joined including women and children. BSWA members went to the police and said this is a miscommunication and there should not be a curfew, and it was lifted. The next day, BSWA put on a 'Peace Mela' (Peace Celebration) on an emergency basis, which brought the local community together and helped further diffuse the crisis. Amun rallies are still held on a regular basis, as shown in Figure 7.4.

BSWA is also involved with skill development and facilitating income-generating activities given their understanding that poverty itself often leads to conflict and violence and that this is an important way to promote gender equity. They set up the Youth Multiple Skill Training Centre in Taluka Kingri to teach various crafts and have organized about two hundred women into the Bhittai Sartyoon Development Cooperative Society. This group now partners with Khaadi, a nationwide popular fashion retailer, to acquire raw materials for women to make baskets and receive training by a Khaadi employee on the designs that Khaadi wants them to make, as shown in Figure 7.5.

Given BSWA's focus on promoting harmony and understanding, we have seen how it has conducted research on timely issues and developed a wide range of activities on the ground. While a decade ago, violence and conflict characterized the interior of Sindh, because of BSWA's actions the area has undergone profound transformation and is largely peaceful today.

The Pashtun Tahafuz Movement (PTM)

The Pashtun Tahafuz Movement (Pakhtun Protection Movement, PTM) was formed to counter violence perpetrated against Pakhtuns and for it to be acknowledged and stopped. The PTM emerged after the extra-judicial murder of Naqeebullah Mehsud, originally from Waziristan, in a police encounter in Karachi on 13 January 2018, prompting demonstrations and protest marches seeking the most basic of rights—the right not to be harmed or killed simply on the basis of ethnic identity—for Pakhtuns. This is comparable to the Black Lives Matter movement in the United States. Naqeeb had been a shopkeeper and an up-and-coming model, and an inquiry team of senior police officers probing the incident concluded that the twenty-seven-year-old father of three was killed in a 'fake encounter' which was 'staged' by police officer Rao Anwar, and that Naqeeb had no links or sympathies with militancy. On 26 January 2018, the PTM began a protest march in Dera Ismail Khan which progressed to Peshawar, winded its way through other cities and then became a sit-in in Islamabad on 1 February, which eventually included over 6,000 protestors outside of the National Press Club. This is a noteworthy location given that the Long March received no mainstream media coverage whatsoever; when I inquired why, journalists told me either that it wasn't an important story or that they were prevented from covering the story.[11] The protestors' demands were,

- Justice for the murder of Naqeebullah Mehsud as well as for all other Pakhtuns murdered extra-judicially in police encounters;
- The formation of a judicial commission to investigate police encounters;
- The de-mining of erstwhile FATA;
- To stop racial profiling of Pakhtuns and to bring Pakhtun missing persons before a court of law—the PTM has compiled a formal list of missing persons with 1,200 names—so that those who are innocent but held could be freed;

- The Pakistan Army should guarantee that they will not abduct or open fire on innocent people in the tribal areas or use violence or collective punishment against entire villages and tribes (this is based on the colonial Frontier Crimes Regulation Act, which was still in force then, but has since been repealed);
- A reduction of military curfews and check-posts in the tribal areas;
- The return of thousands of missing Pakhtuns who are allegedly being held by the army and its intelligence services.

Raza Wazir, a graduate student in Punjab originally from Waziristan, published a powerful article in *The New York Times* in March 2018, in which he sympathized and identified with Naqeebullah Mehsud who like him, 'was trying to build a life in a Pakistani city far from home. Doing that requires acts of will and hope despite an awareness of a history of neglect, prejudice, and violence that the people of the tribal areas share with Pakistan.' He eventually travelled from Lahore to Islamabad to join the PTM sit-in,

> On 8 February, I set out from Lahore in a bus to join them. On the ride, I thought of the personal and political history that had shaped our lives, brought us to the moment when thousands of Pashtuns were gathering in an unprecedented protest to say treat us with dignity and as equal citizens.[12]

He writes of the horrors and tragedies he witnessed in Waziristan and captures what drove other Pakhtuns from all over Pakistan to travel to Islamabad to join the sit-in,

> The murder of Mr Mehsud became the tipping point that compelled young Pashtuns to gather in Islamabad by the tens of thousands to raise our long- suppressed voices, to express the accumulation of pain and frustration over the past sixteen years of war…The protesters chanted the refrain of a song about our status as unequal citizens in the independent Islamic Republic of Pakistan 'What sort of independence is this? What sort of independence is this?' I saw a sea of students, lawyers, professors, and doctors. Young and old, men and women. We shared stories of oppression, abuse, and injustice. All of us had lost a friend or

a relative in the unending war. Arbitrary detentions, extrajudicial killings, enforced disappearances in Khyber Pakhtunkhwa and the tribal areas, multiple displacements, the loss of homes and livelihoods, and the maiming and killing of children by the land mines planted during the military operations had all fuelled despair and anger.[13]

Amir Muqam, a Special Advisor to the Prime Minister at the time, announced the decision of the government and the Mehsud tribal *jirga* on 6 February 2018 to accede to four of the demands: that police officer Rao Anwar be apprehended and brought to justice for the murder of Naqeebullah Mehsud as soon as possible;[14] that the clearing of mines in South Waziristan should be sped up and compensation paid to victims; an Intermediate College be established in Naqeebullah Mehsud's name in Makeen village in South Waziristan; and grievances raised by *jirga* members would be addressed as soon as possible.

In exploring the PTM's activities and its non-violent philosophy— which contradicts all the stereotypes about violent Pakhtuns becoming Taliban extremists—it is using the same expressions of powerful cultural sentiments in *jalsas* (public gatherings) that have long mobilized Pakhtuns into solidarity with one another as it reaches out more widely in the country. The demands of Manzoor Pashteen, its leader born in 1994, are clear and simple, as he told a journalist in a newspaper interview when the movement was barely a month old,

> We are not out here to ask for money, or schools, or even roads, our basic demand is the right to life…This is why we are protesting, we want the right to live without being disappeared, without losing limbs to landmines, without being shot in murky police encounters, without being abused and humiliated at every check-post. Are my demands unconstitutional? Don't *you* already have all these rights?[15]

After disbursing on 10 February 2018, the PTM expanded their efforts and held *jalsas* and other events in Lahore, Peshawar, Dera Ismail Khan, Tank , and in Quetta, Zhob, and Killa Saifullah in Balochistan, Karachi in Sindh, and especially all over social media. It has since held rallies in all major cities throughout the country and abroad in Europe.

Journalist Maham Javaid concludes that 'they have found a leader who looks like them, dresses like them and most importantly, dares to speak their truth.'[16] The anthem of the PTM, 'Da Sanga Azadi Da?' (What Kind of Freedom is This?) powerfully captures the zeitgeist of the movement,

> Our youth is being killed; what kind of freedom is this?
> Our houses are being destroyed; what kind of freedom is this?
> Pashtuns are being ruined; what kind of freedom is this?
> The life boat is being torn apart; what kind of freedom is this?
> When they are denying our human rights, there is a need to start
> a rebellion
> Our brave women are being killed; what kind of freedom is this?
> They are being unveiled; what kind of freedom is this?[17]

The PTM didn't just appear out of nowhere. During the colonial period, the British introduced the Frontier Crimes Regulation (FCR) Act in 1901 in the frontier districts, which became the Federally Administered Tribal Areas (FATA) following independence in 1947, comprised of seven agencies and six tribal areas (Frontier Regions, or FRs). But for the FATA areas, this was hardly actual independence. There was no substantive representation in parliament, people could be arrested without having the crime specified, and it allowed for collective punishment of family or tribal members for crimes committed by individuals. Punishments were to be given out by unelected tribal *jirgas*, not by courts. An example can be seen in events that occurred in November 2016, following the murder of a Pakistani Army major. In response, the federal political agent ordered the demolition of a two-story market in Wana, South Waziristan, citing the clause of collective responsibility and punishment in the FCR. This market had been a popular gathering place for local people. Even though the military had detained the Afghan suspect selling arms, under the FCR's clause of collective responsibility, it still went ahead and demolished the market resulting in all of the business owners, collectively, paying for the crime of a single Afghan national. With the passage of the 25th Constitutional Amendment on 31 May 2018, FATA became subsumed into the province of Khyber Pakhtunkhwa and its agencies became distinct districts within the province.

Waziristan, in particular, was severely impacted both by the ongoing war in Afghanistan and by the Pakistan army's operations seeking to exterminate the Taliban from the area. It is estimated that 2 million people were displaced by the violence in Waziristan. Journalist Aurangzaib Khan, in his tribute to Manzoor Pashteen when he was ranked third in the *Herald's* 2018 'Man of the Year' competition, notes that Pashteen's Mehsud tribe was the first to be uprooted in South Waziristan when the Pakistani state began military operations 'in Taliban-infested regions along the border with Afghanistan, in the mid-2000s.'[18]

Many of the PTM's core members had started out in the Pakhtun Students' Federation (PSF) or the newer Peshawar-based National Youth Organization (NYO) started by the Awami National Party (ANP). The leadership of PTM consists of three principal organizers who had all attended Gomal University and hail from the three main tribes of Waziristan: Manzoor Ahmad Pashteen, Mohsin Dawar, and Ali Wazir (Ahmadzai Wazir). Pashteen had previously used his tribal designation, Mehsud, for his surname and had created the Mehsud Tahafuz Party in 2017 to get landmines removed from Waziristan. Following the murder of Naqeeb, he founded the PTM and changed his surname to Pashteen (the South Waziristan pronunciation of Pakhtun or Pashtun) to reflect that the group's goal was to defend all Pakhtuns (not just Mehsuds). Ali Wazir has lost many family members to Taliban violence, including his father, two brothers, two uncles, and two cousins in a single ambush near their home in July 2005 (he was in prison under the FCR at the time) and the family's businesses were targeted. In the first elections held after FATA was merged into Khyber Pakhtunkhwa, in July 2018, both Mohsin Dawar and Ali Wazir were elected as independent candidates to the National Assembly, Dawar from NA-48 (Tribal Area-IX) and Wazir from NA-50 (Tribal Area-XI).

Bushra Goher, a former leader in the ANP, sees Pashteen as 'actually challenging the state's narrative' and sees him as being,[19]

> a humble, simple person. Down-to-earth, patient. His charisma comes from his patience. He listens patiently, and responds patiently. He takes his time. He takes big ideas, breaks them down and gives examples from his own life, and then gives his opinion.

He wasn't the best of orators during the Islamabad protest—but has really developed since then. He's a common man, his entire persona is that he's one of us. No one talks about him as a supreme commander you have to meet through an appointment. When they talk about him as a person, he's not discussed as someone's son, or being from a certain family, but rather as someone who is very common.

As the PTM built momentum, many of Pashteen's supporters claim him as the true heir of Bacha Khan, as depicted in the artwork of Hamidullah Arbab, in Figure 7.6. While separated by nearly a century, they both attracted thousands of people to *jalsas* speaking of Pakhtun nationalism despite restrictions on reporting on them in the media, as seen in Pashteen addressing PTM supporters in another painting by Hamidullah Arbab, in Figure 7.7.

The PTM has consistently kept to their core demand of essential rights for Pakhtuns. A Baloch member of PTM's central committee told me that he thinks PTM has made its main point clearly: Pakhtun lives matter. He said,

> Before PTM, they were not willing to notice our issues. They were dealing with us differently. We were converted into mere statistics…now they have to accept our identity, our national existence, and that there are Pakhtuns suffering from (counter) terrorism and (in)security.[20]

Ali Arqam, a Karachi-based journalist, considers that the PTM has 'been able to raise the question regarding constitutional rights, specifically about the overarching role of the security establishment.'[21] Hina Jilani, a Lahore-based lawyer and one of the founding members of the Human Rights Commission of Pakistan (HRCP), spoke of the importance of PTM when she reflected on the 10 June 2018 *jalsa* in Lahore,

> After a very long time, we are getting to hear voices that are political, but non-partisan, and entirely in favour of human rights—regardless of whether those oppressed are Pashtuns, Punjabis, Hazara, or Baloch—the PTM is a voice for all…This is why the Human Rights Commission of Pakistan is visibly and vocally supporting the PTM.[22]

Khan Zaman Kakar, a Baloch Pakhtun poet (whose poetry is discussed in Chapter 2), has sought to capture the dynamic of the movement and how it speaks to Pakhtun lives in his poetry,

> I want to block the ways of mullahs' thoughts in our homeland
> That's why I am writing poems in praise of girls' beauty.
> A nationalist is one who wants his/her homeland's freedom
> A nationalist is not someone who just carries a red flag.
> If you're writing our private stories in Punjab's newspapers[23]
> Would you think I would not call you a traitor?

Zaigham Khan, writing in *The News*, underscores the importance and timeliness of the PTM and that it has emerged at a critical moment in Pakistan,

> Pakhtuns are talking and Pakistan must listen. They are talking the language of peaceful protest, the most beautiful language human civilization has invented. In order to make sense of these protests, it is important to understand the medium, the message and the messenger. It is equally important to put the current protests in the perspective…Pakistan is emerging out of a bloodbath. Everyone carries some scar from the period when death stalked us on the streets. Fata suffered the most as it was taken over by terrorists who ran their violent unholy emirate from these areas. The military success against terrorists has revived a sense of normalcy to much of Pakistan.
>
> The people of Fata want to come out of the constitutional limbo and live their lives as normal citizens of the state of Pakistan. They have become weary of the cultural stereotyping they once used to wear as a badge of honour. Their movement is a movement for inclusion, not of exclusion or separation. [24]

PTM supporters claim that Pashteen has no formal political structure to mobilize these *jalsas* for him, but rather people just come to hear him talk. He has been accused of being an agent of Afghanistan and an agent of RAW (India's external intelligence agency, the Research and Analysis Wing), similar to charges that had been levelled against Bacha Khan long ago, but his transparent mode of speaking belies these accusations. The military has frequently spoken out against 'engineered protests' when referring to the PTM; Chief of the Army General Qamar Bajwa was essentially accusing the PTM when he stated that 'some internal and external elements are hell-bent upon harming Pakistan's national security and that our enemies… have subjected us to a cruel, evil, and protracted hybrid war.' He added that these protests have been instigated to undo the gains made by the armed forces in the fight against terrorism.[25] It is because of these views that even talking about the PTM today in Pakistan has become forbidden.

Pashteen and other PTM core leaders speak of the experiences they lived through and experienced firsthand appear to be taking their movement to the national stage so others who have also experienced such struggles can join them. They have taken their voices internationally as well and have held *jalsas* in Germany and London which attracted huge crowds; Pashteen has also spoken to gatherings of Pakistanis in Europe on Skype. After Mohsin Dawar was delayed—nearly stopped—from going to London in March 2019, a student at the University of Westminster who went to attend his speech tweeted about the importance of the message that the MNA came to deliver,

> Kudos to @mjdawar who despite the brief chaos @UniWestminster remained unfazed, strong and calm like the mountains of Waziristan from where he comes. The parliamentarian reiterated that PTM has always been and continues to be a non-violent and pro-constitution movement. While rejecting allegations of so-called foreign backing to his PTM, @mjdawar asked whether one even needs such backing to demand basic human rights like no land mines near your homes, a fair trial?[26]

The PTM's efforts to take a stand and raise their voice to counter extremism and promote peace have touched a delicate nerve in official quarters in Pakistan. By being so public, they enable each member to feel ownership of the movement. Nasar Jamal Khattak, a professor at the University of Peshawar, told me that PTM's adversaries consider that it's 'the singer' who is important, more than 'the song,' given the realities of personalized politics in Pakistan, but they have it wrong about the PTM. While we can say the core leadership of the PTM—especially Manzoor Pashteen, Mohsin Dawar, and Ali Wazir—are the singers, in fact, 'people get together to hear the song.' He offered the example of the huge crowd PTM drew in Karachi when their central leaders were prevented from going there. People came to hear the message, 'the song,' because it is speaking truth to power, which is rarely done in Pakistan.

The international press has started giving PTM coverage. Human Rights Watch in mid-February, 2019, demanded that the Pakistan government should conduct a transparent investigation of the Pakhtun grievances being raised by the PTM.[27] An editorial in the country's most important English newspaper, *Dawn*, commemorating the PTM's first anniversary, concurs with this plea for openness. It observes that the movement has consistently held to its core human rights demands, that its agenda is constitutional and its protest nonviolent. Its message resonates with Pakistani youth who desire 'a more equitable relationship between society and the state.' However, it disdains the state's response,

> For all these reasons, therefore, it is regrettable that, barring some initial steps to address their concerns, the response to PTM by the state apparatus and mainstream political classes at both federal and provincial levels has largely been paranoid and counterproductive...Such heavy-handedness towards the movement can only lead to what is most feared—the hardening of their disaffection and the potential for violent factions to emerge. Pakistan can only benefit from the diversity and plurality of public discourse—even dissenting—but it cannot from further bouts of violence. Instead of attempting to discredit and suppress the PTM, it must be brought into the mainstream through an honest and sincere engagement on issues that require systemic reform.[28]

In his own *New York Times* opinion piece, Manzoor Pashteen speaks to the naysayers of the movement and makes a plea for a truth and reconciliation commission to address what has happened in the tribal areas,

> We are not seeking a violent revolution, but we are determined to push Pakistan back toward a constitutional order. We are drawing some consolation from the recent judgment by Pakistan's Supreme Court telling the military and the intelligence agencies to stay out of politics and media. To heal and reform our country, we seek a

truth and reconciliation commission to evaluate, investigate, and address our grievances.[29]

On 26 May 2019, Mohsin Dawar and Ali Wazir led a group of PTM activists to a check-post in North Waziristan near Miranshah when a clash occurred, resulting in three people being killed and fifteen others injured. The Inter-Services Public Relations (ISPR), the military's media wing, claims that the group violently assaulted the Kharqamar check-post; the PTM leaders, however, have said that they were unarmed, denied that the group opened fire and have accused the army of initiating the violence. Ali Wazir and eight other PTM activists were arrested at once and remanded to a Counter-Terrorism Court in Bannu while Mohsin Dawar turned himself in eight days later so that the curfew imposed in Waziristan and in the area of his native village, accompanied by a large number of security forces in the area, would be lifted.[30] The incident has sparked controversy within Pakistan, prompting some to claim that the PTM are traitors while others claim that the military is seeking to exterminate them and stop the Pakhtun protests. PPP Chairperson Bilawal Bhutto Zardari raised concerns that neglecting PTM's demands will create further conflict,

> I have been saying since day one that you may disagree with them (PTM), you can disagree with their point of view 100 per cent, you can argue with them. But, if you will not engage with the young politicians who come from a place such as FATA, if you will not attempt to reduce their grievances or justify their misperceptions, then we have all seen what used to happen during the Musharraf era in Balochistan. We have all seen what happened with Bangladesh, with East Pakistan, following Ayub Khan's dictatorship. And now, if we will label our own citizens, our own children, our own politicians as traitors when they talk about rights, democracy, civil rule of law, then we will set ourselves on a very dangerous path.[31]

Following the arrests of Ali Wazir and Mohsin Darwar, three other prominent members of the movement were arrested in August 2019 along with dozens of others. Amnesty International called on the Government of Pakistan to end its crackdown against the PTM, stating that 'All activists detained for their peaceful activities must be released immediately.'[32]

While the Counter-Terrorism Court initially imprisoned the two MNAs for eight days, they remained incarcerated until 21 September 2019. Manzoor Pashteen was arrested in Peshawar on 26 January 2020 on sedition charges and amid a great deal of protest was finally released a month later on 25 February 2020.

The PTM, importantly, has captured the attention of millions of people in Pakistan who support constitutional rights through a peaceful process. The PTM has indeed been able to give voice to Pakhtuns who are countering extremism.

Lok Sujag

Lok Sujag has worked for over twenty years with rural communities in ten districts in Punjab in a unique effort to bring about positive change through the voluntary effort of groups on the ground. It is a very different kind of organization than BSWA and PTM already discussed in this chapter as it is part-NGO, part-community organizing and part-social activist focused on and implementing tangible issues.[33] Its priority issues are economic inequality, gender discrimination, religious extremism—really extremism of any kind—and fair, democratic governance.

Lok Sujag's background was that of a loose community of people who were 'committed to working towards a society that ensures equitable access to livelihood resources for all and respects their rights irrespective of race, faith, and gender.' Tahir Mehdi, the senior-most member of the group involved since the early 1980s, recalls how student activists then resisted religious extremism with theatre, what he considers as 'a bold and courageous thing to do at that time.'[34] Members of Lok Rehas, briefly part of Ajoka Theatre Company (discussed in Chapter 3), were writing their own scripts and allowing them to rehearse in their studio. They would also gather in peoples' homes to recite Punjabi and Sufi poetry. For ten years, between 1987 and 1997, they performed plays in various locations. After 1991, when they realized the society was opening up somewhat and they had more cultural space, they started working with various NGOs, mostly women's organizations such as human rights lawyer Asma Jehangir's AGHS and Shirkat Gah, which facilitated their plays.

An unease, however, was developing because many of them were not happy with the lack of seriousness that many communities showed about their performances, and that their audiences were not properly acknowledging what they were doing, taking them as a sideshow or a fun thing. So it was in 1997 that the group formed Lok Sujag: 'Lok' meaning folk, and 'Sujag' being the superlative form of 'jag,' an awakening. Their focus shifted to doing solid community work and early campaigns helped build dairy cooperatives in Okara district in Punjab followed by a health campaign against iodine deficiency that was resulting in goitres in Sahiwal. Lok Sujag volunteers focused on 'organized conscious efforts and by institutionalizing these efforts' from within communities, not from the outside or through legal and administrative efforts alone. They sought to arouse communities to design and implement social, political, and economic interventions 'meant to change the existing systems.' To rectify the iodine deficiency, they launched a health campaign and invited doctors and other medical professionals from Lahore to those areas to help them promote iodized salt. They soon realized there were too many fake iodized salt brands, so they started manufacturing their own. Local salt manufacturers would advertise about adding iodine, but usually wasn't present. When they realized this, Lok Sujag trained the local salt manufacturers on how to iodize salt. Lok Sujag helped a manufacturer set up a new salt mill so they and the local people wouldn't have to go to Lahore for the iodized salt. Then to popularize that salt, Lok Rehas performed a play in different villages. They soon realized that taking the play to villages was very expensive so they instead developed a puppet theatre to communicate the message by a local cadre to local people about the need to consume iodized salt.

They began to expand their research and advocacy work on gender, agriculture, health, and politics/governance, many of these on their own and others in collaboration with some leading civil society organizations. Their mainstay was still volunteer work as they consider volunteering a political act, when people don't expect any financial reward. Lok Sujag's two main projects became conducting basic research about agricultural issues and communicating about them with farmers, and creating an open, communicative environment to learn about local news.

Through conducting basic research on the economy of milk, tomatoes, and potatoes, Lok Sujag could communicate with a wide range of farmers on a level they easily understood. Through simple media like newsletters, they would convey messages to farmers about price volatility, food insecurity and other issues that make farmers aware of how they are being unduly singled out and exploited. Lok Sujag activists claim they aspire for a better economic system to fight against poverty. Kashif Baloch told me that they believe 'that behavioral change is the key; it's only possible when you have a clear sense of history, to convince people that this status quo isn't working. We're addressing this on different fronts.'

Since 2014, the bulk of Lok Sujag's work lies in the provision of news, especially on a very local level. They considered that mainstream media was too urban-centric, run by corporate media focused on elite consumers in the major cities, and due to its historic roots, journalism was not focused on news the masses wanted to hear,

> The development of journalism in South Asia is very different than in the West. In the West, they started from local newspapers that became global. In South Asia, it started as a larger national event either against the British or in favor of them—and also focused on foreign issues, of what was happening in other countries. Our Urdu media draws a lot on that, and for them, local issues are not very important. We wanted to change how that functions.[35]

Lok Sujag's website has an entire section that covers news from different districts in Punjab and has over a thousand users in each district;[36] two districts with their widest coverage are Sahiwal and Faisalabad. Instead of hiring local journalists to write the news articles, they went out and nurtured fifteen to twenty young people to write about their own issues in each district. Lok Sujag develops copious YouTube videos on a wide range of subjects that convey its orientation to over 6,000 subscribers. Its videos are divided into seven categories,

- Khichri: Food for Thought
- Kashif Kahani: Kashif Baloch, one of Lok Sujag's founders, opines on 'whatever is happening in corridors of power'
- Dhaba: An open, public place for people to share informed opinions

- Tund-o-Tanz: Comedies, for people who take themselves too seriously
- Basti Basti: Captures the essence of life in small, rural towns
- March On: Explores various dimensions pertaining to women's rights
- Sports: The conventional (cricket) and the not-so-conventional (kabbadi; the rules of judo)

Its videos, accessible via #SujagVideos, address such issues as 'new media for local democratic discourse in Pakistan,'[37] maize crop farming and related farmers' issues,[38] using street theatre to fight against child marriage,[39] climate change,[40] and to stop Hazara Shia genocide.[41] Each of these videos promote public awareness about issues and, in important ways, are striving to counter extremism. Lok Sujag has also transformed traditional stories into radio programmes. For example, activists translated Maxim Gorky's novel *Mother* into Punjabi and produced it into 135 episodes, each about ten minutes long.

When I questioned the impact Lok Sujag is having on countering extremism in Pakistan, people told me that they they're not just working in an organization. Each person is convinced about the importance of ideology, living to make the world better. They said that they have dedicated their lives to doing this,

> People don't expect the things we say to be on social media. We know it's a long process. We've decided that what we believe is true. The impact we've had—do people get the message? I think I have to say yes. It's only the magnitude of its impact that is the question mark.[42]

Their concern is with building bridges of communication between Punjabi villagers. They bring in income for Lok Sujag when they conduct research work, especially at election time, such as the three-volume reference book on the 2013 Pakistan Elections which they made for the Church World Service. They are also concerned with facilitating people to vote, such as when they helped 80,000 women to get identity cards so they could vote in the 2013 Elections. They leased a Mobile Registration Van for ten to fifteen days a month over two years, and sent the van to public places in

Fig. 7.2: A school created by BSWA in partnership with the Sindh Education Foundation. The warm weather in interior Sindh enables outdoor classrooms. It also promotes sports activities, as seen in posters on the school's interior walls.

Fig. 7.3: Villagers in Sajjan Mahesar meeting with BSWA representatives, retelling the history of conflict resolution efforts there.

Fig. 7.4: BSWA staff organizer of the Sindh Amun Forum with qawwali singers who regularly sing at Sachal Sarmast's shrine, January 2018.

Fig. 7.5: Women in the Bhittai Sartyoon Development Cooperative Society making baskets under instruction by a visiting Khaadi employee, organized by BSWA.

Fig. 7.6: Manzoor Pashteen being compared to Bacha Khan, by Hamidullah Arbab.

Fig. 7.7: Manzoor Pashteen addressing PTM supporters, by Hamidullah Arbab.

villages (e.g., schools, clinics) and made announcements about when they would be registering men and when they would register women to vote.

Volunteers with Lok Sujag consider their greatest challenge, aside from the usual lack of resources, is to overcome people not being ready to hear what is being delivered. In their broadcasts and videos, they make a point not to speak aggressively, to use humour often, and to put their ideas in front of people in 'a very civilized way.' Kashif Baloch said that people in Pakistan are now used to listening to 'jingoism' on media, and don't like listening to people talk about minorities' rights or challenges confronting women. They hope to do this effectively on a regular basis and spread their ideas more widely, building a sense within rural communities that they will all stand for one another. In southern Punjab, this is proving to be a highly effective way of countering extremism.

Orangi Pilot Project (OPP)

The Orangi Pilot Project (OPP) is deeply committed to countering extremism in the Orangi slum area of Karachi through engaging local people to make a difference in their physical environment and view themselves as empowered by doing so. Established by Dr Akhtar Hameed Khan in April 1980 by an agreement with Agha Hasan Abidi, then chairman of the Bank of Credit and Commerce International (BCCI) Foundation (now known as the Infaq Foundation), OPP sought to develop models of community participation and local resource mobilization prioritizing low-cost sanitation, housing, health, education, and credit to establish micro-enterprises. In other words, according to its own website, OPP decided to strengthen people's initiatives with social and technical guidance.[43] Anwar Rashid, long-time OPP worker who became director after former OPP director Parween Rahman was killed in March 2013, sees OPP's programmes as providing people with the tools to join them together.[44] Arif Hasan, noted Karachi architect, social activist and mentor to Parween Rahman, observes that structured weekly meetings enabled the knowledge and vision of Akhtar Hameed Khan to be transferred to the OPP staff and community leaders. In the process, 'social organizers became technicians and technicians became social organizers.'[45]

Anwar Rashid said that OPP, from the outset, would begin their activities by talking with members of communities, asking questions and then determining what programmes are required. They would then seek out to identify local activists, people who have already been involved in some action in their own community and need some guidance. They then set out to provide them with training and then with a small amount of support from OPP's Core Fund to help them get started.

In 1988, OPP was upgraded into four independent institutions: the OPP-Research and Training Institute that focuses on low-cost sanitation, housing, education, research, documentation, and advocacy; the Orangi Charitable Trust that operates a microcredit programme; the Karachi Health and Social Development Association which runs a health programme in Orangi; and the OPP Society, a conduit for charitable contributions to the other three entities.[46] Five years later, in 1993, OPP initiated its Youth Training Programme (YTP) to train local young people in surveying, documentation, designing, estimation, construction work, on-site supervision, and community mobilization for the sanitation programme in their respective settlements. Youth were sent out to document water and sanitation needs in their informal housing settlements (*katchi abadis*) and details of land-use, and helped implement solid waste disposal programmes. Many also took the initiative to begin tree plantation programmes in their communities.

Parween Rahman was central to all of OPP's activities. A few months after receiving her architecture degree, she joined OPP along with Rashid Anwar when it was still being run by its founder, Dr Akhtar Hameed Khan, in 1982. She became deeply dedicated to working in the urban slum of Orangi, meticulously tracking land records and helping poor residents to get their land reinstated after it had been illicitly taken, and engaged on a daily basis with a wide array of local people. She was threatened, for years, by various entities seeking to stifle her, to stop her from standing up for local people's land, but she shrugged off the threats. Finally, she was gunned down in her car, returning from work on 13 February 2013. Rashid Anwar, soon after her death, described her as 'a courageous and brave lady. She was a true pupil of Akhtar Hameed Khan who worked in an environment where most people will avoid to work.'[47] She gave local people hope that someone was standing by their side as they would seek 'to fight city hall.' The result was not simply a development project, but something socially transformative that was of interest to and engaged everyone in the community. NED University of Engineering and Technology's Noman Ahmed aptly characterized the special nature of what Parween Rahman did when he said that she became personally involved and empowered communities,

> She involved communities in development work and her cautious endeavour was to empower people and lessen their sense of deprivation. Her motto was way forward. She saw it as a defeat to terrorists by not changing her routine to help people.[48]

While the Orangi area is surrounded by a great deal of violence, the locales within OPP's projects exude tranquillity rarely present in working-class slums.

Today, OPP has become a multi-faceted enterprise in Orangi. The Kitchen Garden programme, with a vision of food security for all in the local community, teaches people how to grow their own food in container gardens, how to recycle water using broken buckets and bottles, and overall how to work to become self-sufficient in food. OPP provides local people with seeds—one person grows spinach, another person grows something else—and they encourage them to trade with each other. They also have an organic farm and the vegetables they grow are half the price that are sold in the market. OPP is also bringing art education into local schools in various towns within a half hour from Orangi. Aquila Ismail, Parween Rahman's sister who has helped run OPP with Rashid Anwar since her sister's death, says that they have become involved in art education because 'it gives people creative thinking, brings people together, and they express themselves, talk with each other.'[49] OPP is now extending their outreach to areas that have been most affected by violent extremism such as Ghotki, Obaro, Shikarpur, and Khairpur in Sindh and Jang, Rajanpur and Layye in southern Punjab.

The importance of the OPP development model as a means to counter extremism is captured by OPP's board member, Arif Hasan, who writes,

> Development does not take place with funds alone. It takes place through the development of skills, self-reliance and dignity. The

three are closely interlinked and follow each other in the order in which they are mentioned. They make relationships within community, and of communities with government agencies, more equitable. This change in relationships brings about changes in government planning procedures and ultimately in policies.[50]

The power of OPP's Youth Training Programme is an example of how to channel the frustration that young people experience when their communities have neither clean water nor sanitation, and come to see themselves as social actors making a difference. The reverberations of the OPP model have been felt throughout Pakistan as other NGOs have sought to imitate it. It's not just self-help or giving people hope: it's teaching them about what they can do to make a difference and facilitating them to do so.

When queried about how he sees OPP countering extremism, Anwar Rashid said that they are making deliberate efforts in their work to convey what it means to be secular, liberal, and progressive. He observed,

> Women from nearby villages come here, mill around—we want the ones who killed Parveen to see this, to see the freedom here. This all is to counter it too. We show Parveen's killers that you have not killed our spirit or what we stand for. You will kill one Parveen, a thousand will rise.[51]

He asserted that the outreach they do in small towns and villages—'neglected areas'—is proving to be very effective as OPP's programmes are 'tools for joining people together' and are the best way to counter extremism.

Khwendo Kor's Viable Village Project

The final organization we discuss in this chapter that is engaged in communal and social activism is Khwendo Kor (KK), which in Pashto means 'Sister's Home.' This participatory development initiative was registered in February 1993 in Khyber Pakhtunkhwa (then the Northwest Frontier Province) and in June 2012 in FATA and remains active wherever health, education, and income generation facilities are either non-existent or dysfunctional and women and the poor are marginalized.[52] It avers that it is, one of the oldest and biggest women-led and women-managed NGOs in this region, well reputed for its service delivery and values in commitment, accountability, integrity, and mutual respect. At present, KK implements projects under the thematic areas of Civil Rights, Health, Education, Economic Empowerment while Humanitarian Response is dealt as a social responsibility.[53]

It has significantly expanded from a small women-oriented NGO to a multi-faceted development organization active in over 250 villages in Khyber Pakhtunkhwa, Sindh, and the former FATA area, operating through eight regional offices which enables it to cover a wide range of remote areas. In all of its work, Khwendo Kor remains deeply committed to its vision of a compassionate society where women live with dignity and self-reliance which is only possible when it is accepted by both men and women in the society alike.

In the areas when Khwendo Kor operates, NGOs have historically been deeply distrusted and often seen 'as disseminating a degenerate western culture.' Given this, Khwendo Kor acknowledges,

> The most difficult part of development work in such areas is gaining access to local people (particularly women) and establishing the trust which will allow the work to begin. It is wasteful and potentially counter-productive to then use such access and trust to deliver only one type of aid and the costs of monitoring, accounting, and reporting can be disproportionately high. Most importantly, such piecemeal aid does not educate the villagers in how to sustain their own development when the project money ceases or security concerns interrupt the flow of aid.[54]

This has motivated Khwendo Kor to engage with villagers in the locales where they work to determine priorities. Khwendo Kor finds that these participatory discussions 'reduce distrust, give confidence and valuable experience to the villagers, provides models which other villages wish to copy, and identifies issues that need to be tackled at a wider policy level.'[55] Khwendo Kor personnel then reach out to politicians and government offices to build on this success, which enables it to be sustainable and to spread.

Over time, Khwendo Kor activists realized that while they were able to succeed in distinct projects, this was not enough to bring in the long-term societal transformations they had hoped for. In 2013, Khwendo Kor's strategic plan recommended adoption of the Viable Village approach which seeks to reconstruct social relations from the ground up in villages where it operates. A Viable Village 'is characterized by a community especially women who own and take the lead to identify, prioritize, and develop potential partnerships to address their issues and needs, on a sustainable basis.'[56] It also aims to make these villages 'viable' so that they have access to basic services and are able to develop these further on their own.

The approach begins with baseline data collection about the needs and issues of the village. Khalid Usman, head of Khwendo Kor's Viable Village initiative said that they endeavour to have women take the lead in this to identify and therefore work to solve their own issues. They then organize both men and women in groups to facilitate developing the capacities of men and women in an area. Importantly, and uniquely, they focus on educating men about the needs of women and the challenges women face, 'embedding and negotiating all these things in different activities' such as when meeting with the community and talking about women's rights issues and other things come out which concern future visions. In addition, they try to include people who the villagers are fearful of, be they religious leaders, local extremists, or others who the villagers perceive have opposed them. Therefore, when Khwendo Kor now begins to work in a village, it agrees on an agenda for change with the local people and negotiates its activities to do six things,

1. Forms local village groups which can identify development needs and help with staff recruitment, monitoring, and supervision. In some areas, it is possible for these groups to mix men and women, but in others it is necessary to form different groups with special objectives but in all areas the participation of women is essential;

2. Sets up a minimum of basic services in each village (e.g., maternity services, education including education for women, microcredit or village banking, again, with priority given to women and disaster management plans which are sensitive to women's needs);

3. Increases local voter registration and helps local people to use their political voice to sustain these services after Khwendo Kor withdraws (again with the priority being to reach women who are traditionally underrepresented in these areas);

4. Shows them how to access other NGOs or government agencies for services which do not fall within Khwendo Kor's areas of expertise;

5. Provides examples of successful practices which appeal to nearby villages and which leads to demands for similar work there, and

6. Works with politicians and line departments of local government to ensure that they become more receptive to local demands, which ensures that the work is neither short-lived nor limited to a particular area.

An example can be seen in the outcome of Khwendo Kor's work on the protection and promotion of women's and children's rights,

> As a rights-based organization, KK has used its basic education, health, and livelihood activities to increase the communities' awareness of their rights, encouraging them to act together and with government to achieve favourable structural changes. At the level of the family, KK has been targeting a campaign at community and religious leaders and relevant government officials. The campaign seeks to make them aware of women's rights to inherit, to give or withhold consent to marriage, and to be free from Gender Based Violence. In collaboration with another partner organization, KK has worked with local organizations and traditional *jirgas* to form Masalihati Anjuman, a body which aims to resolve family disputes. Overall therefore, KK can claim substantial experience of setting up organizations designed to help grassroots communities especially women to claim their rights and substantial experience in campaigns on behalf of women and their children.[57]

The priority, therefore, is no longer just provision of basic services, but an ideology of sharing and mutual empowerment—for men and women alike—that goes along with it. Khwendo Kor has found that this approach yields sustainable, cost-effective, and holistic development and can be scaled up to cover wider and wider areas that promote resilient communities and empowered women. It emphasizes that it works *with* people, not *for* them, involving them in decisions about what should be done, forming committees of men and women to manage services among other activities. Khwendo Kor has seen that local people want development interventions and given that it's a result of their own efforts, can easily accommodate women's involvement in various activities. Khalid Usman says that the understanding gained from all of these encounters is transformative, changing the power configurations within families, within villages, and facilitating them to become viable, peaceful locales that are no longer plagued by violent extremists seeking to break them down.

SMALL GROUPS AND INDIVIDUAL INITIATIVES

There are countless efforts being done on a daily basis throughout Pakistan by small groups or by individuals to counter violent extremism. While the previous section highlights five movements that are seeking to bring about long-term societal transformation, the three initiatives featured here are far more modest in scope and impact. Indeed, the first two projects to be discussed have ceased to exist, at least temporarily, and I'm not sure about the longevity of the third. But I have chosen to include them because of their ingenuity as well as the hope and promise I see within them.

CFX Comics' *Paasbaan* (*The Guardian*) comic books contain critical thinking messages promoting youth to make choices in thinking about violent extremism. The idea behind *Paasbaan* came from an experience of one of its key founders, Gauher Aftab, when he was a 9th grade student at Aitchison College in Lahore in 1996.[58] At the time, as a thirteen-year-old boy, he was enthralled by stories his Islamic Studies teacher would tell them about his experiences fighting with the mujahideen against the Russians in the 1980s; it was an easy transition for him to become enthusiastic about going to Kashmir to fight the new 'jihad.'[59] His family serendipitously ended that plan, and on reflection he realizes how misguided he had been and how close he had come to joining violent extremists,

> I was made to feel disdain against those who chose 'inferior' beliefs; I dehumanised those I wanted to fight, and I belittled the act of taking a life to the point where it seemed like nothing at all—like

brushing away a troublesome insect. When I realised that I had once walked a dangerous path, filled with both darkness and light, I tried to read and learn as much as I could to answer my questions and seek out the truth. I must report that every answer has led me to even more questions, and I have learned just enough to know that I know nothing.[60]

In effect, he realized how quickly young people can be persuaded to hate and engage in violence. He was very concerned about the escalation of violence in Pakistani society and felt that it was just a matter of time before people he knew would be getting shot. In early 2013, such a tragedy took place very close to home as one of Gauher's students lost a father and a brother to a brutal sectarian killing. The incident moved him to believe that the very fabric of Pakistani society could disintegrate if the surge of radical ideologies was left unchecked. Shortly thereafter, he began a youth platform to promote critical thinking and debate skills so that students could learn to evaluate arguments based on logic and evidence rather than be indoctrinated by violent extremist narratives. After the 2014 attack on the Army Public School in Peshawar, he and his associates did a lot of soul-searching. They felt that Pakistan was careening into the fractured space of militancy and they needed to make a difference. They decided to start CFX Comics in early 2015 as a publishing label for youth comics. Gauher thought to use debates and critical thinking skills as a template for the kind of programming, he and his colleagues wanted to promote: active citizenship, positive values and to be able to dissect someone else's argument using empathy and critical thinking.

Gauher's new mission was to address the problem of religious extremism in society through comics. He and his colleagues decided to embark on developing a comic series for schoolchildren and adolescents focused on religious extremism so that children would reject 'the toxic hatred' they saw permeating society. Their goals for the project are captured on the back cover of the *Paasbaan* comic book,

> The aim of this project is to encourage and promote democratic values and peaceful civic engagement as a means of promoting social change through positive role models. The project discusses, through its storylines and messages, in detail the role of citizens in

a democracy and how they should participate in the democratic process.

In January 2015, Gauher began writing the *Paasbaan* story, Yahya Ehsan started drawing the illustrations, and Mustafa and Rebecca Husnain set out to create an app (computer program) for reading the comics online. In March 2015, the award-winning Pakistani writer Amjad Islam Amjad joined them to translate the stories into Urdu. The resultant first issue of *Paasbaan* tells the story of five college friends, all relatable to young readers, and two other evil characters full of rage, willing to strike out in vengeance and having no qualms for being recruiters for violent extremists. The story introduces us to the students, their aspirations and everyday challenges, but then one of the five friends, Asim, goes missing. The story then shifts to how the students brainstorm on finding their friend. The next issues of the comic series show how innovative and creative young people can be in the wake of encountering evil, and how the friends finally stand up for their principles.

When they started to print *Paasbaan* in June 2015, they distributed copies of six issues to 5,000 students in public and low-income schools in Lahore, Multan, and Lodhran districts in Punjab. The CFX team would visit the schools and talk with students about the choices that they would make if faced with such a dilemma. Gauher talks about his experiences when he goes to the schools and tries to draw parallels to the students' own experiences and encourages them to talk about them. He encourages the students to trace through the storyline, engage with the actors involved, address how the actors make moral choices, see what happened to the man who always strikes out in rage, but also to see that everyone is redeemable. Gauher queries them if the fire can be extinguished, can someone reclaim their humanity when they've done so much and killed so many? Many of the students told the CFX Comics team that they have met people like the provocateurs in the stories. For example, during a discussion about the characters and the book, a girl told him about her nine-year-old cousin who had attended a madrassa after school. Some older boys there recruited him to go with them to fight jihad, and he soon went missing, a likely victim of organ harvesting.

The CFX Comics team encountered some backlash at a few schools, but mostly people were enthusiastic about the project. The second year, they expanded their distribution to Muzaffargarh and Bahawalpur. They did surveys and focus groups to see if there were any changes in perception about violent extremism after reading the comic books and found a couple of important impacts. First, students noted that there was a change in how they regarded religious leaders; they realized that they have to think about what religious leaders are saying and can't just accept everything at face value, as it was a sham religious leader who had misled Asim in the story. The second observed change in students' attitudes was how they thought about violence. They had previously thought that if someone doesn't agree with you, you have to fight them, but afterwards, at least half of them changed the way they looked at this.

This inspired the CFX Comics team to explore new opportunities. They started brainstorming on how to get into the debates on jihad and 'mujahid' (one who wages a jihad), and decided to write a series named *Haider*, about various war heroes of Pakistan. They first highlighted Major Aziz Bhatti, the most celebrated war hero of the 1965 war, and then Squadron Leader Sarfraz Rafiqi who is known for having said that it gave him no pleasure to shoot down Indian pilots. Aziz Bhatti became the voice of what is an honourable jihad and who is a 'mujahid' following an argument with another major who denigrated Indians, and articulated what principles they were actually fighting for. The final product that CFX Comics launched, was *Khiladi,* a cricket-themed series, in February 2016 so they could move into conversations about social values, something that rarely occurs in Pakistan.

By this time, *Paasbaan* had nine issues, *Haider* had four, and then they developed four issues for *Khiladi*. All of these animated comics pull readers in and then take a subliminal 'hearts and minds' approach to counter radicalization. But they gave the comics to students for free and despite periodic funding from NGOs and other donors, the effort was not financially viable. The principals had to bring in an income, and the effort was shut down in 2018, though with the hope that they may be able to restart it in the future.

The second initiative to be discussed here is Aghaaz-e-Dosti's efforts to promote understanding between Pakistani and Indian children. Aghaaz-e-

Dosti—the Beginning of Friendship—sought to build bridges in creative ways to foster long-term attitude changes about each other. Its materials state that it is 'a joint initiative of Mission Bhartiyam (India) and Hum Sab Aik Hain (We Are All One, Pakistan) [that] seeks to create unwavering bonds of peace and friendship between India and Pakistan.' Aghaaz-e-Dosti began in India in 2012 and expanded into Pakistan in 2017, conducting 'peace education activities that are aimed at facilitating people-to-people contact, challenging stereotypes, creating a culture of peace, understanding, and faith in dialogue for conflict resolution.'[61]

At the heart of Aghaaz-e-Dosti's efforts are three activities it conducts in schools. It has published eight calendars—the most recent was in 2020—that show the artwork each month of O-level and A-level students. Six of the monthly pictures are from students in India, six from Pakistan, and they all are messages for peace. Ten schools in India, five in Pakistan, and one Indian school in Oman participated in the Aghaaz-e-Dosti initiative and submitted pictures for the 2018 calendar.[62] A sampling of messages written on these pictures are 'Say no to war, we are peace loving nations,' 'India-Pakistan, Stronger Together,' 'We choose Love,' and 'Peace.' The themes invariably show young people reaching out to each other across borders, with flags hanging together. The calendars avidly spark students' interests, and a girl I met at a Bacha Khan school in Peshawar very proudly turned to the month where her picture was showcased.[63]

The second activity that Aghaaz-e-Dosti conducts in schools are letter exchanges. I was shown a number of huge piles of these letters in the Lahore office that were waiting to be distributed to the thirty-one schools participating in the pen pal exchanges in Pakistan that had been sent by students in India, each starting off with 'Dear Unknown Friend.' They were sent in colourful—and coloured—envelopes, some with stickers and glitter, and all conveying a sense of a child writing to a prospective friend.

The third activity in which they engage is classroom to classroom video-links. For a couple of years, Aghaaz-e-Dosti sought to hold a video-link at least monthly between different schools, though they were sometimes held more frequently. In November 2017, I witnessed a video-conference at an upscale Beaconhouse School in Lahore with a school in Delhi, India. The excitement in the 4th grade classroom was palpable as the teachers tried to get the Skype connection working. I chatted with the students—twenty-four in the classroom—and learned that most had been to the US, mostly New York and California, but other places as well. After the connection was made and introductions were completed, the children were invited to come to the microphone and ask a question to the other classroom's students. A student on one side asked what their favourite food was and the other side called out in unison, 'biryani!' The children on both sides began cheering, shouting that everyone loves biryani. A student from the other side came to the microphone and asked what their favourite sport was; the unanimous cheer from the other side was 'cricket!' and again, everyone started celebrating their love for cricket. Other questions ensued, and I became increasingly impressed with the effortless way that children on both sides came to realize the similarities they shared. After the Skype engagement ended, the children in Lahore shared their impressions of their Indian counterparts with me, saying:

'Now we know that they are friendly, they are respectful.'
'They were very patient. They were kind. We like the same sports.'
'They were trying to give us as much information as they could.'
'We are very similar.'
'Their language was different. I think they use British English, which is a bit different.'
'Our national sports are the same. They like cricket.'
'Some of them are vegetarian, and we are not.'

What Aghaaz-e-Dosti is trying to accomplish—promote greater understanding and friendship between children in India and Pakistan—was clearly accomplished that day as these children had a positive experience communicating with one another. I heard from others associated with Aghaaz-e-Dosti that similar kinds of experiences occurred at other schools when teleconferences occurred. Promoting greater understanding between Indian and Pakistani children can certainly go far in countering extremism in the long-term as members of neither side will likely provoke hatred between the two groups in the future.

However, Aghaaz-e-Dosti has ceased to function in a substantive capacity in Pakistan (although it continues to function in India). Merely a month later its main convener, Raza Khan, 'disappeared' late at night from the Aghaaz-e-Dosti office in Lahore (mentioned earlier in Chapter 4). He was released some eight months later and soon after left Pakistan. No one else has stepped forward to run the organization from the Pakistan side, causing it, essentially, to shut down in Pakistan.

The final effort to be discussed in this section is that of the Taangh Wasaib Organization (TWO) in Sargodha. This initiative begun in 1998 by university and college teachers, students, social workers, and local activists aims to promote communal harmony, gender equality, respect for human rights, and peace. It is an independent, not-for-profit non-governmental organization that mainly operates through engaging volunteers and local fundraising. In a relatively short period, the TWO has grown into a vibrant network of linkages with more than fifteen hundred volunteers from Sargodha as well as from Khushab, Mianwali, Mandi Bahauddin, Jhang, Jhelum, Bhakkar, Chiniot, Sialkot, Gujarat, Chakwal, Lahore, and Peshawar.

Current executive director Rubina Feroz Bhatti is a founding member who was a chemistry lecturer and member of the Professors Union in 1998.[64] She recalls that she and her colleagues were outraged when Tajammul Hussain, a Shia Commissioner in Sargodha, was assassinated in 1997. The faculty came together to discuss how they could talk with students regarding what happened which could help them prevent further violence. The founding chairman, Dr Mohammad Ahmed Khan, began to hold study circles with students and faculty where they talked about sectarianism and how radicals recruited students, and they discussed their ideals of communal harmony. They all talked about how the real fight is for human rights, where no one lives in fear. Eventually, they called the study circles 'Dialogue of Life,' with the goal to promote interfaith harmony. They never discussed any particular scripture or theology, but rather just met and discussed general issues like why there aren't adequate roads, why schools perform poorly, etc. Rubina Bhatti recalls that after sometime, other NGOs encouraged them to form their own NGO. The TWO board members didn't want to take money for the organization from outside donors, so they donated their own funds for the group to run.

One of their first activities after becoming a formal group was to organize students to put on street theatre to bring the message of communal harmony literally to the streets. They were more active in the summers when there were school vacations, though they also performed on 8 March, International Women's Day, and on other days celebrating peace. The students would decide when they wanted to put on a certain kind of performance, either a dramatic performance, singing, or even doing mime. The students also decided where they would perform, and often wanted to put up street theatre in the villages where they were from. That they performed in places where they had strong roots in the local community helped as the local community would then organize the space. The plays always promoted social issues, emphasizing interfaith harmony, culture, and promoting peace. Wherever they performed, they invariably generated new volunteers.

TWO built a Peace Garden in the middle of Sargodha to have a place where they could rehearse their plays and gather. They started it on one *kanal*[65] of land in Sargodha that was donated by Father Sohail Patrick. They soon expanded its usage to public gatherings and even rallies. An INGO from Holland gave them a bit of money to create a boundary wall, and the Peace Garden is now six *kanals* in size.

They thought this was a great strategy to create the Peace Garden, which sets TWO's work apart from other NGOs'. Everyone sits on the ground and talks about a wide range of issues with local people. At these gatherings, they question what peace is, the nature of conflict and contradiction, and other social issues that may arise. They encourage differences of opinion so people can understand one another, which finally leads towards peace-building. Some of the sessions are very general while others are with community workers, widows, divorcees, violence survivors, and other groups. The park grew into a site where the local community frequently gathers together, resolves conflicts, and speaks out for peace. Once a year, they used to hold a big event, the Volunteers Convention, at the Peace Garden to appreciate hundreds of volunteers who supported TWO.

They began to engage in other communal activities to promote cooperation and understanding, such as setting up a *chaki* where women can grind flour and make *rotis* together. Rubina Bhatti sees this too as peacebuilding, 'how we meet together within the context of our culture.' They also sat with women in the Peace Garden and distributed colouring tools to make art so 'they can use colours to express the events of their lives' and also provided legal counselling, when necessary. She said that the Peace Garden has become like a *chopaal*, a place to meet in a village.

Rubina Bhatti sees what they were doing as being within an integrated framework, from personal development to economic development. She said that her vision is that,

> Extremism is not just in the use of a gun. Extremism is not accepting others. We have to accept diversity if we want to promote tolerance.

TWO's activities changed after 2008 (a decade after it started). An Irish charity, Trócaire, whose mandate is to support the most vulnerable people through working with local partners, gave them funds for empowering violence survivors. In the conservative environment of Sargodha, this did not go well with the larger community, and Rubina Bhatti started to receive threats that they should cease this activity. In August 2016, an inspector from the Ministry of Interior in Lahore met with her that they had received complaints that she and TWO was preaching Christianity and defaming Pakistan. Rubina Bhatti rejected these allegations and provided details about TWO's activities, particularly its long-term efforts to promote peace and interfaith harmony. This was occurring in a context, in Sargodha, where sectarianism and anti-Ahmadi activities were escalating. For the past decade, local mullahs frequently have tried to stop celebrations on the basis that Islamic culture is opposed to these.

However, local police at the behest of the provincial government went to TWO's office in Sargodha on 1 September 2016 and stated they were there to shut down the office. The staff asked the police to show orders to this effect, which they did not. The police locked TWO's offices and temporarily detained eight staff members—Naveed Sardar, Mohsin Noor, Azeem Khan, Zaib Nawaz, Ijaz Ahmed, Haider Ali, Muhammad Shafique, and Meherban—in the Sargodha police station. The police asked staff members to tell them Rubina Bhatti's whereabouts and said that all of their concerns were related to her activities.[66]

The day TWO was closed, personnel from the Punjab Human Rights ministry came to Sargodha and showed support for them, writing an affidavit that this organization was not engaged in anything wrong.

The local community didn't understand on what basis TWO had been shuttered. Rubina Bhatti, inspired by all this support, sought out human rights lawyer Asma Jehangir to help them, and TWO was reinstated nine months later, on 22 June 2017.

Taangh Wasaib Organization's activities have been fairly limited since they were reinstated, mostly involving functions at the Peace Park. TWO volunteers told me that they felt they were living in uncertain conditions and were reluctant to engage in some of their former work such as holding meetings, promoting interfaith harmony, or being involved with survivors of violence. Rubina Bhatti still periodically brings a team of volunteers, lawyers, and social workers to the Peace Park to review local people's concerns and complaints, such as a woman in need of financial support from her ex-husband to a man involved in a property dispute.[67] TWO has laid a foundation for how they intended to counter extremism, and all involved with the organization hope they can resume all of their former activities again soon.

ACTIVITIES TO RECLAIM AND CREATE CULTURAL SPACE OCCURRING AT PUBLIC VENUES

In many parts of the world, it has become common practice for people to meet at public venues such as coffee shops, bookstores, or similar locales to discuss myriad political, social, and cultural issues. Areas like Soho in Lower Manhattan, the West End in London, and the salons of Paris became famous for such cultural activist activities a century ago, but such activities continue to occur in urban areas throughout the world today. However, they are very limited in Pakistan.

In Pakistan, such venues have usually been founded by social activists and are located either in bookstores or coffee shops. The four best known existing venues in Pakistan are The Second Floor (T2F) in Karachi, Khanabadosh in Hyderabad, and Books n' Beans and the Last Word in Lahore. Kuch Khaas had existed for many years in Islamabad, though closed when its owner passed away; Sattar Buksh in Islamabad has tried to fill the cultural gap left by Kuch Khaas' closing but is still in a very preliminary stage of doing so. The Multan Tea House also welcomes anyone to come and assemble and talk in an open, free atmosphere with no limitations though like Sattar Buksh, is still in the initial stage of doing so. The Pak Tea House in Lahore had been famous as a gathering place for poets and journalists half a century ago, but recent visits have shown that today it capitalizes more on advertising its past than actually holding events.

T2F and Khanabadosh are true gathering places, where coffee and snacks complement the occasional public programmes and daily 'salonesque' conversations. The founder of T2F, Sabeen Mahmud, desired to create an open platform not controlled in any way; she didn't want a guarded space.[68] She wanted to create 'an inclusive space where different kinds of people can be comfortable.'[69] She writes that her motivation to start was,

> I started fantasizing about creating a public space for free speech and creative expression. I had long conversations with myself: How could we become agents of social change if our theatre practitioners had no rehearsal spaces, if our underground musicians had no venues to perform in, if our emerging artists had nowhere to hang their work? How could creative dissidents even learn of each other's existence, let alone build and cultivate a community, without physical spaces where people could talk politics? In fact, years of military rule, terrible violence, and a range of other events had stripped people of their political will and the desire to be the change they wished to see. I had grown up hearing stories about Pakistan's teahouses where poets and revolutionaries would gather, and I had seen countless photographs of inspirational leaders from the women's movement being tear-gassed for demanding their rights. What would it take to create a space that espoused liberal, secular values through its programming and projects? I wondered if I could create a minuscule postmodern hippie outpost, a safe haven for artists, musicians, writers, poets, activists, and thinkers— essentially anyone who wanted to escape the relentless tyranny of the city for a little while. If I built it, would anyone come?[70]

With hardly any money, she created the NGO PeaceNiche in 2007 and the flagship project of PeaceNiche was T2F. This was the open space, reclaiming culture that she had wanted to create,

> On the one hand, here it was—her community space, her field of dreams. She had built it and they were coming. Their first event was an Open Mic, hosted by comic Saad Haroon, followed by a

reading by poet Zeeshan Shahid, and it just went on from there. There were book readings and lectures on evolution and tabla players and indie rock concerts and art exhibitions and discussions on climate change.[71]

T2F survives on monies generated by the café as well as events, though they try to keep half of them free. When they do charge admission to an event, they give over two-thirds of the funds generated to the performing artists. But it was barely enough for T2F to survive, so its Board reached out to private benefactors and prospective donors to keep it going.

While youth came to T2F in droves, not everyone wanted such an institution, even in Karachi which many people claim is the most cosmopolitan of Pakistani cities. Sabeen began to receive threats—death threats, rape threats, and messages inciting violence against her and other civil society activists—and she took them in stride, refusing to stop doing what she deeply believed in. However, it was on 25 April 2015 that T2F hosted a discussion on Balochistan that other locales had refused to hold. Titled 'Unsilencing Balochistan,' it comprised various Baloch activists including Mama Qadeer, Farzana Baloch, and Mir Mohammad Ali Talpur who spoke of the struggle for an independent Balochistan. That night, after leaving T2F and driving home with her mother, Sabeen Mahmud was shot dead; the murderers are still at large.

After the shock and dismay of her death felt by her fellow civil society activists and T2F's supporters abated somewhat, they rose to the occasion to keep T2F in operation. Marvi Mazhar, an architect and otherwise close friend of Sabeen's, agreed to take on being the interim director of T2F to keep Sabeen's vision alive. She continued to encourage creative programming—especially in music and dance—as well as the social activism that Sabeen had nurtured. For example, they held a programme 'meet your candidates' where politicians contesting an upcoming election from a wide range of parties were invited to sit down together and talk to each other, therein providing space for mature discourse. She also organized sessions on anti-encroachment drives, science for the people, a philosophy circle, the Mother Earth project, among other topics. But running T2F was always meant to be a temporary position for her, as she aspired to return to her architectural career.

Arieb Azhar, who had been well known for organizing cultural musical performances in Islamabad and had performed at T2F during Sabeen's lifetime, came on as the T2F director in May 2018. He has tried to revive T2F since coming to head it, introducing new programming, but told me of the challenges he faces there,

> It's a mission to make this place sustainable. If there was a successful formula to run a cultural café/art gallery/performance venue/a place for discourse, and alternate artistic expression, then there would be more places like this around Pakistan. There are no grants for arts and culture through the government. And given the security threats still existing in the country…you have to be very careful how you put things out.

He has introduced monthly *qawwali* performances and drum circles. He said that only after he had taken charge has he realized the depth of connections T2F has in Karachi. He said, 'There are so many people who feel that their purpose in life started at T2F.' He finds it challenging to retain its flavour of the 'underground resistance' alive while at the same time trying to keep an ideological balance to get people to come to programmes and speak to each other.

In the future, he intends to do more with music—it's personal to him, but also to do more through T2F. He had previously run the Art Langar festival in Islamabad, and intends to transfer it to Karachi as a product of T2F. He wants to expand T2F's presence in social media and get more people involved, from all parts of the political spectrum, that would truly live up to Sabeen's initial dream of creating a public space 'for free speech and creative expression.'

Not very far from Karachi—about two hours north on the Expressway—is the provincial city of Hyderabad which houses another place seeking to reclaim and create cultural space, Khanabadosh. The founder, University of Sindh professor Amar Sindhu, designed it as a meeting place for intellectuals, feminists, journalists, and other cultural activists who can assemble for various activities in this distinct space nestled near the Sindh Museum.[72] Meaning 'vagabond' (in Amar Sindhu's words), Khanabadosh was launched in May 2015. While she and others had realized for some time that they had no place in Hyderabad to gather—'no neutral space where they could mix and talk, sit and share'—the big motivator was the Women's Action Forum (WAF) chapter in Hyderabad that included some very good women writers, poets, and professors. They determined that women's space had been shrinking and they began to feel the need for a writer's café. So finally, in 2015, they created Khanabadosh.

The big annual event that Khanabadosh hosts is the Ayaz Melo, a week-long memorial to the late Sindhi poet, Shaikh Ayaz. Its popularity has grown tremendously and it has recently incorporated musical performances as well. Amar Sindhu recounts that Khanabadosh's success is 'even beyond' her imagination, given the acute problems she has faced just in running the café especially financially, in management, and the lack of cooperation of the Sindh Provincial Culture Department. But she had not thought about all that they could do with youth. She had thought they were making this for writers, but now many youth, both male and female, come to attend Khanabadosh's events. She hadn't thought it would build its own identity, but it has. Importantly, it has moved the dialogue between writers and others forward, and involved youth extensively in those conversations. So despite the shrinking of public space elsewhere in the area, Khanabadosh provides a sort of cultural haven where writers, progressive politicians, and youth can meet.

Aside from being a café that is open daily, Khanabadosh is open for groups to hold meetings there. In addition, it hosts two or three 'Meet the Authors' and/or performers each month. People come from all over Sindh to attend events there. It has become common for Khanabadosh to host the first performances of Sindhi performers before they reach out and go to Islamabad or Karachi. Amar Sindhu said, 'It's like before they go to Coke Studio, they come here.' Lok Sujag, featured earlier in this chapter, made a video of Amar Sindhu and Khanabadosh to spread the word in local areas regarding this unique cultural site.[73]

There are other efforts creating similar kinds of cultural spaces in Lahore, such as Books n' Beans bookstore and coffee shop in Gulberg, and the Last Word bookstore in Defence. Najam Sethi, founder of Vanguard Books (bookstore and publisher), *The Friday Times*, television commentary host, occasional politician (including a stint as interim Chief Minister of the Punjab preceding the 2013 elections), and erstwhile Chairman of the Pakistan Cricket Board, was seeking to do 'exactly that' and create a distinct cultural space in Lahore.[74] For this current site, he founded a relatively small bookstore but designed it a bit 'off the beaten path' to be more of a space for conversations. It holds weekly seminars, debates, and group talk sessions organized by different schools, culture and art groups. He said, 'We encourage them to come here, and it's a free space. Every week, on a Saturday or Sunday, there are thirty to fifty people here. We cover everything—politics, history, sports.' He said the café doesn't make any money and even the bookstore is usually 'in the red,' but he opened it because he is passionate about creating cultural spaces. He recounted that one of the reasons he went into publishing and book-selling over forty years ago was to create a new dimension in terms of culture in Pakistan. He saw that all the bookstores at the time were selling textbooks; they weren't selling books to give people ideas. He set up a bookstore selling progressive books, Vanguard, in the 1970s. He became used to his office being 'a cultural haunt of writers, poets, etc.,' and he missed that when he was no longer going there. So when he established *The Friday Times*, the bookstore became an extension of that. He began it right after he had completed overseeing the Punjab Provincial Elections in 2013 and had returned to working in media.

Aima Khosa began voluntarily organizing talks and discussions at Books n' Beans in 2015, mostly with student groups, the Awami Workers Party, and other progressive organizations. Najam Sethi hired her to do this fulltime in January 2017. She has arranged for a wide variety of people to talk there including philosophers, writers, authors, academics, and people from NGOs. She says that 'The whole point is to encourage critical discussions and debates.' They have held talks about *katchi abadis* (informal living settlements), the controversial Kalabagh Dam, pollution, labour rights, an awareness session on Thalassemia, and about other issues for which there are no locales in Lahore where people can easily come together and discuss these things. When asked about the extent of Books n' Beans activities, Aima Khosa said,

> We have public events—progressive discussions—and have held
> private events as with *Good Times* magazine. We sometimes have
> ticketed events like Aurat Naak, the comedy group, and Shehzad
> Ghias, another comedian; or a book launch. When we have to

charge for an event, we make the tickets affordable, not more
than Rs500-600. Most of the proceeds go to the artists; we only
keep about 10% towards our costs. The whole point is to bring
people together. Actually, the more divisive the event is, the more
people come. We can fit 80 people comfortably, and can stretch
it to about 100 people.

She has established a people's solidarity forum comprised of a women's
collective, a labour group, and a progressive students collective that hold
events at Books n' Beans. They have also held career guidance workshops,
but they were not very popular. She says that the feminist talks are the most
popular, because people have fights over them. In the summer of 2017, they
organized a summer colloquia series starting with 'Unpacking Masculinity',
then 'Unpacking Feminism,' then 'Unpacking Revolution' which was very
popular. When asked what she was providing to the audiences that come
to the bookstore to participate in the various programmes, she said,

> Conversations and discussions that they would not usually have
> in their classrooms, living rooms, etc. These discussions are to
> question everything they have become used to. When people ask
> questions and it gets interactive, it's a good way for people to get
> together. There are *no* spaces, no alternative spaces for young kids
> to do things.

She stated that there are other venues which have started to emerge to
reclaim some cultural space, but they have been problematic. For example,
there is another Lahore locale, *Punj Vehra*, a restaurant in Barkat Market,
that has set aside a bit of space with *charpais* and a small theatre room that
was starting to develop some programming. She also noted that the well-
known Gulberg bookstore, Readings, had tried to organize some talks but
as they didn't hire a person dedicated to doing this, they stopped and so
they just sell books.

The Nawaz Sharif government in 2013 had tried to restart the Pak
Tea House but, in Aima Khosa's opinion, it is no longer conducive for
such events because the available space is too small and they had negative
interactions there with people fighting. Indeed, the foundation in Lahore
for claiming a cultural space was that which had once been provided by

the Pak Tea House. It had provided a vibrant environment where left-leaning writers, scholars, and others could meet and talk over cups of tea. Founded by a Sikh family in the early 1930s and named India Tea House, it came under the control of the YMCA in 1940. The YMCA later leased it to Sirajuddin Ahmad who, after 1947, gave it the well-known name, Pak Tea House. In its heyday, it catered to intelligentsia in the Progressive Writers' Association and became a site where people with all viewpoints were welcome. It gained a reputation where people could voice their opinions in a non-judgmental atmosphere, an epitome of efforts to reclaim cultural space as seen in the activities of other entities covered in this chapter. But that was in the past, and Pak Tea House, today, is a shell of its former cultural strength. When you walk in the front door, it feels like a tea shop frequented mostly by men. Walking upstairs on the long, winding staircase, you come upon the large room where special meetings are occasionally held. Otherwise, the room is reminiscent of a Gulberg coffee shop: women and men meeting over tea or coffee, though not talking with each other as a group. On Wednesday, Friday, Saturday, and Sunday evenings, various groups meet there, but it's not the open atmosphere other entities seek to create.

Elsewhere in Lahore, Ayesha Raja had always envisioned running a bookshop where people could meet and discuss 'books with meaning' and related social concerns.[75] She started a small bookstore in 2007 above The Hot Spot in Qaddafi Stadium. At the time, she was working as a publicist for authors and then started a second small bookshop in Islamabad at Kohsar Market. In 2014, she realized she wasn't doing what she wanted to do and decided to open a proper bookstore in Lahore and founded The Last Word, initially in Gulberg and then shifted to Defence in 2018. She regards 2014 as having been an important moment for Pakistan. She said that Pakistan was a horribly traumatized nation after the APS attack, but that also prompted people to start addressing serious issues in public forums and 'terrorism wasn't sucking up all the air, all the time.'

The Last Word holds frequent events about social concerns, such as the annual pollution that engulfs Lahore in the wintertime, and otherwise holds book readings that spark lively conversations. Today, the two most popular issues they address at The Last Word's events pertain to women's rights and the environment. She and others at The Last Word are very cause-driven, not motivated by profit, which is why Ayesha Raja says the shop works well as a community space. For her, the more she can give a platform to writers, the better. Through The Last Word, she has been able to establish a sort of counter culture, an alternative to the mainstream information people usually get which she considers is consumption-based and often reactionary. But she adds that the point of having a bookshop, at the end of the day, is for someone to pick up a book and learn something. She makes the environment at The Last Word as inviting as possible to bring people into the store. Anyone who has a computer can sit down and work here. She estimates that by the fourth time they come to her store, they finally look at books on the shelves, and by the sixth time, they actually buy some books.

When we met again in mid-January 2019 at the relatively new DHA location, she said that it was only a bit different from the Gulberg one. They have a slightly younger clientele, more professionals, millennials, and youngsters coming to the shop and its events. While they were closed, people were supportive and were ordering books online. She said that The Last Word is 'a loved destination now,' that their reputation in Defence has become larger since it's a sanctuary, there's a sense of calm, where patrons can get away from their daily stresses. All of their events are mainly focused around books: in 2019, they held a book launch on nuclear proliferation, another one on feminism in Islam, and another one on a new book on the Pakistani middle class. Children-focused events have included a craft workshop that showed kids how to make bags and rucksacks from recycled materials, a creative writing workshop with Sonia Rehman, a drawing workshop, and an art history workshop. They have started a monthly 'open mic' where a lot of people talk about their experiences and share prose.

She sees their activities as very different from Books n' Beans as The Last Word attracts a much younger demographic and one not so politically-focused. She aspires to make The Last Word very personal, a place where people are able to share their stories regardless of class background. She especially wants to make it a safe space for women so they feel comfortable talking, such as at one open mic event that was about women in public spaces, and everyone shared about how they feel going about alone in public.

The Last Word is designed with younger people in mind, very bright colours and airy. Ayesha Raja gets frustrated by events like the Lahore Literary Festival which is designed for older adults, because she sees that the future resides with the young. She told me that if she 'is doing something anti-extremist, it's to try to sell books. Just providing a space for cultural activities is countering extremism.' She considers that growing the number of people who read books and buy books is countering violent extremism.

Indeed, each of the entities reviewed in this section are doing just that with their public efforts to reclaim and create cultural space.

Notes

1. Her efforts to counter violent extremism, as a dancer, are discussed in Chapter 3: Music and Performance.

2. Women Action Forum activists in Hyderabad shared their experiences with me in January 2018. The full story is recounted in 'Sheema Kirmani defies act of terrorism, performs at Lal Shahbaz Qalandar's shrine,' *Dawn*, 21 February 2017, accessible at: https://images.dawn.com/news/1177132.

3. Haroon Khalid (2016, p. 87) defines *dhamaal* as a Sufi devotional dance involving frenzied and ecstatic swirling of the head and body into a hypnotic trance, accompanied by the beat of a *dhol*, drum. It is often performed at Sufi shrines, and frequently at Lal Shahbaz Qalandar's shrine in particular.

4. All of the information on BSWA is based on extensive conversations with Khadim Hussain Mirani and other BSWA staff and volunteers held in January 2018 as well as first-hand observations of their projects and engagement with its literature.

5. These are laid out in the BSWA blog accessible at: http://bswakhairpur.blogspot.com/p/articles.html.

6. Hassan Nasir Mirbahar, 'Tribal Trouble: Economic, Social and Cultural Impact of conflicts in north Sindh,' BSWA, 2012, p. 5.

7. More information on Peace My Right campaign as a strategy to counter conflict is in Khadim Hussain Mirani, 'Conflict Transformation Analysis & Strategy for Peace My Right Campaign,' BSWA, 2015.

8. Sindh has a tradition at the local level of *katchahries*, community meetings (different from the Urdu term *katchery* meaning 'court'). The *katchahri* brings the community together to make particular decisions without any pre-planning. Most rural Sindhis prefer a community *katchahri* over a *jirga* as they believe it includes everyone and intervenes in a positive way based on the group's preferences and priorities.

9. An FIR—First Investigative Report—is the first action that occurs when a crime is allegedly committed. Anyone, whether a witness or not, can lodge an FIR with the police. That an FIR has been created is irrelevant to the guilt or innocence of anyone named in the FIR. I was accompanied to Taluka Kingri by BSWA Executive Director

Khadim Hussain Mirani and other BSWA staff who translated responses from Sindhi to Urdu for me.

10. Ashura, held annually during the 8th, 9th and 10th of the Muslim month of Muharram, is a Shia festival that commemorates the martyrdom of the Prophet Muhammad's (PBUH) grandson Hussain, at the battle of Karbala in Iraq. In this area, the typical practice is that men publicly perform *maatam*, self-flagellation with knives, evoking passion as if they were experiencing the tragedy themselves. Ashura is a time when Sunni-Shia conflicts sometimes emerge in Pakistan, but in the interior of Sindh, other religious groups have traditionally facilitated the event.

11. I spoke informally with a journalist in Islamabad at the time who struggled to have a straight face as she told me that her editor didn't consider the PTM sit-in to be important and she should instead cover other things. I spoke informally with a number of other journalists as well between February and March 2019 about coverage of PTM events.

12. Raza Wazir, 'To be Young and Pashtun in Pakistan', *The New York Times*, Opinion, 9 March 2018, accessible at: https://www.nytimes.com/2018/03/09/opinion/pashtun-pakistan-young-killing.html.

13. Ibid.

14. While this did occur, Rao Anwar has subsequently been released on bail—rare for a murder suspect in Pakistan—and retired from the Sindh Police Department on 1 January 2019.

15. Maham Javaid, 'First among Equals', *The News on Sunday*, 25 March 2018, accessible at: http://tns.thenews.com.pk/first-among-equals/#.XE6NySenf_Q.

16. Ibid.

17. This translation of *Da Sanga Azadi Da?*, originally written and sung by Shaukat Aziz from South Waziristan, is by Ghulam Dastageer, 'The Pashteen Question: the Making of a new nationalist movement,' *The Herald*, vol. 52, no. 5, May 2018, p. 53.

18. Aurangzaib Khan, '#3: Manzoor Pashteen, for leading the fringe to the Center,' *The Herald Annual*, vol. 53, no. 1, January 2019, p. 84.

19. Bushra Goher communicated her views about Manzoor Pashteen to me in a meeting on 22 January 2019.

20. This was confidentially conveyed to me in an interview in Islamabad in March 2019.

21. As quoted in Sarah Eleazar and Sher Ali Khan, 'Grounded: Anatomy of a Political Moment: How a democratic movement is challenging Pakistan's Status Quo,' *Himal Southasian Magazine*, 15 June 2018, accessible at: https://himalmag.com/pasteen-tahafuz-protection-movement-rally-manzoor-pashteen-pakistan-rights/.

22. Ibid.

23. He explained to me that this is a reference to Pakhtuns' strong storytelling tradition, and that their stories of their homeland should be told first among their own people, not broadcast on global media by outsiders who don't understand them.

24. Zaigham Khan, 'Listen to the Pakhtuns,' *The News*, 5 March 2018, accessible at: https://www.thenews.com.pk/print/288442-listen-to-the-pakhtuns.

25. Zamir Akram, 'Engineered subversion: As a nation we should recognize the critical need for all of us to be on the same page,' *Express Tribune*, Opinion, 22 April 2018, accessible at: https://tribune.com.pk/story/1691015/6-engineered-subversion/.

26. This tweet, the author of which shall remain confidential, was tweeted at 4pm on 15 March 2019.

27. Brad Adams, 'Pakistan Should Address Pashtun Grievances: Conduct Transparent Investigation into Activist's Death', accessible at https://www.hrw.org/news/2019/02/15/pakistan-should-address-pa (though subsequently removed).

28. Editorial, 'Genuine Engagement,' *Dawn*, 24 January 2019, accessible at: https://www.dawn.com/news/1459471/genuine-engagement.

29. Manzoor Ahmad Pashteen, 'The Military Says Pashtuns Are Traitors. We Just Want Our Rights,' *The New York Times*, Opinion, 11 February 2019, accessible at: https://www.nytimes.com/2019/02/11/opinion/pashtun-protests-pakistan.html.

30. News coverage of the event and its aftermath can be found at Sirajuddin, '3 People Killed, 5 soldiers injured in exchange of Fire at check post in north Waziristan,' *Dawn*, 26 May 2019, accessible at: https://www.dawn.com/news/1484709/3-people-killed-5-soldiers-injured-in-exchange-of-fire-at-check-post-in-north-waziristan, and at Sirajuddin and Javed Hussain, 'MNA Mohsin Dawar arrested from North Waziristan, remanded in CTD custody for 8 days,' *Dawn*, 30 May 2019, accessible at: https://www.dawn.com/news/1485493.

31. Sirajuddin and Javed Hussain, op. cit.

32. Abubakar Siddique, 'AI Calls On Pakistan To Halt Crackdown On Pashtun Rights Group,' *Gandhara*, 29 August 2019, accessible at: https://gandhara.rferl.org/a/ai-calls-on-pakistan-to-halt-crackdown-on-pashtun-rights-group-/ 30136534.html.

33. All information and quotes are from extensive interviews with various members of Lok Sujag in Lahore and Sahiwal in October and November 2017, and reliance on a variety of Lok Sujag publications including but not limited to 'The Political Economy of Milk in Punjab: a People's Perspective,' 2003, *Farmer Report*, September 2008, and various websites including: https://pakngos.com.pk/ngo/punjab-lok-sujag.

34. Stated to me by Tahir Mehdi in Lahore on 28 October 2017.

35. Based on a discussion with Tahir Mehdi, one of the original founders of Lok Sujag, in February 2017.

36. *See* http://sujag.org/.

37. *See* https://www.un.org/democracyfund/news/new-media-local-democratic-discourse-pakistan

38. *See* https://www.youtube.com/watch?v=b19cliCZSZ8

39. This can be found at https://vimeo.com/69325754 and also at https://dailytimes.com.pk/296390/sujag-theatre-raises-awareness-about-child-marriages-in-sindh-2/.

40. *See* https://www.youtube.com/watch?v=3pBy5nZi-mE

41. *See* https://www.youtube.com/watch?v=-NKsmSWlF7c&list=PL045zYIRNXyJgQU vNMI9D3xKsZlnvx0JX&index=5&t=0s.

42. Based on an interview conducted with Kashif Baloch in the Lok Sujag office in Lahore on 17 October 2017.

43. *See* OPP's website: http://www.opp.org.pk. As it is not the purpose here to provide a complete history of OPP and of all of its activities, but rather to focus on how OPP uniquely works to counter extremism, for more details on OPP *see* Akhter Hameed Khan, *Orangi Pilot Project: Reminiscences and Reflections*, Karachi and New York, Oxford University Press, 2005; Arif Hasan, *Participatory Development: the Story of the Orangi Pilot Project Research and Training Institute and the Urban Resource Centre, Karachi, Pakistan*, Karachi, Oxford University Press, 2010; and Ismaïl Serageldin (ed.), *The Architecture of Empowerment: People, Shelter and Livable Cities*, London, Academy Editions, 1997.

44. This and other reflections on OPP's activities and impact were shared with me by Anwar Rashid, OPP Director, at the OPP offices in Orangi, Karachi, in February 2017.

45. Arif Hasan, *Localizing Habitat Agenda Research Project: A Case Study of the Orangi Pilot Project Research and Training Institute*, Karachi, 2003, p. 80.

46. Ibid., pp. 1–2.

47. 'Parveen Rehman: a fighter for the poor silenced,' *Dawn*, 14 March 2013, accessible at: https://www.dawn.com/news/792501/parveen-rehman-a-fighter-for-the-poor-silenced.

48. Ibid.

49. This was told to me by Aquila Rehman at the OPP offices in Orangi, Karachi, in February 2017.

50. Arif Hasan, *Localizing Habitat Agenda Research Project: A Case Study of the Orangi Pilot Project Research and Training Institute*, Karachi, 2003, p. 95.

51. This was told to me by Anwar Rashid, OPP Director, at the OPP offices in Orangi, Karachi, in February 2017.

52. Information on Khwendo Kor is based on numerous interviews I had with its founder and now CEO Maryam Bibi, the head of its Viable Village project Khalid Usman, other Khwendo Kor personnel, and numerous pamphlets, reports, and online information Khwendo Kor personnel provided to me between 2017 and 2019 at its head office in Peshawar. For more information *see* Friends of Khwendo Kor UK (FROK) website: https://ukfrok.wordpress.com/about-khwendo-kor/.

53. 'KK Profile: An Introduction to Khwendo Kor' pamphlet, 2017.

54. Khwendo Kor, 'Outline Concept Paper: The Viable Village,' 2017, p. 2.

55. Ibid.

56. 'KK Profile: An Introduction to Khwendo Kor' pamphlet, 2017.

57. 'KK Profile: Achievements: Civil Rights' pamphlet, 2017, p. 6.

58. This section is based on extensive conversations with Gauher Aftab and others in Lahore involved with CFX Comics between 2017 and 2019.

59. He has discussed his experience with his Islamic Studies teacher that changed his life in 'How I almost joined a 'jihad' training camp', *Dawn*, 25 July 2016, accessible at: https://www.dawn.com/news/1272244 and he presented a TedX Lahore talk using scenes from *Paasbaan*. *See* 'Making a Terrorist,' 24 March 2016, accessible at: https://www.youtube.com/watch?v=GMFNTkN2jHA.

60. Gauher Aftab, 'How I almost joined a 'jihad' training camp', *Dawn*, 25 July 2016, accessible at: https://www.dawn.com/news/1272244.

61. This is written on Aghaaz-e-Dosti's 2018 Indo-Pak Peace Calendar.

62. In India, there were three schools in Delhi, two in Karnataka, two in Uttar Pradesh, and one each in Gujarat, Jharkhand, and Uttarakhand. In Pakistan, there were two schools in Lahore, one each in Rahim Yar Khan and Karachi, and the Bacha Khan school in Nauthia, Peshawar.

63. A comprehensive history of the Aghaaz-e-Dosti calendars can be found at: https://aaghazedosti.wordpress.com/our-initiatives/peace-education/indopakcalendar/.

64. This section on TWO is based on interviews I had with Rubina Bhatti and other longtime TWO members in Sargodha in December 2017 as well as a number of press reports about the organization.

65. One *kanal* of land is roughly 605 square yards.

66. This was conveyed to me by Rubina Bhatti and others involved with TWO. More information is accessible at: https://www.frontlinedefenders.org/en/case/harassment-dr-rubina-feroze-bhatti-and-closure-her-organisation on what occurred.

67. I attended a meeting at the Peace Park in December 2017 and heard these individuals raise their concerns to Rubina Bhatti and her team.

68. This section on T2F is based on interviews with the former director, Marvi Mazhar, Sabeen's mentor Zaheer (Zak) Kidvai, and current T2F director Arieb Azhar, on-site visits, and numerous articles about T2F and circumstances surrounding Sabeen's murder.

69. As quoted in Qasim Makkani, 'The reluctant non-conformist: the director of T2F, Sabeen Mahmud, in profile,' *Aurora*, July–August 2013, accessible at: https://aurora.dawn.com/news/1141129/.

70. Sabeen Mahmud, 'Creative Karachi; Establishing an Arts & Culture Center for the World's Most Rapidly Growing City, Case Narrative: PeaceNiche and The Second Floor', *Innovations*, vol. 8, no. 3/4, 2013, pp. 28–9.

71. Qasim Makkani, 'The reluctant non-conformist,' op. cit.

72. This section on Khanabadosh is based on extensive conversations with Amar Sindhu, Arfana Mullah, Zakia Aijaz, and others involved with Khanabadosh between 2017 and 2019. Photographs of its activities can be found on its Facebook page, accessible at: https://www.facebook.com/khanabadosh/.

73. *See* video at: https://www.facebook.com/1875658202672246/videos/1401628906666268/UzpfSTkwNDk4MDA1NjIzMjIyODoyNDc3NTY0ODc1NjQwMzk3/.

74. This section on Books n' Beans is based on conversations held with Najam Sethi and Aima Khosa, his special assistant for organizing events at the bookstore, in 2017–18.

75. This section on The Last Word is based on conversations with Ayesha Raja in Gulberg and Defence in Lahore between 2017 and 2019.

Afterword

When I set out to research this book, I had great expectations but no real idea of what I would find. Now with the supposed finish line in sight, I realize that what has captivated me these past four years truly has no end. I feel we have explored so much about Pakistan that has hardly received attention anywhere else, but there's so much more to discover about this multi-faceted, vibrant, ever-changing, and still hopeful society. This is what sets Pakistan apart from many other countries: while few are actually optimistic that change will really happen in the future, many remain hopeful and passionate despite obstacles that may arise.

I opened a door, and it is my hope that others will venture into it further to investigate each of the categories explored in this book. Poetry remains popular and celebrated throughout the country in ways many in the West would find alien. I realize it is often written today as a way to have a political voice in these socially and politically changing times. In my research, I only just touched the surface of Pakistan's poetic traditions; its legacy lives on in dynamic ways throughout the country in Balochi, Punjabi, Kashmiri, Burushashki, and other languages unexplored in these pages. The same can be said about music and performance: there was so much to choose from to include, and what I have written about is just a small sample of the dynamism that is emerging today.

Much of the public art I discovered, photographed, and wrote about in this book was completely unexpected. For the purposes of this project, I shied away from 'art for art's sake' given that I, being the sociologist who I am, was intent to explore how art is used as social expression against violence and extremism. Here too, I only touched on the metaphorical tip of the iceberg as I'm sure different manifestations of what can be deemed 'social art' exists still unexplored throughout Pakistan. I had expected to write more about the Karachi Biennale and the Karachi Conference but somehow, at the end, I felt they were less compelling to the focus of this book as they are seemingly elite projects with limited impact on countering extremism. A telling conflict emerged during the latest iteration of the Karachi Biennale in October/November 2019 when Adeela Sulaiman (she of the 'Reimagining the Walls of Karachi' initiative discussed in Chapter 4) created 'The Killing Fields of Karachi' installation, a reflection on the violence that Karachi has undergone in the past decades. It had featured symbolic gravestones representing the 444 people allegedly targeted in extra-judicial killings under the supervision of police official Rao Anwar, the man held responsible for the killing of Naqeebullah Mehsud (discussed in Chapter 7). The Karachi Biennale organizers shut it down deeming it incompatible with the event's theme of 'Ecology and the Environment' and social media virtually exploded with criticism of this action. That so many people rose up to find their voices, however, is promising, proof of the growing numbers of people who are becoming aware of the social power of art.

I am so honoured that religious leaders from a wide spectrum of creeds welcomed me into their lives and shared their stories of how they are seeking peace and harmony between disparate groups. I could only write here about a small number of those I met as I sought to portray a representative sample of what is happening in the country. I would welcome the opportunity to find out more, to walk into small towns and villages where local religious leaders have been able to bring people together, to inform each other about their traditions and values, and through doing this extremists can have no point of entry into a community. There is dynamism within many religious leaders that I hadn't expected to find, which again bodes well for Pakistan's collective future. When Maulana Zubair Ahmad Zaheer, the *Naib Ameer* of the Markazi Jamiat Ahl-e-Hadith Pakistan in Lahore, related to me how he had been imprisoned a number of times defending Christians' rights (discussed in Chapter 5), I immediately connected that this was indeed 'an act of the Pakistan I knew' (as raised in the Preface) and a prime example of how Pakistanis were 'standing up all over the country for what was right, just, and authentic.'

I have spent a great deal of time in Pakistan over the past forty years and have visited many primary and secondary schools as well as colleges and universities throughout the country. When I have asked students, especially those from more challenged socio-economic backgrounds, about their dreams for their future, I have often come up against blank stares, for their futures were not in their own hands. But the first time I went to a Bacha Khan school—the one in Mingora, Swat—I was stunned by the self-confidence and enthusiasm these working-class students had that they could make their mark on Pakistan's future. I found this exciting: they had the belief inculcated in them that they were important players in Pakistan and could work towards building a positive future for everyone. This proved true throughout the Bacha Khan School System, even in places where extremists had gained a strong foothold. Dr Khadim Hussain must be commended for what he has accomplished: the promotion of critical thinking along with the values of nationalism, communal harmony, and peace. Students in the Zoya Science Schools shared these principles. I look forward to hearing about other school systems elsewhere in Pakistan that offer outstanding academics while also instilling these values.

I hope the final chapter, Chapter 7, makes as much sense to readers of this book as it makes to me. I wanted to include the activities of NGOs and small groups of people, but capture local initiatives, not ones instigated by external groups or donors. I believe I have, and hope that this list also keeps growing despite that some of them have had to shut down. I will admit I was disappointed to find the number of entities seeking to reclaim cultural space in public venues declining—I still mourn the closing of Kuch Khaas in Islamabad—but am enthusiastic about all of the ones I discovered. Khanabadosh is such an unexpected gem in Hyderabad, remaining true to its syncretic Sindhi roots. I hope that Pakistanis of every ilk will discover the ones I have written about and create more, speckled throughout the country.

There were other themes I had explored while conducting research for this book but finally decided that while they were important issues, they were veering further away from the focal theme of people's actions to counter violent extremism. The two most notable were efforts to keep the Internet open (and accolades to 'Bytes for All' and 'Bolo Bhi' for all that they do in this regard) as well as news reporting to ensure open communication and alternative narratives to violence. I appreciate all the journalists and news reporters who met with me, especially Imtiaz Alam at SAFMA, Raziuddin in Multan, Malik Achakzai and all he revealed to me about reporting about Balochistan, and the many journalists who discussed their involvement with the Cultural Journalists Forum in Peshawar. They conveyed much about the context for many activities about which I was writing. However, in the end, I couldn't pinpoint what all I would write about in a chapter devoted to media and open communication, and hope that someone with more insight into this than I have, will write about it in the future.

I remain even more hopeful and enthusiastic today about Pakistan's future than I was when I set out to write this book. I hope that you, having finished reading it, feel the same.

Bibliography

ABBAS, QAISER, 'Cultural Identity and State Oppression: Poetic Resistance to Internal Colonialism in Pakistan,' *Pakistaniaat: A Journal of Pakistan Studies*, vol. 6, 2018, accessible at: http://pakistaniaat.org/index.php/pak/article/view/353.

ABRO, JAMAL, *Pirani & Other Short Stories*, Karachi: Oxford University Press, 2017.

ADAMS, CHARLES J., 'Mawdudi and the Islamic State,' in *Voices of Resurgent Islam*, John L. Esposito (ed.), New York: Oxford University Press, 1983, pp. 99–133.

AGENCE FRANCE-PRESSE, 'Artists Reclaim Karachi Walls from Hate Graffiti,' *Dawn*, 25 July 2015, accessible at: http://www.dawn.com/news/1196150/artists-reclaimkarachi-walls-from-hate-graffiti.

AHMAD, MUMTAZ, 'Islamic Fundamentalism in South Asia: The Jamaat-i-Islami and the Tablighi Jamaat,' in *Fundamentalisms Observed*, Martin E. Marty and R. Scott Appleby (eds.), Chicago: University of Chicago Press, 1991.

AHMAD, SALMAN, *Rock & Roll Jihad: A Muslim Rock Star's Revolution*, New York: Free Press, 2010.

AHMED, ZAHID SHAHAB, 'Idealism Versus Pragmatism in Teaching Peace in Pakistan,' *Peace Review: A Journal of Social Justice*, vol. 30, 2018, pp. 331–8.

AKHTAR, AASIM, 'Islam as Ideology of Tradition and Change: The "New Jihad" in Swat, Northern Pakistan,' *Comparative Studies of South Asia, Africa and the Middle East*, vol. 30, no. 3, 2010, pp. 595–609.

ALI, ASHRAF, 'Violent Extremism: Changing the Social Values,' *Tigah: a Journal of Peace and Development*, FATA Research Centre, vol. 1, no. 1, Summer 2012, pp. 1–26.

ALI, MUBARAK, *Pakistan in Search of Identity*, Delhi: Aakar Books, 2011.

ALIF AILAAN, '25 Million Broken Promises: The Crisis of Pakistan's Out-of-School Children,' Islamabad: Alif Ailaan, 2014.

AMAN, SHAHIDA AND MUHAMMAD AYUB JAN (eds.), *Conference Proceedings: Dynamics of Change in the Pak–Afghan Borderland—The Interplay of Past Legacies, Present Realities and Future Scenarios*, Third International Conference, Islamabad: Hanns Seidel Foundation, 2014.

AMIN, HUSNUL AND MARYAM SIDDIQA (ed.), *Pakistan Countering Terrorism: Challenges and Prospects*, Islamabad: Iqbal International Institute for Research & Dialogue, IIU, 2017.

AMIN, HUSNUL, *Post-Islamism: Pakistan in the Era of Neoliberal Globalization*, Islamabad: Iqbal International Institute for Research & Dialogue, IIU, 2016.

AMJAD, AMJAD ISLAM AND GAUHER AFTAB, *Haider: 5 Days of Glory: Maj. Raja Aziz Bhatti*, vol. 1, parts 1 & 2, Lahore: CFX Comics, 2015.

AMJAD, AMJAD ISLAM AND GAUHER AFTAB, *Paasban, The Guardian: Darkness & Innocence*, Lahore: CFX Comics, 2014.

AZIZ, SHAIKH, *Palatial Tales from Sindh*, Jamshoro: Sindhi Adabi Board, 2013.

BALA, SRUTI, 'Waging Nonviolence: Reflections on the History Writing of the Pashtun Nonviolent Movement Khudai Khidmatgar,' *Peace & Change: a Journal of Peace Research*, vol. 38, no. 2, April 2013, pp. 131–44.

BANERJEE, MUKULIKA, *The Pathan Unarmed: Opposition & Memory in the North-West Frontier*, 2nd edn., Oxford University Press, 2017.

BASIT, ABDUL, 'Countering Violent Extremism: Evaluating Pakistan's Counter-Radicalization and De-radicalization Initiatives', *IPRI Journal* XV, no. 2, Summer 2015, pp. 44–68.

BENNOUNE, KARIMA, *Your Fatwa Does Not Apply Here: Untold Stories From the Fight Against Muslim Fundamentalism*, New York: W.W. Norton & Company, 2013.

BHITTAI SOCIAL WATCH AND ADVOCACY (BSWA), *Citizen's Report on Economic, Social and Cultural Rights*, Khairpur Mirs: BSWA, 2012.

BHITTAI SOCIAL WATCH AND ADVOCACY (BSWA), *Constitutional Rights in Pakistan: Training Manual*, Khairpur Mirs: BSWA, n.d.

BHITTAI SOCIAL WATCH AND ADVOCACY (BSWA), *National Plan of Action on International Covenant on Economic, Social and Cultural Rights (ICESCR)*, Khairpur Mirs: BSWA, 2014.

BOKHARI, FARHAN, 'Saudi Arabia gives Financial Aid to Pakistan,' *Financial Times*, 14 March 2014, accessible at: https://www.ft.com/content/d40980deaa88–11e3–9fd6-00144feab7de#axzz3sFxTtR1S.

BUNERI, SHAHEEN, 'Poetry Fights Back,' *Boston Review*, January/February 2012, accessible at: http://bostonreview.net/archives/BR37.1/shaheen_buneri_afghanistan_pakistan_pashtun_poetry.php.

CHANNAN, FR JAMES, *Christian-Muslim Dialogue in Pakistan*, Lahore: Multimedia Affairs, 2012.

CHANNAN, FR JAMES, *Path of Love: a Call for Interfaith Harmony*, Lahore: Multimedia Affairs, 2014.

COLL, STEVE, *Ghost Wars: The Secret History of the CIA, Afghanistan, and bin Laden, from the Soviet Invasion to September 10, 2001*, New York: Penguin Books, 2004.

CONSTABLE, PAMELA, *Playing with Fire: Pakistan at War with Itself*, New York: Random House, 2011.

DAWOOD, N.J. (trans.), *The Koran: A New Translation*, London: Penguin Books, 2006.

DEVJI, FAISAL, *Muslim Zion: Pakistan as a Political Idea*, Cambridge, MA: Harvard University Press, 2013.

EASWARAN, EKNATH, *Nonviolent Soldier of Islam: Badshah Khan, A Man to Match His Mountains*, 2nd edn., Tomales, CA: Nilgiri Press, 1999.

FATA RESEARCH CENTRE, *Impact of War on Terror on Pashto Literature and Art*, Islamabad: FATA Research Centre, 2014.

FAZAL, FAZAL KHALIQ, *Barbarism in Disguise of Patriotism*, Mingora, Swat: Shoaib Sons Publishers & Booksellers, 2009.

GOVERNMENT OF PAKISTAN, MINISTRY OF FEDERAL EDUCATION AND PROFESSIONAL TRAINING, *Pakistan Education Statistics 2016–17*, Islamabad: National Education Management Information System, Academy of Educational Planning and Management, March 2018.

GOVERNMENT OF PAKISTAN, *Pakistan Penal Code (Act XLV of 1860), October 6th, 1860 (with Amendments)*, 2012, accessible at: http://www.pakistani.org/ pakistan/ legislation/1860/actXLVof1860.html.

GUL, AYAZ, *Mysticism, Sindh and Sachal Sarmast*, Khairpur: Sachal Chair, Shah Abdul Latif University, 2011.

GUNERATNE, ARJUN AND ANITA M. WEISS (eds.), *Pathways to Power: The Domestic Politics of South Asia*, Lanham, Maryland: Rowman & Littlefield, 2014; South Asia edn. Orient BlackSwan, India, 2015.

HALL, STUART, 'Cultural Identity and Cinematic Representation,' *Framework: The Journal of Cinema and Media*, no. 36, 1989, pp. 68–81.

HAQQANI, HUSAIN, *Pakistan: Between Mosque and Military*, Washington, DC: Carnegie Endowment for International Peace; Distributor, Brookings Institution Press, 2005.

HARLOW, BARBARA, *Resistance Literature*, New York: Methuen, 1987.

HAROON, SANA, *Frontiers of Faith: Islam in the Indo-Afghan Borderland*, New York: Columbia University Press, 2007.

HASAN, ARIF, *Localizing Habitat Agenda Research Project: A Case Study of the Orangi Pilot Project Research and Training Institute*, Karachi, 2003.

HASAN, ARIF, *Participatory Development: The Story of the Orangi Pilot Project Research and Training Institute and the Urban Resource Centre, Karachi, Pakistan*, Karachi: Oxford University Press, 2010.

HASHMI, SYED MASROOR ALI AKHTAR, *Muslim Response to Western Education: A Study of Four Pioneer Institutions*, New Delhi, India: Commonwealth Publishers, 1989.

HOODBHOY, NAFISA, *Aboard the Democracy Train: A Journey through Pakistan's Last Decade of Democracy*, London: Anthem Press, 2011.

HUSSAIN, AZHAR, AHMAD SALIM, AND ARIF NAVEED, 'Connecting the Dots: Education and Religious Discrimination in Pakistan: A Study of Public Schools and Madrassas,' Washington, DC: United States Commission on International Religious Freedom (USCIRF), November 2011.

HUSSAIN, FAHMIDA (ed.), *Selection of Verses from Shah Jo Risalo*, trans. Sirajul Haque Memon, Fahmida Hussain, Amjad Siraj Memon, and Naveed Siraj Memon, Karachi/Hyderabad: Siraj Institute of Sindh Studies, 2018.

HUSSAIN, KHADIM, *Rethinking Education: Critical Discourses and Society*, Islamabad: Narratives, 2012.

HUSSAIN, KHADIM, *The Militant Discourse: Religious Militancy in Pakistan*, Islamabad: Narratives, 2013.

HUSSAIN, ZAHID, *The Scorpion's Tail: The Relentless Rise of Islamic Militants in Pakistan—And How It Threatens America*, New York: Free Press, 2013.

IQTIDAR, HUMEIRA, *Secularizing Islamists? Jama'at-e-Islami and Jama'at-ud-Da'wa in Urban Pakistan*, Chicago: University of Chicago Press, 2011.

ISPAHANI, FARAHNAZ, *Purifying the Land of the Pure: A History of Pakistan's Religious Minorities*, New York: Oxford University Press, 2017.

JAFFRELOT, CHRISTOPHE, *Pakistan: Nationalism without a Nation?* London: Palgrave Macmillan, 2002.

JAFFRELOT, CHRISTOPHE, *The Pakistan Paradox: Instability and Resilience*, trans. Cynthia Schoch, London: Hurst & Co., 2015.

JAMAL, ARIF, *A History of Islamist Militancy in Pakistani Punjab*, Washington, DC: Jamestown Foundation, 2011.

JAN, MUHAMMAD AYUB AND SHAHIDA AMAN (eds.), *Conference Proceedings: The Dynamics of Change in Conflict Societies—Pakhtun Region in Perspective*, Annual International Conference, Islamabad: Hanns Seidel Foundation, 2013.

JASAM, SAIMA, *Militancy and Tehriq-i-Taliban Pakistan: Historical Overview*, Pakistan: Heinrich Boll Stiftung, 2012.

JASAM, SAIMA, *Pakistan from Radicalism to Terrorism: A Historical Journey*, Pakistan: Heinrich Boll Stiftung, 2014.

JASAM, SAIMA, *Reporting Conflict: Traditional & Social Media Narratives in the Baluchistan Conflict*, Pakistan: Heinrich Boll Stiftung, 2012.

JOYO, MUHAMMAD IBRAHIM, *Shah, Sachal, Sami*, trans. S. Noorhusain, Karachi: Culture & Tourism Department, Government of Sindh 2009.

KADOOS, ABDUL, '*Pakistan Mei Intiha Pasandi ke Rujhanat ki Wujuhat aur Tadaruk ke Liye Tajaweez ka Mukalama*' ('The Causes Behind the Rise of Terrorism in Pakistan and Prospects for Alleviating It—an Essay'), unpublished manuscript, n.d.

KANAANEH, MOSLIH, STIG-MAGNUS THORSEN, HEATHER BURSHEH, AND DAVID A. MCDONALD (eds.), *Palestinian Music and Song: Expression and Resistance since 1900*, Indiana: Indiana University Press, 2013.

KHADIM, MEHR, *Sachal Sarmast's Urdu Kalaam*, Bahawalpur: Saraiki Adabi Majlis, 2005.

KHALID, HAROON, *Beyond the 'Other': Roots of Religious Syncretism in Pakistan*, Lahore: Faiz Foundation Trust, 2016.

KHAN, AKHTAR HAMEED, *Orangi Pilot Project: Reminiscences and Reflections*, Karachi: Oxford University Press, 2005.

KHAN, AURANGZAIB, '#3: Manzoor Pashteen, for leading the fringe to the Center,' *The Herald Annual*, vol. 52, no. 1, January 2019.

KHAN, HAMID, *Constitutional and Political History of Pakistan*, 2nd edn., Karachi: Oxford University Press, 2001.

KHAN, MOHAMMAD SOHAIL, *Bacha Khan's Vision of Alternative Education*, Mardan: Bacha Khan Chair, Abdul Wali Khan University, 2018.

KHAN, MOMINA AND ALI HUSSAIN, 'In Karachi: When Hate on the Wall Disappears,' *Dawn*, 25 May 2015, accessible at: http://www.dawn.com/news/1184142.

KHAN, NAVEEDA, *Muslim Becoming: Aspiration and Skepticism in Pakistan*, Durham, North Carolina: Duke University Press, 2012.

KHAN, TALIMAND, 'Putting the "verse" back in "subversive",' *The Friday Times*, 12 June 2015, accessible at: http://www.thefridaytimes.com/tft/putting-theverse-back-in- subversive/.

KIDWAI, SHAFEY, *Cementing Ethics with Modernism: An Appraisal of Sir Sayyed Ahmed Khan's Writings*, New Delhi: Gyan Publishing House, 2010.

KILCULLEN, DAVID, *The Accidental Guerrilla: Fighting Small Wars in the Midst of a Big One*, New York: Oxford University Press, 2009.

KUMBAR, KHALIL, *The Intense Pain of Broken Bones*, Hyderabad: Sarangana Publishers, 2018.

LAMBRICK, HUGH T., *Sind: a General Introduction*, Hyderabad: Sindhi Adabi Board, 1986.

LELYVELD, DAVID, *Aligarh's First Generation: Muslim Solidarity in British India*, Princeton, N.J.: Princeton University Press, 1978.

LIEVEN, ANATOL, *Pakistan: A Hard Country*, New York: PublicAffairs, 2011.

LODHI, MARYAM SIDDIQA, *Politics of Madrassa Reforms in Pakistan: Islamization and Enlightened Moderation*, Iqbal International Institute for Research & Dialogue, IIU, 2017.

MAHMUD, SABEEN, 'Creative Karachi; Establishing an Arts & Culture Center for the World's Most Rapidly Growing City, Case Narrative: PeaceNiche and The Second Floor,' *Innovations*, vol. 8, no. 3/4, 2013.

Malik, Hafeez, *Sir Sayyid Ahmad Khan and Muslim Modernization in India and Pakistan*, New York: Columbia University Press, 1980.

Masud, Muhammad Khalid, 'Analysis Paper: Religious counter-narratives against violent extremism,' Pakistan Peace Collective, Federal Ministry for Information, Broadcasting and National Heritage, Government of Pakistan, 34 pp., n.d.

McDonald, David A., *My Voice is my Weapon: Music, Nationalism and the Poetics of Palestinian Resistance*, Durham and London: Duke University Press, 2013.

Mirani, Khadim Hussain, 'Conflict Transformation Analysis & Strategy for Peace My Right Campaign,' Khairpur Mirs: BSWA, 2015.

Mirbahar, Hassan Nasir, 'Tribal Trouble: Economic, Social and Cultural Impact of Conflicts in North Sindh,' Khairpur Mirs: BSWA, 2012.

Mustafa, Daanish and Katherine E. Brown, 'The Taliban, Public Space and Terror in Pakistan,' *Eurasian Geography and Economics*, July–August, vol. 51, no. 4, 2010, pp. 496–512.

Nadeem, Shahid, *Selected Plays*, trans. Tahira Naqvi, Khalid Hasan, Shahid Nadeem, and Naila Azad, Karachi: Oxford University Press, 2009.

Nayyar, A.H. and Ahmad Salim (eds.), *The Subtle Subversion: The State of Curricula and Textbooks in Pakistan (Urdu, English, Social Studies, and Civics)*, Islamabad: SDPI, 2005, accessible at: https://www.sdpi.org/publications/files/State%20of%20Curr&TextBooks.pdf.

Noorhusain, Saleem (ed. and trans.), *Ayaz: Songs of Freedom*, Jamshoro: Sindhi Adabi Board, 2006.

Obaid-Chinoy, Sharmeen, 'Living in the Shadows: A Man from the Hazara Community Finds Solace in Poetry,' *Dawn*, 2 August 2015, accessible at: http://www.dawn.com/news/1197617.

Pape, Robert and James Feldman, 'Pakistan' *Cutting the Fuse: The Explosion of Global Suicide Terrorism and How to Stop It*, Chicago: University of Chicago Press, 2010, pp. 138–166.

Paracha, Nadeem Farooq, *Points of Entry: Encounters at the Origin—Sites of Pakistan*, India: Tranquebar, 2018.

Pirzado, Anwer, *Cultural Heritage of Sindh*, Karachi: Anwer Pirzado Academy, 2015.

Qaiser, Shahzad, *Culture & Spirituality: the Punjabi Sufi Poetry of Baba Farid-ud-Din Masud Ganj-i-Shakr*, Lahore: Suchet Kitab Ghar, 2017.

Rais, Rasul Bakhsh. *Imagining Pakistan: Modernism, State, and the Politics of Islamic Revival*, Lanham, Maryland: Lexington Books, 2017.

Rais, Rasul Bakhsh. *Islam, Ethnicity, and Power Politics: Constructing Pakistan's National Identity*, Karachi: Oxford University Press, 2017.

RANA, MUHAMMAD AMIR, *The Militant: Development of a Jihadi Character in Pakistan*, Islamabad: Narratives, 2015.

RASHID, AHMED, *Descent into Chaos: The U.S. and the Disaster in Pakistan, Afghanistan, and Central Asia*, Penguin Books, 2008.

RASHID, AHMED, *Jihad: The Rise of Militant Islam in Central Asia*, New Haven: Yale University Press, 2002.

RAZA, AAMER, 'Voices of Resistance: Pashto Poetry as Bulwark against Extremism,' *The Dynamics of Change in Conflict Societies: Pakhtun Region in Perspective*, Peshawar: Peshawar University and Hanns Seidel Stiftung, 2013.

RAZA, SYED SAMI (ed.), *Conference Proceedings: The Dynamics of Change in the Pakistan–Afghanistan Region: Politics on Borderland*, Islamabad, Hanns Seidel Foundation, 2015.

REAT Network, *REAT Network Progress Report 2013–15*, Islamabad: REAT Network, n.d.

RIZVI, HASAN ASKARI, *The Military & Politics in Pakistan, 1947–1986*, Lahore: Sang-e-Meel Publications, 2000.

ROGHANI, ABDUL RAHIM, *Da Ranra Saskey 'Drops of Light'*, Peshawar: Aamir Print & Publishers, 2014.

ROGHANI, ABDUL RAHIM, *Selfish: A Book of Humour, Fun and Advice, based on the Harsh Realities of Life*, Mingora, Swat: Shoaib Sons Publishers & Booksellers, 2017.

RUMI, RAZA, *Being Pakistani: Society, Culture and the Arts*, India: Harper Collins, 2018.

SAHIBZADA, IMTIAZ AHMAD, *A Breath of Fresh Air. Abdul Ghani Khan: Speeches and Interventions in the Debates of the Central Legislative Assembly of India 1946–1957*, Islamabad: The Army Press, 2016.

SAIL, REHMAT SHAH, *The Beauties and the Spring Breeze*, Peshawar: Mangal Kitab Kaur, 2009.

SAIL, REHMAT SHAH, *Za da Khazan da Panrey Panrey Sara Orajedam*, Peshawar: Mangal Kitab Kor, 2018.

SALEEM, AGHA, *Introduction to the Poetry and Mystic Thought of Shah Abdul Lateef Bhittai*, Karachi: Culture Department, Government of Sindh, 2012.

SAMPSON, ROBERT AND MOMIN KHAN, *The Poetry of Rahman Baba: Poet of the Pukhtuns*, Peshawar: University Book Agency, 2010.

SAYED, DURRE-SHAHWAR, *The Poetry of Shah Abd Al-Latif*, Jamshoro/Hyderabad: Sindhi Adabi Board, 1988.

SCOTT, JAMES C., *Weapons of the Weak: Everyday Forms of Peasant Resistance*, New Haven: Yale University Press, 1985.

SENGUPTA, ASHIS (ed.), *Islam in Performance: Contemporary Plays from South Asia*, London/New York: Bloomsbury Methuen Drama, 2017.

SERAGELDIN, ISMAÏL (ed.), *The Architecture of Empowerment: People, Shelter and Livable Cities*, London: Academy Editions, 1997.

SHAH, AQIL, *The Army and Democracy: Military Politics in Pakistan*, Boston: Harvard University Press, 2014.

SHAHZAD, SYED SALEEM, *Inside Al-Qaeda and the Taliban: Beyond Bin Laden and 9/11*, London: Pluto Press, 2011.

SHAIKH, FARZANA, *Making Sense of Pakistan*, New York: Columbia University Press, 2009.

SHINWARI, SHER ALAM, 'Pashto writers craving for Peace,' *Dawn*, 31 December 2014, accessible at: https://www.dawn.com/news/1154226.

SIDDIQUE, ABUBAKAR, *The Pashtun Question: The Unresolved Key to the Future of Pakistan and Afghanistan*, London: Hurst & Company, 2014.

SULTANA, BUSHRA, *Leading Lights: The North Stars of Pakistan's Marginalised Religious Communities*, Lahore: Faiz Foundation Trust, 2016.

SUSTAINABLE DEVELOPMENT POLICY INSTITUTE (SDPI), 'Research & News Bulletin: Governance and Empowerment in South Asia,' vol. 22, no. 4, 2015, 69 pp.

SYED, JAWAD & EDWINA PIO, TAHIR KAMRAN, AND ABBAS ZAIDI (eds.), *Faith-Based Violence and Deobandi Militancy in Pakistan*, London: Palgrave Macmillan, 2016.

TENDULKAR, DINANATH GOPAL, *Abdul Ghaffar Khan: Faith is a Battle*, New Delhi: Gandhi Peace Foundation, 1967.

ULLAH, HAROON K., *Vying for Allah's Vote: Understanding Islamic Parties, Political Violence, and Extremism in Pakistan*, Washington, DC: Georgetown University Press, 2013.

VASWANI, T.L., *A Voice from the Wilderness (A Voice from the Desert)*, Khairpur: Sachal Chair, Shah Abdul Latif University, 1996.

WEAVER, MARY ANN, *Pakistan: In the Shadow of Jihad and Afghanistan*, New York: Farrar, Straus and Giroux, 2002.

WEISS, ANITA M. (ed.), *Islamic Reassertion in Pakistan: The Application of Islamic Laws in a Modern State*, Syracuse, New York: Syracuse University Press, 1986; Lahore: Vanguard Publications, 1987.

WEISS, ANITA M. AND S. ZULFIQAR GILANI (eds.), *Power and Civil Society in Pakistan*, Karachi: Oxford University Press, 2001.

WEISS, ANITA M., 'A Provincial Islamist Victory in NWFP, Pakistan: The Social Reform Agenda of the Muttahida Majlis-i-Amal,' in John L. Esposito and John Voll (eds.), *Asian Islam in the 21st Century*, New York: Oxford University Press, 2008, pp. 145–73.

WEISS, ANITA M., 'Crisis and Reconciliation in Swat through the Eyes of Women,' in Magnus Marsden and Ben Hopkins (eds.), *Beyond Swat: History, Society and*

Economy along the Afghanistan–Pakistan Frontier, first published in the UK by C. Hurst & Co. (Publishers Ltd.), 2013; New York: Columbia University Press, 2013, pp. 179–92.

WEISS, ANITA M., 'Surviving in Pakistan's Cities: A Complex Web of Challenges and Alternatives,' *Arena Journal*, no. 41/42, 2013–14, pp. 260–77.

WEISS, ANITA M., *Interpreting Islam, Modernity and Women's Rights in Pakistan*, US: Palgrave Macmillan, 2014.

YUSAFZAI, ROHAN, *The Dream of Light*, Peshawar: Bacha Khan Research Center, 2012.

ZAIDI, HASSAN JAFAR, *State & Religion in the Perspective of Muslim History*, Lahore: Idara-e-Mutalaa-e-Tareekh, 2015.

ZAMAN, MUHAMMAD QASIM, *Modern Islamic Thought in a Radical Age: Religious Authority and Internal Criticism*, Cambridge: Cambridge University Press, 2012.

Index